HOPE IN HELL

HOPE IN HELL

90 DAYS OF ADDICTION
TREATMENT AND RECOVERY

VALERY GARRETT

Garrett, Valery.
    Hope in Hell: 90 Days of Addiction Treatment and Recovery/ Valery Garrett.
    p. cm.
    Includes resource information and bibliographical references
    1. Drug Abuse—Treatment. 2. Alcoholism—Treatment. 3. Substance Abuse—Treatment. 4. Drug Rehabilitation—California. 5. Drug Abuse Programs.

Library of Congress Control Number 2014907495
CreateSpace Independent Publishing Platform
North Charleston, North Carolina USA

Cover Design by Jeanne Kaye

ISBN-13 978-1499218749
ISBN-10 1499218745

To my parents, Diane and Tom Eves

CONTENTS

PHASE III

ABOUT THE BOOK

This book is a nonfiction account of individuals striving to overcome drug addiction. No people or events were invented or revised. Nor have I attempted to alter the addicts' raw feelings or attitudes in portraying their journey through treatment. Though most individuals undergoing treatment asked that I use their real names, I opted to change them.

I spent several weeks at the Acton Rehabilitation Center, conducting dozens of interviews and observing the interactions of residents, counselors, and staff. I also attended classes, Twelve Step meetings, and counseling sessions. I was candid about wanting to document their lives, and as a result people quickly became at ease with my presence, allowing me to crouch on dormitory floors or sit in the rear of classrooms unnoticed, scribbling notes of what were often spirited and emotional interactions.

As much as possible, I use the language of the participants to describe their thoughts and the actions as they unfolded. Accounts of individual drug histories and past experiences are as they were told to me; I performed no independent verification.

My hope is that this intimate portrayal of the Acton experience provides insight into the substance abuse recovery community, where there is hope for all and redemption for those who choose it.

PREFACE

My first experience with drug treatment was when the director of the Acton Rehabilitation Center asked me to write its history. As an unpublished graduate student, I accepted eagerly, even though it meant spending much of the summer in the blistering desert heat. I looked upon the project as a way to do some serious research and produce a publishable historical piece. I had no clue that my undertaking would introduce me to a world wildly different from mine.

I shared a garage, converted to an office of sorts, with two fascinating residents. Joe and Al, who were working on the sporadically published Acton Rehab newsletter, immediately began vying for my attention. Joe, a burly black man with one glass eye and riotous gestures, was eager to absorb everything I knew. He was more passionate about learning than any of my students or fellow grad students. Joe had grown up in an institution after his prostitute mother was imprisoned for murder. He didn't learn how to read until age twenty-five, after spending time in prison and losing an eye in a brawl. He seemed to be making up for lost time because by the time I met him, Joe was a sponge for information; he read more widely than most people I knew and loved discussing classic literature or debating philosophy.

Al, a slight, middle-aged white man, saw himself as my protector. He followed me from the office to the cafeteria to make certain that the rough elements at Acton didn't harm me. Al was a television writer and considered me the only other person of intelligence at the center. An alcoholic, he was in the minority among Acton's hard-core drug-users. He felt out of place because of that and also was dismayed at what he saw as an obnoxious emphasis on Christianity.

Each time I returned to my college campus I missed my conversations with these two very different men. I soon realized that Acton was friendlier than my university community. At Acton, people frequently greeted me or initiated conversations. On my campus, people seemed engrossed in their own tiny worlds, often too focused on exams or papers to acknowledge each other. My friends, though, always wanted to hear stories about Joe and Al and anyone else I met. The world of recovery was foreign to them, but they were eager to know the backgrounds of these addicts and how they fared.

Once I finished the research and published an article, I thought I had left the drug treatment world forever. But Joe and Al and the amazing staff at Acton remained on my mind. After finishing my doctoral studies, I decided to return to Acton. Writing a history of the facility and American drug treatment policy was not enough. I needed to witness how addicts recovered and learn how Acton inspired recovery. I knew it was a unique facility, but I wanted to understand how it helped people—and how the counselors could continue working day after day when they saw so many addicts fail. Also, I was curious about why some addicts were successful at recovery their first time and others returned to treatment programs again and again.

I wondered, though, if going back to Acton would be disappointing. What if I didn't meet people as intriguing as Joe or Al? What if the residents refused to talk to me or let me observe their activities? What if the counselors didn't want me studying them or their classes? My excitement soon outweighed my doubts and I arranged to return, this time to research people rather than policies.

BEGINNINGS

1

ARRIVAL

On a scorching summer afternoon, I returned to the Acton Rehabilitation Center. A fire had erupted in the nearby desert. Orange flares rimmed the hills and black soot shot upward, dirtying the horizon. The smoke formed a gauzy veil in the sky. Most of the 234 men and 75 women residing at the remote Los Angeles County drug treatment facility had no idea how lucky they were that the hot winds pushed the conflagration north, where it consumed three thousand acres of scrub brush. The blaze could have traveled a short distance south through the tumbleweed town of Acton and then to Acton Rehab, a sprawling camp dotted with decades-old wooden cabins and other tinderbox structures. The center's acres of cacti and unpainted split-rail fences would have offered no protection from the inferno.

Twenty hours later, most of the flames had been reduced to smoldering ash, and it was a normal Monday morning at the drug treatment center. Eddie was the first addict admitted to Acton that week. He stood inside the Admissions Office, one of the many sun-bleached buildings at the facility. Desks cluttered the room. Two windows relieved the boredom of the off-white walls. An air conditioner, one of the few at Acton, choked out lukewarm air.

As a gesture of courtesy, Eddie had removed his baseball cap, exposing stubby, graying hair. He was stationary and silent, his brown eyes lifeless, much like one of the charred rattlesnakes left in the wake of the recent fire. Every molecule in Eddie whimpered failure. Until recently, he had been proud of two years of sobriety. He had kicked his habit, religiously pursued the Twelve Step program originated by Alcoholics Anonymous, and developed armor strong enough to resist the temptation of heroin. But Eddie made a common mistake by thinking that his only demon was heroin. On his first unescorted trip away from the Clare Foundation, the Santa Monica treatment center he called home, he stopped for a beer, believing that he would be fine with a drink or two.

He was wrong. Two brews quickly led to several more.

When Eddie wandered into an alley outside the Hollywood bar, he probably looked like what he was: a fifty-one-year-old Hispanic drunk. Taking him for an easy mark, a young punk slugged him, broke his dentures, and tried to steal his money. But even wasted, Eddie wasn't going down without a fight; his old street gang experience kicked in and he swung back, landing enough punches to whip the kid's ass. Leaving the would-be thief crumpled on the ground, Eddie somehow found his way back to the Clare Foundation. A self-professed liar, the best shucker and jiver, that day Eddie felt compelled to tell the truth and confess his relapse. He didn't expect forgiveness from the people at Clare. He knew he didn't deserve it and doubted he could even forgive himself. But Eddie did want understanding and was disappointed that the Clare Foundation wouldn't let him stay after detoxing.

So there he stood, in the middle of the Acton Admissions Office, burning with anger at the Clare Foundation, at himself, at Acton. Thinking only of his failure, Eddie barely registered the chaos around him.

That day, Rico, the staff member in charge of admissions, had abandoned his office for the upheaval of the main room. Rico was an owl of a man, his bronze eyes ever watchful, vigilant against his own relapse as well as the misbehavior of residents. The wisdom etched on his ebony face was matched by an ageless body well-toned by lunch-time jogs and a diet of fruit and granola. He wore immaculate clothing and a gold chain displaying the recovery symbol, a triangle inside a circle, as a talisman against his own descent into drug hell.

Rico dominated the front desk, phone glued to his ear, pen in hand. He introduced himself by his first name and shot quick questions to a caller attempting to get into the program: "What's your phone number? Date of birth, Sharon? Social Security number? What city do you live in, Sharon? Sharon, do you have any ID? You need something to show an L.A. County address. Have you ever been to Acton or Warm Springs before?"

Scribbling the answers while continuing the interrogation, Rico asked, "When was the last time you drank or used? Are you currently receiving an income? On SSI? Probation or parole? Ever register as a drug offender?

Done community service? Are you a diabetic? Are you taking any medications? Ever been to a psychiatrist before? Do you need any medical or dental work in the next ninety days? Do you have any court dates? Are you aware that the county will bill you for your stay here? No one is ever denied admission for lack of funds, and you may be eligible for county assistance which can be applied to your stay, but when you leave here you might have a bill. How soon are you trying to get in?"

There are several types of treatment, from outpatient to long term residential facilities. Callers sometimes request information about Acton's program, but more often they have heard about the center through word of mouth. Acton is known in the Southern California area as a low cost alternative to pricey Malibu facilities. Rico's caller wasn't inquiring about the program, so he questioned her to find out if she was eligible for admission and to determine if Acton was the type of program she needed.

Never showing a sign of the heat, Rico swiveled toward a big board against the east wall. Under each dwelling name was a slot for each bed in that building. Names covered almost every space, indicating that most of the four-bed cabins and twenty-four-bed dormitories were full. There was one opening in the women's dorm, but Rico knew that there were several women languishing in the county jail, waiting for a place at Acton. He couldn't give up the spot.

Meanwhile, Rico's assistant, Jackie, searched Eddie's bag for contraband—drugs, weapons, or food. The satchel and its meager contents were the only things he owned, aside from his hat, blue jeans, the ring in his left ear, a nasty scar circling his right index finger, and a series of tattooed naked women that started at his wrists and disappeared into the short sleeves of a T-shirt displaying the Clare Foundation logo.

Jackie's gloved hands pulled a pair of long, thin scissors with a rounded tip out of Eddie's bag. She held them up to Rico and asked if she could let Eddie keep the potential weapon.

"What are they for?" Rico asked, now off the phone.

"Moustache and ears." Eddie barely opened his mouth in an effort to conceal his missing teeth.

"He can't keep them," said Rico. Before Jackie could put the scissors away, to await Eddie's release from the program, Rico spotted Lynne, the assistant administrator, across the room and nodded at her. To Jackie, he said, "Ask Lynne."

Lynne crossed the room and took the scissors. "What are they for?"

Eddie repeated his answer, displaying both resignation and hope. He was resigned to giving his life over to Acton, to these people he had never met, yet the scissors allowed him a small measure of independence and he needed to be in control of something, even if it was simply the neatness of his moustache.

"What cabin are you in?" Lynne asked.

"T."

Lynne examined the scissors and thought about it for a few seconds; Eddie didn't seem like a rabble-rouser and his cabin was small and the others in it weren't trouble-makers.

"Okay," Lynne said, handing them to Eddie. She turned from him and showed Rico a letter she had picked out of the incoming mail. It was addressed to a current resident.

"Look at the return address." Lynne pointed and read, "Your soon to be husband Randy. It's to Sheila. They were here at the same time." Strict Acton policy prohibited residents from forming relationships while at Acton, but the letter appeared a blatant announcement that Randy, who had already gone home, and Sheila, who had not yet left Acton, had ignored the rules.

Rico shook his head at the many possible infractions the couple broke while together at Acton and picked up the phone. His words resonated across the center-wide public address system: "Attention male residents. May I have one volunteer, one male volunteer for escort service. First come, first served. Thank you."

Within seconds, a man raced into the room.

"Volunteer, please introduce yourself to . . . Eddie?" Rico looked more intently at Eddie. "You look familiar. Where do I know you from?" Rico religiously attended Narcotics Anonymous meetings in the Los Angeles area and spoke at dozens of panels, so he knew many people in recovery.

"Clare, maybe," Eddie said.

Rico nodded. Eddie picked up his bag, and the volunteer hefted the allotted bedroll. It was official: Eddie was an Acton resident. But he took no joy in the fact that he had a bed for the next ninety days. Eddie's sole concern was staying out of trouble so he could get back to the Clare Foundation—his real home.

A few hours after Eddie's entrance to Acton, another newcomer, Patty, danced in the middle of the Admissions Office, her low-waisted blue-jeans dress swaying as she rocked from foot to foot, the silver anklet above her left sandal bobbing with each movement. The thirty-two-year-old moved like a teenager, but the youthful image vanished when she smiled broadly, exposing the gaps between her teeth. Patty's heavy mascara and thick eyeliner did nothing to disguise the lines around her mouth and eyes. Her decaying gums and wrinkles showed the physical ravages common to drug addicts. A flattened nose was a gift from her boyfriend.

Evelyn, a bird-like senior citizen, entered the room and introduced herself to Patty. She had volunteered to escort Patty to the facilities office so she could get her hair dryer and electric curling iron approved for use with the center's ancient electrical outlets.

As they burst out the front Admissions door, both women talked at once, barely listening to what the other was saying. Even the shock of ninety-five-degree air failed to slow their words.

"Call me Granny," Evelyn said. "Everybody does. Everybody comes to me and cries on my shoulder and it doesn't get around." Evelyn's grandmotherly appearance masked her past. No one would guess by looking at her that she had burned through seven husbands, performed strip-teases for strangers, often wound up in unfamiliar places after a night of boozing, and once had been beaten with beer bottles by two businessmen and, as she put it, dumped for dead.

"I only have five days sober," Patty said. She was happy to be at Acton, but still felt pickled. "I called for six weeks to get in here and then came in last Thursday, but I wasn't sober and they wouldn't let me in. I asked to have a bed saved. Rico said I need to stay sober. I had a backpack and everything. My mom said it wasn't to be."

"I've been here five weeks and I'm learning acceptance," Evelyn said, sparkling with the zeal of someone who has recently seen the light. Evelyn had over sixty years of experience with alcohol. Her father, the town drunk, often became violent and, at a very young age, Evelyn, her father's pet, learned to induce him to leave the house so that her mother and siblings could escape his brutality for a few hours. Later, she had tried pot, cocaine, a crack pipe, and acid but always returned to beer, just like her father. After four arrests for DUIs and countless blackouts, Evelyn found Acton and loved it.

"I'm an artist," Evelyn continued. "I have oils. I've been sketching. It helps me learn acceptance."

Patty also kept talking. "I asked for them to save me a bed. I went to church and prayed to God. Now I'm here. I was saved last Thursday." Patty longed to be saved permanently. Her alcoholic father had put down his bottle fifteen years ago and didn't understand why Patty couldn't quit as easily. She knew her father had the grace of God and hoped she, too, could gain His favor. She believed that spirituality was important and she wouldn't succeed unless she clung to God with all her might. So she prayed that the Lord would take away her craving and hoped it would happen soon.

"God works in mysterious ways," Evelyn said. "When we're drinking we feel like dirt, but here it only takes one week and you don't have feelings of low self-esteem."

Patty's appliances passed the electrical test. They were tagged and returned to her. Back in the Admissions Office,

Patty retrieved her belongings and the standard issue of bedding and toiletries. A new escort, Olivia, showed her to her cabin. Olivia, a squat Hispanic woman, was also a resident. She volunteered in the Admissions Office and was one of the six people staying in V cabin, the same place Patty had been assigned.

Once inside the cabin, Olivia pointed to each of the single beds, beginning with the one to the left of the door and continuing clockwise, "Janice, Vicky, Karla, me, Linda, and you." Although the dorm was not artificially cooled, two women had escaped the harsh sun by retreating inside. Vicky sat on her cot, watching Patty. Linda was lying down, pretending to read. Though the others weren't present, their beds and the surrounding areas bore evidence of occupation; photos and homemade drawings commandeered wall space while other knickknacks rested on tiny nightstands. Patty's area consisted of a naked mattress supported by an iron frame that looked old enough to have been in the cabin since it was built in the 1930s. Patty flung her possessions onto the pallet.

Olivia continued the introduction, first showing Patty her assigned locker and then leading her through a curtained doorway into the sitting area. A sagging couch and green vinyl chair roosted on the worn linoleum. To the right was a bathroom without a tub. Instead, it housed two showers, two sinks, and a toilet. On the other side of the sitting room was another curtained doorway, hiding cabin W, a mirror image of Patty's new dwelling.

"I don't mind work," Patty said when Olivia mentioned the cleaning schedule for all cabin residents.

The short tour completed, Olivia departed.

Patty immediately moved all her things off the bed and started setting up her temporary quarters. As she reached for the plastic bag containing the linens, she announced to no one in particular, "I'm really glad I got this place. I have four kids. Three girls. One boy. Someone took three packs of my cigarettes. I had a carton, I took one, now there's six packs, so someone took three. Granny said it was one of the new people. I let it go already."

"I quit everything," Linda said, peering over her book.

"I gave my heart to the Lord Thursday night," Patty said. "I haven't drank or ate anything since then. I'm going to quit smoking, too."

"I got nothing to do, so I smoke," Vicky said.

"If I don't use, I don't smoke," Linda said.

Patty began making her bed. Her thoughts were disjointed, but she didn't mind sharing them with her new cabin mates. "I did speed. I'm a tweaker. And alcoholic. I did a little meth two months ago and lost my apartment. I'm doing this for me. I just got a haircut. What do you think of it? My thirteen- and fourteen-year-old daughters took me in and got me a haircut."

"I haven't seen my kids in six months," Linda said. "I've been here ninety days and was locked up for three and a half months before that."

"I cried leaving my baby girl. She's three." Patty's heart ached at the thought of her daughter. But she was happy that the baby's father was with her. The toddler loved her father so much. And Ned was Patty's soul mate; he made her complete. He knew what Patty thought before she even thought it. She loved him with all her heart and was happy that he wanted to marry her. She remembered how gentle he was, even crying when apologizing for his violence. When sober, he was wonderful. And he'd been clean longer than Patty.

"I have a three-year-old, too." Linda said. "Stress on it for a day and then concentrate on yourself. You can't afford to think about anything else for a while."

"Granny told me about the Saturday night rock concerts. Are they good?"

"Really good," answered both Vicky and Linda.

"If you want to go to church," Vicky said, "we have Bible studies every day at six in the morning. There are meetings all day."

"I prayed to get into the right program," Patty said. "I checked out three different programs, but they wouldn't take me—and they were mission programs."

"When I got here I did cartwheels," Linda said. "I was court-referred. I wanted to go to Tarzana, but I'm glad I'm here. A lot of programs, you do what they want between eight and five and then you're free. Here there's only one class a day on weekdays, ten meetings a week. In between, you do what you want."

"This isn't my first rehab. Maybe God is with you the third time around. If it don't work now, kiss it." Patty emitted a big raspberry, her bubbly mood visibly dissipating.

"Never give up," Linda said.

Patty finished tucking in the blanket provided by the center. She added a blue-and-white checked bedspread, making the area a bit less institutional looking. Her face flushed from the heat and exertion, she announced, "I hate making beds."

"I got my life back after twenty-seven years," said Linda.

Patty wasn't listening to Linda. Instead, she deposited her suitcase on the bed and began putting her clothes in the locker. Suddenly she perked up. "When I got here today, I was dancing around, happy, smiling. Everyone was commenting on how much I was smiling. They were even calling me Smiley. I don't talk like this all the time. Sometimes I do shut up."

To prove her point, Patty stopped talking.

Linda filled the sound vacuum, taking it upon herself to explain how the center worked. "Diane is the cabin counselor. She's cool. She's not a user, but she's cool. You have to ask to do the Steps. But she doesn't have a packet. I went to Stella. Stella's cool. One of the best counselors is David. Are you going to do AA or CA or NA?"

Alcoholics Anonymous, AA, is both a philosophy and a recovery plan well-known even to individuals who have never been in rehab. Many people have heard the story of Bill W. and Dr. Bob, who in the 1930s co-founded the group that has become a worldwide organization open to anyone seeking recovery. Bill W. wrote *Alcoholics Anonymous*, the "Big Book" as AA members call it, to tell how he overcame his prejudice against the God of formal religions and recognized the idea of a force greater than himself. By believing in such a Higher Power, he began to battle his addiction. Through trial and error, AA pioneers created a Twelve Step program run solely by addicts.

Alcoholics Anonymous first appeared at Acton in the late 1940s, and though a resident-driven program, it is a vital adjunct to Acton's treatment program. Narcotics

Anonymous (NA) and Cocaine Anonymous (CA) are off-shoots of AA, using the same text and tenets, but also integrating ideas and meeting styles responsive to an individual's drug of choice. Many Acton residents belonged to both AA and a second group.

Patty didn't need an explanation of the Twelve Step programs. She declared that she would attend AA and NA.

"NA Newcomers is Wednesday," Linda said. "You can go to AA anytime."

Patty held up a sedate-looking dress. "Can you tell that my mom helped me pack?"

Intent on teaching Patty about Acton, Linda ignored the question. "They're really strict about talking to guys, which I think is kinda crazy. They stick us together for everything. What do they expect? After five and on weekends, they don't get picky, but you can't sit real close."

Linda didn't mention something that soon became apparent to Acton newcomers: the fact that there were three times more men than women created a large population of needy males who pounced on the new females before they had a chance to unpack. Married or single, it didn't matter, testosterone ruled and every woman became instant prey. Greasy hair, missing teeth, and sickly bodies failed to impede the crude courtship of the desperate at Acton.

"I flirt too much. I have to learn how not to flirt," Patty said. She had been at Acton less than an hour, and yet she had already responded to the attention of Owen, the older man who had dubbed her Smiley. She quickly dismissed that issue and pointed to the vase on Linda's nightstand. "Where'd you get the flowers?"

"I picked them." Linda resumed her instruction. "PE is Wednesday and Friday mornings. Program Review is Monday and Friday mornings."

"I'm an airhead," Patty said, without the slightest bit of embarrassment.

"We all are," Linda said. "The outside panel meetings here are good."

"You know what that's from, don't you," Patty said. "It's from methamphetamine. I came here last Thursday and wasn't detoxed enough. They wouldn't let me in."

Linda gave up. Patty had finally deterred her from the lecture. Instead, she began to get competitive, informing Patty, "I was on a speed high for nine and a half years. I detoxed in jail, just slept a lot."

"Meth, you don't detox hard," Patty said. "I'm not going back to it. My mother said don't tell anybody about this, but the father of my baby shoved my face into the ground last Christmas Eve. Mom picked me up at Christmas and everyone had to see me like that. And my house burned down that day."

The Christmas Eve brawl was the final punch, but Patty's life had begun its descent toward hell much earlier. She had been using for years but seemed to be doing okay, even with the scumbags hanging around her home. Her drug dealer's mother had a condo and Patty used five hundred of her welfare dollars to rent the place. Patty's face turned ugly whenever she thought of her sister Tammy, the speed freak. Tammy had taken Patty's check to buy a half ounce of dope which she claimed she would sell and double the money. Tammy bought the dope and then partied out the "investment." Tammy left, the dope was gone, the bucks evaporated, and the rent was due. Patty never recovered.

Similar to other addicts proud of their war stories, Linda seemed to think that her hit-bottom tale topped Patty's. After all, she had been arrested and spent time in jail. She wasn't at Acton by choice—unless one hundred twenty days at Acton was one choice and three years in the penitentiary a second choice. Still, she claimed that she didn't think about using and said, "I got a six-month chip," rewarded for remaining drug-free for six months.

"What's your drug of choice?" Patty asked Vicky, who had been mutely listening to the conversation.

"Alcohol."

"Us drug addicts drive her crazy," Linda said. "I spent a year and a half drunk."

Patty looked at her neat area. "Am I getting organized here?"

"Too organized. It took me two days and I didn't have anything."

"That's why I prayed to God," Patty said. Ignoring the nearby door which might burst open at any moment, she shed her sweaty dress, revealing a white bra and blue panties. "I'm glad I didn't come here from a jail cell. I had a DUI four years ago and I didn't want to get into the court system."

Giving into the energy-sapping heat, Patty donned a pair of black shorts and a black-and-white striped T-shirt. "I'm comfortable here, girls."

Getting into Acton had required so much effort that Patty hoped the hard part was over. Now it seemed that to succeed all she had to do was avoid drinking and using. After the other rehab programs, she thought she understood what she needed to do and planned to use Acton as a refresher course. She didn't even intend to stay the full ninety days. Sixty, she thought, should be enough to completely dry out and get her health back.

What Patty didn't realize was that Acton's definition of success required her to remain at the center for the entire three-month program and, perhaps, internalize some of its lessons. Americans at large had another gauge of success: forever foreswearing drugs and becoming a productive member of society. Whether attempting to achieve the goals of Acton or society or even if she followed her quest to pray away her addiction, Patty had some rough weeks ahead of her. The program demanded focus and introspection while Patty usually darted from one thing to the next without forethought or hindsight. This time, though, she was determined to stay clean. She understood the stakes of her recovery: she could lose her children, her health, or even her life.

There were many reasons why addicts went to Acton. Some people, like Patty and Eddie, wanted to get clean. Others, like Linda, were sent by a court. Jason's impetus was somewhat different: he was trying to stay one step ahead of his parole officer—and keep his parents off his back.

Jason exited the car driven by his father and found his way to the Admissions Office. His beard and scraggly ponytail, held back by a rubber band, seemed to insulate him from his surroundings. Likewise, his clothes—baggy blue jeans, plaid shirt, and dirty three-tone ski vest—hid the shape of his body. By appearance alone, his age was difficult to pin down; he looked anywhere from twenty-five to forty. In fact, he was chronologically twenty-eight but psychologically still fourteen.

Oblivious to the heat, Jason concentrated on quelling his twitchy body. He had been clean only one day and was still wired. He worried that someone would recognize his withdrawal symptoms and refuse to let him stay. Stressful situations like this one were the reason that he took drugs; they were his crutch in coping with people and new situations.

Jason tried to hide his jumpiness while filling out the admissions forms. He lied about how long he had been clean and kept praying that no one would notice. Once finished with that test, and seeming to escape detection, Jason followed instructions and walked to the dispensary. Paying little attention to his surroundings, he could think of only one thing: What if the nurse "stuck him" and learned that he was still high? The butterflies in his belly seemed to flap faster and faster.

He took a seat in the dispensary and tried to calm his stomach. A young man on the other side of the window that divided the examination area from the waiting room leaned toward Jason. "You'll like it here. It's a safe haven for people like us. It's all right. You only get what you want out of it."

Jason nodded, but didn't speak. He had been in and out of institutions for seventeen years and wasn't sure how Acton would compare, though he knew it wouldn't be as confining as prison. His first stint in a lock-up situation was at a camp in San Dimas when he was eleven. There, he sniffed glue and took PCP to fit in. Later, he learned that to survive it was necessary to impress the other guys, get a little respect, acquire some clout so he could ask a favor if he needed it. He knew he could never appear timid. Since he was smaller than most men, he cultivated a reputation as a crazy type of guy and was proud of his nickname, "Psycho."

Another lesson he learned behind walls was to stay with his own kind. He talked only with his own kind; he ate only with his own kind. He claimed that was the law of the land. For survival he hung out only with whites and, if he saw others breaking the code, he was happy to fight them.

Two male residents came into the dispensary and introduced themselves. One man said that he volunteered in rehab services. The other man worked in the kitchen.

"Come talk to us if you need a counselor," the first man said.

"Or get bored," added the second man.

Suddenly excited about the possibilities at Acton, Jason asked, "You got a library?"

The men nodded.

Jason's anxiousness flooded back when called for his exam. But the nurse didn't test him for drugs. She merely took his medical history and sent him back to the Admissions Office.

Relieved that he had been accepted by Acton, Jason decided that he'd better embark on his next task: making friends with his counselor. His primary concern was to avoid being sent back to prison. He recently had three dirties, tests indicating that he still used drugs, and had missed two weeks of testing—which was the same as having dirties—and he was afraid that his parole officer was planning to send him back to prison for failing the drug checks. In an attempt to stall the parole officer, Jason had left a phone message on her answering service, saying that he had enrolled himself into a treatment program.

Jason got an escort to his cabin. After tossing his things onto the bed, he immediately looked for the rehab services building and signed in to see his counselor. Several people crowded into the tiny waiting room. The six chairs were taken and five additional people hovered wherever they found space.

Jason was too nervous to stand still or be silent. "What do you do all day?" he asked a man standing next to him.

"After I get up, I . . . sleep," the man said.

Not knowing what else to do and feeling uncomfortable without noise, Jason launched into a summary of one of his favorite Stephen King thrillers. Jason loved books with an unsettling atmosphere and stories that could take him out of the hellish boredom of everyday life and give him a glimpse of real terror.

Jason talked out of the side of his mouth, his voice emitting a slight lisp, his whole body moving as he recounted the tale. With each detail that he revealed, Jason swayed from left to right, leaned forward, gently pounded his hand into his fist, or smoothed his hair behind his ears. His rendition sucked the other residents into a world of demonic situations and they listened intently. When he finished, no one spoke.

A few seconds later, his counselor came into the room and asked Jason to follow her. He trailed behind the woman and, once inside her office, carefully sat down in the visitor's chair. He leaned forward and in a polite, measured voice introduced himself.

"You came in this morning?" she asked.

"Yes, ma'am."

She handed him a program card and said that he should start it tomorrow. The program card, labeled "Phase I," spelled out the classes required for the first month at Acton. The first week included three orientations, three chemical dependency education classes, and a literacy test. In addition to the daily classes, the counselor explained that Jason was required to go to PE twice a week and attend ten Twelve Step meetings a week. Attendance at all functions was mandatory and there were spaces on the reverse side of the card where counselors or meeting chairpersons initialed completion of the class or meeting.

Jason looked at the card and said, "I've been to walk-in meetings before." He waited for a response. He was expecting the counselor to tell him everything about Acton, everything that was required of him. He understood structure and liked to know the rules. Armed with that information, he thought he would be set. But the counselor seemed to be looking at him like she didn't know why he was there. All he wanted was serenity. But it didn't seem as though she was even going to speak again. Finally, Jason asked, "So, I could go to the library today?"

The counselor said yes and told him to ask other residents where things were located. "They'll point you in the right direction," she said. "Make friends. You won't remember everything so use your program card."

Jason needed more help than that. He didn't know what to do, where to go next. Surely the counselor could give him some idea of how he should spend the afternoon. Grasping for some way to prod her into aiding him, Jason said, "I'm sure there's somebody else from the Valley here."

When she didn't respond, he seized on a subject guaranteed to draw her out, asking, "What percentage of people recover?"

"I can't give percentages," she said. "What really matters is you putting your best foot forward."

"I'm tired," Jason said. "I think getting clean is a matter of willpower. With or without a program doesn't matter much. It's your life. You make your own bed."

"The desire to stay clean is important," she said. "We hope we do. What we first need is to admit total defeat."

"Yes, ma'am," Jason said. He stood up and politely thanked her. He wondered if she liked him. That was important, especially if he needed her to write letters to his parole officer.

When he exited the building, brilliant sunlight temporarily blinded him. He blinked, but continued forward. He was thinking only about his next tasks: checking out the library for Stephen King novels and trying to get some clout.

2

COUNTY JAIL

It was night and an eerie stillness pervaded the medical pod of the Twin Towers Correctional Facility in downtown Los Angeles. The television was silent. The inmates' usual shouts, insults, and jockeying for power had been hushed by the mandatory bedtime curfew. The only sounds were involuntary ones: snoring, troubled moaning, and the rustling of sheets, as the women tried to get comfortable on unyielding metal shelves, only a thin pad separating them from hard steel. Each pie slice-shaped cell contained four beds and a metal sink and toilet unit. Makeshift bunks spilled out of the cells and into the day room.

Deborah, a forty-six-year-old inmate, was crammed into the lower half of one bunk, her ponytailed head resting at the foot of the bed so she could take advantage of the constantly burning lights. When the others slumbered, Deborah came alive. Her chocolate eyes, intense behind a pair of black-rimmed glasses, darted across the pages of a romance novel, absorbed in the flirtation between an average woman and her prince. Deborah enjoyed the fictional characters in books almost as much as she hated the tedium of her confinement. Night was the only time that she could retreat from the reality of her situation without fear of interruption.

Yet Deborah's withdrawal from prison life was as tenuous as it was temporary. Despite her fantasies about tall, dark, and handsome white men, she knew that the only males in her life were the guards monitoring her movements. Deborah and the others were on constant display. A thirty-foot-high soundproof glass separated the prisoners from their jailers. Deborah could discern little on the other side of the window, but she knew that the darkened guard station displayed the activities in the cells through a closed-circuit television system. The officers could both see and hear each inmate, ruling them with a touch of a button at their Orwellian controls. Twin Towers was a maze of catacomb corridors and frequent reinforced steel doors that allowed no escape. Viewed from above, the two eight-story octagonal buildings connected by a three-story concourse resembled a pair of the world's largest handcuffs. The fortress filled ten acres in downtown Los Angeles, but the city was only a dream to its thousands of inmates.

Deborah was anxious for her release. She hated the inactivity of the med dorm; all she did was eat, sleep, and read. After five weeks of incarceration, the 5'7" inmate was no longer a skinny 125 pounds and her usual broad grin had gone into hiding. Worse than her actual confinement was the fact that she didn't know how long she had to remain sealed in the Twin Towers tomb.

Deborah had landed in jail on what she considered a bogus charge. She had been apprehended in Hollywood while walking with a guy carrying a pipe used for smoking dope. The cops found a broken codeine tablet in the bottom of her purse and claimed that she possessed a controlled substance. The district attorney rejected the case, but Deborah continued to be held as a probation violator on a previous drug possession conviction.

The original conviction was solid. Deborah had used drugs and had been caught. Long ago she had dedicated her life to the pursuit of pleasure. She chose not to have children so she could concentrate on fun and that included frequent cocaine use. She first tried weed but rejected it after ending up in a 7-Eleven with twenty dollars worth of Ding Dongs. She didn't understand how people could use marijuana or any drug that produced hallucinations. But cocaine was totally different. That drug made her happy. It made her laugh, tell jokes, even think in German. Cocaine was the perfect drug for her; it took her effervescent personality and amplified it, elevating her into the life of any party and the star of her own cheerful dramas.

Prostitution was another choice. After blowing an inheritance from her father, Deborah decided hooking was a good way to earn money to support her habit. She enjoyed sex and claimed that if she was going to lie on her back anyway, why not use that ability to make money? She counted her days as a hooker from her first conviction—when a cop popped out of the trunk after Deborah propositioned his partner—but she was an accomplished "amateur" for several years before that. Previously, after she had been arrested at Jack in the Box for driving without a

24

license, Deborah used her jail time to learn the tricks of the trade from a plump white girl. Soon she was standing at the corner of Sunset and Western, waving down customers like a pro and getting her fair share of takers. White men, Deborah had observed, enjoyed tall, black girls with big tits.

By the end of the twentieth century, though, the world of prostitution had changed—and not for the better, Deborah thought. Phone sex and the Internet played parts in diminishing Deborah's client base. Lots of men continued to crave warm flesh, but some men with the means to afford expensive pay-by-the-minute calls or pornography turned in other directions. Deborah also found it impossible to compete with drug addicts who exchanged blow jobs for a hit. And then there were Deborah's problems with the police. By the time of her last arrest, she couldn't walk down the street without cops asking for her ID. She concluded that there was a need to fill recently built jails.

The make-up of the prison system appeared to confirm Deborah's assumptions. By 1999, more than thirty times as many drug offenders were sentenced to prison in Los Angeles County as in 1980. In the 1990s, California had implemented a harsh law enforcement strategy based on the belief that imprisoning drug offenders would both diminish drug use and reduce crime. However, by the late 1990s, more than half of California's drug arrests were for low level offenses, like Deborah's. That meant that a large percentage of drug manufacturers and traffickers escaped penalty while punishment for the possession of small amounts of drugs became California's primary drug prevention policy.

———

In her first two weeks in the regular jail dorm, Deborah had problems with ignorant, aggressive inmates who thought she was too smart for her own good and made them look stupid. Deborah tried to avoid confrontations by being the most entertaining woman there, hoping that the others would hang on her amusing stories and defend her when necessary. But humor didn't work with everyone and Deborah couldn't muzzle her sarcasm against stupidity, even knowing that most people in jail would rather get hit than be made to look foolish by someone with a caustic tongue. One inmate threw window cleaner at her after Deborah corrected the woman's grammar. Luckily, Deborah was wearing her glasses.

That incident didn't dampen her arrogance. Deborah was smart and didn't mind showing it. The girls called her "Miss Jeopardy" because whenever the television game show aired, she kicked ass. It amazed her that most women in the dorm didn't know the answers to simple questions; she claimed that they didn't realize that Picasso was the most important artist of the twentieth century or that Shakespeare had written thirty-seven plays. Even more astonishing to Deborah was that many of the women couldn't read. She discovered that when she enabled the television's closed captioning so she could follow the programs above the noise in the dayroom. Most of the others couldn't decipher the words on the screen or were too slow to keep up.

Deborah was mystified by the gangs of dumb women who thought that getting into fights with the deputies made them look cool. Those idiots didn't mind the extra charges, longer sentences, or confinement to the hole so long as they thought they had the respect of other inmates. Deborah's attitude was totally different: she treated the deputies with humor and humility. She told them that she knew they were in charge. She wasn't there to argue or be difficult. She just wanted to follow the rules, do her time, and get out.

Luckily, Deborah was promoted to the kitchen dorm where her upbeat personality fit in. Instead of the two-person cells of the regular dorms, there were two floors with double- and triple-tiered bunk beds, housing approximately one hundred fifty women. The layout made their incarceration seem like a communal experience, one conducive to camaraderie, rather than the more isolated existence of individuals constantly trying to prove themselves. The women in the kitchen dorm were allowed to keep the lights and television on until midnight and had access to the telephone far later than the other dorms. Plus, they were permitted to linger in bed until it was time to go to work. The women there appreciated Deborah's funny stories and she always had a witty reply to others' tales. She sang the lyrics to *West Side Story* with some of the younger girls while dancing like the Jets or Sharks in between the rows of bunks. Deborah even liked her job cleaning pots. She enjoyed the physical labor and became adept at keeping deputies away from her area by ricocheting water from the hose off a pot or cookie sheet and toward anyone who got too near.

Unfortunately, her stay in the kitchen dorm was short. She developed a horrible toothache and for days quelled the pain using Tylenol hoarded by her new friends from their two-a-shift limit. Since Deborah had no money she also relied on her fellow dorm mates to buy painkillers for her from the commissary. But, one night her toothache became so painful that the women in her dorm used the intercom to call the deputy, an action forbidden except in emergencies. The result was a visit to the dentist who prescribed an antibiotic, which meant that Deborah had to move to the med dorm. Although she needed the medicine, Deborah was sad to leave her friends and missed the fun.

During Deborah's weeks in jail she departed the facility only once, to go to court. She was escorted to a pre-arraignment hearing during which the judge ordered a probation officer to determine whether or not Deborah would remain in jail on the latest, her second, violation. The woman who interviewed her felt that Deborah's education (she claimed a bachelor's degree in history from UCLA) and background (she was an Army brat who once had a successful career working for an engineering firm) were more conducive to rehabilitation than imprisonment. The interviewer called her an intelligent addict and recommended that she be sent to Acton. The public defender accepted the probation officer's advice and the judge sentenced her to ninety days at the rehabilitation facility. The problem was that she was at the mercy of Acton to find a bed for her. In the meantime, she vegetated.

Deborah was released from jail into Acton's care on a Tuesday. After breakfast, she and several other women had exchanged their uniforms for the unwashed clothes they wore when arrested. Deborah had gained so much weight that she was given a pair of men's white shorts to match her

V-necked T-shirt. Around her waist was a black fanny pack, still containing the sixteen condoms she possessed when arrested.

The women were then crowded into a small holding area while awaiting the Acton van that would transport them to their new home.

At Acton, the van rested in front of the Admissions Office. The weather forecast predicted highs in the mid-90s for the Antelope Valley, but it was only 9:00 A.M. and the full strength of the sun was not yet in evidence. The stagnant air hovered between early morning coolness and the searing heat of desert afternoons. The county driver exited the Admissions Office, followed by three recently arrived female residents. The women piled into the back of the van, bumping into each other in their excitement to leave the facility for a few hours. Three weeks ago they had been desperate to depart Twin Towers, and now they were ecstatic to be returning to the county jail, knowing their visit would be short. They were allowed to make the trip because when they had been released there had been no time to collect money held on account for them.

The fifty-mile trip to downtown Los Angeles took an hour. The driver parked in a "No Parking" zone on Bauchet, directly in front of the jail entrance. The women hopped out of the vehicle. Two of them excitedly pointed to the tiny jail windows, trying to pinpoint where they had resided in the massive structure.

Inside the forbidding building, the quartet trooped up the wide, concrete stairs leading to the second floor waiting area. Once at the top, the driver headed toward a bulletproof window and deposited a list of prisoners bound for Acton. The three women scattered. One grabbed a receiver off the nearest phone in a long bank, hoping to reach her boyfriend. The other two lined up in front of the cashier's booth, intent on retrieving their money.

None of the women from Acton paid attention to their grim surroundings or the tired people awaiting the release of friends and relatives. Children, parents, and grandparents sat on hard concrete slabs or stood listlessly. Whether they looked inward, toward the bulletproof cashier's booth and county guards, or outward, toward the smoking area on the other side of the large windows, the view was unappealing. A grayness hovered over the entire area. Even the softly droning television contributed to the impersonal sadness of the room.

Not long after the Acton group arrived, a door near the cashier's booth opened. A scraggly line of men emerged. They ranged from teenagers to senior citizens, but all looked alike: tired and deflated by the system. Many carried cardboard boxes with plastic handles—the prison equivalent of a suitcase. Some found a waiting relative. A few even found the energy to hug their rescuers. Most of the newly released vanished quickly, not wanting to endure another minute within the spirit-draining building.

By the time the Acton group picked up their money, they were as subdued as their environment. After the first rush of excitement at seeing their old jail, the bad memories bubbled to the surface and everyone was ready to leave. It seemed like an eternity before a guard announced the Acton-bound prisoners.

Eight bedraggled women, including Deborah, crowded into the waiting room. The Acton driver stepped forward to claim them. Not giving them time to talk, he quickly led the group out the door and down the stairs.

"Can we smoke?" asked one ex-prisoner.

"Can we buy cigarettes?" asked another.

The driver didn't answer. He marched forward, leading his charges away from the jail, trying to shepherd his new flock to the van before they realized how easy it would be to walk away and quickly disappear into the bowels of Los Angeles. As soon as the group reached the van, the driver opened the door and tried to herd everyone inside.

By then, one woman had lit a cigarette and offered it to the others. Suddenly the women balked against the driver's attempts to whisk them away, indignantly declaring, "We're smoking!" The solitary cigarette quickly made the rounds; except for Deborah, each ex-prisoner took a hurried puff and passed it on.

The driver impatiently waited for the cigarette to expire.

"What happens if we don't go with you?" Deborah asked.

"We'll turn your name over to the judge. When you get picked up, you'll get double your sentence," the driver said. He wasn't going to force them into the van, but he wanted them to have an idea of the consequences. The women exploded with more questions.

"What about court dates?"

"How long will it take to get processed in?"

"Who's got a soda?"

"My mother sent me a box—"

"Okay, ladies," the driver said, indicating that it really was time to go.

The cigarette had been smoked and the butt tossed. They had no more excuses. Each woman inhaled one last breath of freedom and climbed into the van. The ex-prisoners filled up the back rows while the other three again took their places directly behind the driver, who immediately fired up the van, cranked up the air conditioning, and headed toward Acton.

For most of the ride, the new people were quiet, somberly staring out the window as the van headed away from Los Angeles. The only new rider who showed any signs of life was Deborah. When the radio played a song she liked, she quietly sang along. The other three African-American women had their armor intact, shielding them from others. Nancy, dressed in masculine clothes, wondered if she made the right decision by getting in the van. She was glad to be out of jail, but didn't know what to expect from Acton. Uta, a light-skinned black woman wearing a shapeless shift, appeared drugged; she moved slowly and others' comments took a moment to register. Helen had a definite "'tude"—her angry face was enough to keep people away and that is what she thought she wanted.

The three Hispanic women, Ana, Yolanda, and Inez, were stone silent. Ana was small and with her hair pulled into a ponytail looked like a teenager, even though she had recently turned fifty. Yolanda was too chubby to be wearing hot-pink shorts cut so high that her underwear showed. Her heavy make-up, including bright blue eye shadow, added to the cheap effect. Inez's charcoal eyeliner emphasized her cheerless dark eyes and thick eyebrows.

Marissa, the only white woman, contrasted her pale skin with short, unnaturally colored black hair, an all-black wardrobe, and bright red lipstick.

Within half an hour, signs of the city faded as the county vehicle snaked through desert-like lands punctuated with huge tan-and-pink housing subdivisions placed improbably among the cacti. Soon, even the suburbs vanished. The driver exited south at Crown Valley Road, passed a gas station, several ranch houses, and within five minutes reached the town of Acton. The town's main intersection, a dusty crossroads without a signal, contained a development on only one corner: a tiny strip mall, resembling a facade in a western movie. Ironically, the last building on the road to the treatment center was the Forty-Niner, a saloon announcing spirits for sale. The van zipped through town, paused at a stop sign, and crossed the railroad tracks. It turned left onto a smaller road and then left again at the entrance to Acton. A heavy gate, permanently open, stood by a yellow tank, bearing a hand-lettered sign: Welcome to the Acton Rehabilitation Center.

The Twin Towers group filled out forms at the Admissions Office and then trooped into the sweltering midday heat for a short walk to the cooled dispensary waiting room where they completed more paperwork. Uta wrote slowly and took long pauses between letters. Every few minutes she asked how to spell a new word. Marissa, perched next to Uta, sped through her own pile, but patiently answered all Uta's questions.

A male resident poked his head inside the door, grinned mischievously, and said, "Welcome to Acton, everybody."

A staff member shooed him away and the women continued writing. Another man entered the room and handed eight sack lunches to the staff member, who then distributed them to the new residents. Marissa wrinkled her nose when she pulled out a peanut butter sandwich and quickly traded it to Nancy for ham and cheese. Most of the women ate the potato chips but ignored the apple.

Once the forms were finished, the women had quick medical check-ups and were soon out the door, heading toward a task that excited them immensely: picking out clean clothes. The donated clothes were in a small, dark room. In addition to a cosmetic kit—consisting of a towel, toothbrush, soap, razor, deodorant, three pairs of new underwear, and a bra—the women were permitted to choose four pants and four shirts. They crammed into the tiny room, rooted through shelves of clothes, and chose items they hoped would fit. Like mini-tornadoes, they attacked, swooped up outfits, and disappeared. Only Deborah and Marissa took their time.

All the garments draped over Marisa's arm were black or white. She was having a difficult time deciding which pants to choose. Stalling, she looked through a box of belts and selected two. She then moved to a box marked "vests" and rummaged through it. Next, she spotted a wool jacket, one that no one else wanted during the unbearable summer heat, and talked the staff member into letting her take it. Marissa said thanks and walked out with a large stash of clothing.

Meanwhile, Deborah was having fun selecting her wardrobe. It was the first time she had been "shopping" in months. She spotted a section of shoes and asked if she could have a pair.

"You find a pair, take 'em," was the reply.

Deborah instantly grabbed a pair of cowboy boots decorated with red swirls and rhinestones against a black background. She dubbed them "hooker boots."

The fun part of her introduction to Acton over, Deborah now needed to learn how to fit in at the treatment center.

3

ADDICT STREAM

Just like there was a constant stream of addicts entering Acton, there were people departing almost every day. Some people left because they couldn't stand the rules, others were kicked out after breaking the rules, and some individuals deserted because their interest in getting clean was fleeting. Almost half of the residents completed their 90-day stay—or sometimes 120 days if court-ordered to rehabilitation—and went through a graduation ceremony, held once a week.

Fridays were always electric with anticipation. Those graduating buzzed around the center, borrowing clothing and accessories for their big day. Others cleaned their cabins to compete in weekly prizes.

I really enjoyed graduations—or completion ceremonies as they were officially known. They were always upbeat and seemed to encapsulate the sentiment of a former director who said that Acton is like a small village where the sick find health and the miserable find hope.

On graduation days, hope permeated the center. The ceremony held immediately after Patty and Eddie arrived was especially interesting to me because I had gotten to know some of the newcomers along with one person who was graduating.

I had met Danika soon after I arrived at Acton. She and Tiffany had approached me, wanting to know who I was and what I was doing. After I told them, they asked if they could help. By then I was overwhelmed by the number of residents who were eager to talk to me and wanted to "be in the book." Although I enjoyed listening to each person's story, I didn't have time to talk to everyone and had decided only to follow the few people that I first encountered during their admission process. But Danika and Tiffany seemed more lively and interesting than many of the others, so I broke my self-imposed rule and said I would interview them. Tiffany had just entered Acton, which meant that I was able to follow her throughout most of her journey. I was only able to talk to Danika that week, near the end of her stay.

During the one time that we spoke at length, we sat at a picnic table in an area usually considered out of bounds to residents. The air was pristine. The sun was blazing in a brilliant azure sky. A distant hill dotted with scrub brush and topped with four trees rose an additional 1,000 feet beyond our 2,620 foot elevation. Danika was drinking from a soda can and eating Cheetos. Her long, bleached-blonde hair swayed as she softly called to a blue jay in a nearby tree, her tongue ring softly clicking against her teeth.

"In the morning," she told me, "I say hi to all creatures when I take my meditation walk."

The blue jay cocked its ear and then flew directly to the table. Danika's eyes, brown with blue contacts, danced in delight as she held out a Cheeto. The bird snatched it from her fingers, dipped its head, as if in gratitude, and soared back to its branch. Danika's gentle laugh tinkled into the atmosphere.

Her laugh was pure and musical, as if in defiance of all the dark things that she began to tell me. "My father abused me, he abused my mother and sisters. I left home three days after my eighteenth birthday. My sisters were taken by child protective services and I wondered, 'What about me?' My sisters got help and they're totally normies, got married, et cetera. I have had little contact with my family. My parents divorced and I missed my mother's remarriage. I haven't seen my father. He denies what he did. He molested me when I was young and stopped when I was almost five. It was just touching, but later there was physical, emotional, and mental abuse.

"I drank at age three. Family members at Christmas parties gave me drinks. They all laughed . . . At eighteen, I was an alcoholic . . . I went to college for three years, doing business and accounting, then nursing and then I decided that sick people drove me nuts."

Soon after that, life changed dramatically for Danika.

"I was caught shoplifting. The man who caught me offered forty dollars for a blow job. I asked if he had a condom. I dropped out of college and became a prostitute and drug addict. I was living with a guy and his wife, supporting them and my husband . . . I don't want to support anyone . . . I went from prostitution to being a call girl to stripper. I do adult movies. I was slamming speed and weighed eighty-nine pounds. I thought I looked great. I was losing a cohesive grip with reality. I was really out there.

"I was making an average of five thousand dollars per movie and on weekends I went to Las Vegas to perform at bachelor parties. I would come home and have free time, so I used. When I had a bad experience on the set or didn't feel like I measured up, I used . . . My lifestyle spoiled me. There was always more."

For Danika, it was more alcohol, more speed, more crack. She took a deep breath and slowly exhaled. "This is my sixth program, my second time in Acton. The first time I was sent by the court I completed, but no one helped me after I left. This time, I checked myself in here. The difference now is that I have a sponsor and I'm really doing the work.

"Acton was a great eye-opener," she said, leaning forward to emphasize her point. "People thought I was spoiled, not realizing that I work hard for what I get." Nor did others realize that there had been times that she ate little to retain the figure she needed for work. Spoiled or not, well-fed or not, Danika knew that she didn't want to live like most of the people who came to Acton. "I'm not better than them, but see a vicious cycle and I don't want to be sucked into it . . . It's awful. I've made friends and seen them screw up. It's not the way I want to live.

"I'm going to UCLA extension to become a licensed therapist so I can work with kids. I decided that here. I asked God, my Higher Power . . . I want to serve Him and others . . . I want to serve women and children. Because bad things happened to me, I have a good idea of what it's like . . . I read about success: if you can make a difference in one person's life, that's success." Of course she'd go to a sober-living home, a group house inhabited by addicts serious about recovery, and work, really work with her sponsor.

"I'm facing myself in a real way, but I know that when I leave Acton, that's when things will get real. When I leave, I'll do Internet stuff and get $3,000. It's a safe environment. I'll relax and work on Step Four. It will be out in the middle of the desert. They spoil us there. I'll work from ten to eleven, doing a tease. At one and four, I'll chat. Seven to ten is the main show. My husband is going to help me do it. There won't be just toys and stuff."

She rationalized the gig by telling herself that it would give her money for a sober-living place. She figured that if she were frugal she could live off the money for six weeks. She said that she might do more Internet shows or movies, but she also knew that movies "could lead me back out." Internet porn seemed safer.

Danika glanced at my watch, asked what time it was, then told me she wanted to pick up her mail. I walked with her.

"I'll be twenty-nine tomorrow," she said. "I wasted my twenties loaded. I don't like getting older. Life is passing faster and faster. I don't want to look up and be fifty and see life has passed by me."

Several people stood in a ragged line outside the door of the dirty white building that served as the mail dispensing room. They were chattering about letters or packages they hoped to get. When Danika reached the front, she received five envelopes. The first was a birthday card from an FBI agent. "I picked him up as a trick two years ago.

Last summer I said I wouldn't sleep with him and he began stalking me. He constantly called me, showed up on my boat. He has a wife and children. Now he writes me and showed up here on a non-visiting day."

She shuffled that card to the back and opened envelopes from friends while saving her husband's for later. Danika then insisted on leading me to her dorm to say hello to someone. On the way, she said, "I had a Christian baptism while here. I'm getting committed, washing my sins away."

"What sins?" I asked.

"Using, cheating on my husband, flirting with other men, robbing, stealing, hurting people, prostitution, dreaming of having sex with the devil."

Danika's area of the dorm was a tribute to her commitment to changing her life. There were several self-help books, the Big Book, a Narcotics Anonymous text, and a Bible. Dried flowers poked out of one of the iron bedposts. She pointed to the small dream catcher at the head of her bed. "I thought it would help with my nightmares . . . It doesn't."

She picked up a small stuffed bunny. "My mother got Bun Bun before I was born and put him against her stomach. He played a lullaby originally, but needed heart surgery when I was tweaking. I had to be out of the room when they removed the old music box and put in a new one. He pulled through . . . He's always been my faithful friend."

Her sweet laugh echoed through the room and then died.

"I would wind him up after a beating, curl in a ball, hide in my room, and he would soothe me."

———

For the completion ceremony, held soon after my afternoon with Danika, an outdoor auditorium had been set up near the canteen, a structure once used to sell snacks and personal items. I sat in the middle of a row of folding chairs, trying to avoid the smoke from numerous cigarettes held by residents sitting or standing between the canteen and the string of nearby cabins. The wind rustled through the trees, but the summer heat remained stifling. A nearby air conditioner purred.

Most of the residents appeared to be present, lolling on the grass, perching on chairs facing the podium, leaning against trees, or parked on fence posts. Mr. Clark, the Acton administrator, stood at his weekly spot to the side of the podium. Also in the audience were groups of families or supporters of those finishing the program at Acton. Many of their bodies seemed tense with worry for their loved ones. No doubt they were hoping that the program had succeeded, that this would be the last time drugs shadowed their lives, that this would be the breakthrough allowing them to have their child, parent, lover, or friend back. Danika's mother and stepfather were present, sitting on a bench under a tree.

Newcomers sat at the front. Danika and the other graduates faced the audience. As befitting a formal ceremony, the graduates were dressed up in an attempt to set them apart from their usual scraggly appearances and to exhibit the solemnity of the occasion and their pride in making it through the Acton program. The California state flag, topped by the U.S. flag, blew in the background.

The ceremony began with introductions. Members of the Acton Center Resident Counsel stood to be recognized: the secretary, mail committee, welcoming committee. Next, the newcomers, who had been arranged in the front rows near the outside guests, were asked to stand and introduce themselves. They did so in quick succession.

"My name is Patty. I'm an alcoholic-addict."

"Matt, addict."

"My name is Harold. I suffer from multiple addictions."

While the others were introducing themselves, Eddie stayed seated, unwilling to talk in public.

The Cabin of the Week was awarded to the cleanest cabin. This weekly competition was a serious affair. The larger dorms, those occupied by the women and the "old-timer" men's dorm, were not as involved, but the men living in the cabins took pride in fixing up their dwellings. Some men tried to keep their space neat on a daily basis, but Friday mornings were the time of the real work. Not only was the inside scrubbed, with cleaning agents and mops from housekeeping, but many men spent hours outside their cabins designing elaborate dirt or rock gardens.

The next award went to the Female of the Week, a woman "faithful to Bible study every week. She's come a long way!" The Male of the Week award went to a man who "goes the extra mile in giving to others."

The crowd offered enthusiastic support for each of the winners.

Danika had been selected to do the traditional reading of the Twelve Steps. She moved to the podium, looking soft and vulnerable in a black dress suited more to a ballroom than to a dusty desert setting. Her extremely high heels made her look thin and waif-like. Her hair was swept up in a sophisticated coiffure, held together by sparkling pins shaped like stars and butterflies. A choker and sunglasses completed her wardrobe.

As Danika started to recite the Twelve Steps, someone from the back yelled, "Who are you?"

"My name is Danika and I'm an addict in recovery until the day I die." She then recited Step One. The crowd yelled, "TWO!" Danika recited Step Two and the crowd erupted in a "THREE!" and so on.

When she finished the twelfth step, Danika sat down. The male resident sitting next to me said, "She made it. That's great."

The first completer approached the podium. A trans-sexual, Jeri had had a difficult time at Acton. But that day he stood proud. His long hair flowed freely over a dark blue, Kung Fu-type jacket. He leaned toward the podium. "Hi, I'm Jeri and I'm an addict. Thanks to God. Thanks to a good friend, my counselor, and dorm members, and . . . that's about it."

The following completer said, "I've heard this is the best recovery center in the state and I believe it. I'm glad I was one of the chosen few to be here. Some of us used so many drugs in one day we're surprised that we didn't have a heart attack or stroke. We are among the chosen few."

The nearby air conditioner gasped off.

Tiffany sat on the porch of Z dorm with three other residents. As Danika glided back to the lectern, Tiffany leaned forward.

Danika placed her speech on the podium and began to read it. "Hi. I'm Danika and I'm an addict-alcoholic. Until the day I die I'm in recovery. Thanks for the second chance. The man who started this program is Dr. Richard Rioux. He had a dream of a million people marching in recovery. Let's give a moment of silence for Dr. Richard Rioux."

Richard Rioux had not started the program at Acton, but he was an influential administrator who had recently died. Although Danika had never met him, many of the counselors knew him well and some considered him their mentor.

Danika continued. "Thanks to a higher power in God and chaplains. Thanks to counselors David and Cassandra—they brought sanity to the world. And to Mike who made me get real. A shout-out to L dorm. To dear friends, those who have gone home, and STUART who *will* make it. My sponsor who cares."

She paused for a moment and looked at her mother. "Mom, I love you. Thank you for trusting me again. I will always be your little Sue Sue. To my grandmother who has eleven years sober at seventy-five. If she can do it, you can do it."

Danika turned to the newcomers. "Learn the Twelve Steps. Remember this is a threefold disease of the body, mind, and spirit. You will be amazed at what you learn without realizing it . . . I want something better. I have begun to love myself . . . one day at a time. I wrote this poem back in my addiction. It shows that I wanted something better." Danika read from a poem that she titled "Reflection of Life":

Looking into the eyes of the reflection
Into the soul of a mirror image
 A copy? or
 A clone?
Can it be equal if it is the counter balance?
Can it be the same if it is the opposite?

Or just the revealing of another facet
Or the other opposite the complete self?
Conscious and unconscious

When the self,
Freed from the limits of limiting awareness gains
 mind
 soul
 emotion
In union as well as only a stepping stone
To the existence beyond current reality
And its confines achieving finally
The ultimate destination of purpose
In the copied reflection of the mirror image we call
LIFE

Danika ended with a soft, "Thank you." She quickly sat down and lit a cigarette.

The man sitting next to me said, "I wish her well, but I don't see how she'll be able to move on. I've seen her movies. They're B grade and they'll haunt her the rest of her life. She'll never be able to pretend that she's not a porno star."

The next graduate sang "Amazing Grace" without accompaniment. The sweet sounds of the song filled the air. Mr. Clark bowed his head. Some people were tittering as the singer belted out, "I was lost, Lord, but now I'm found." People began cheering, but the singer continued with the next verse. By then, one or two people were chiming in. Finally, the words tailed off and he said, "I can't continue."

"Please don't," muttered one person near me.

Soon the graduates introduced their visitors, the friends and family members who had patiently listened to the upbeat speeches. Next, a few Acton alumni spoke. One said, "Acton is a wonderful place. It gave me humility and turned out to be a pilgrimage. If you're new and you're shaking in your boots, like I was, just hang in there. It does get better. Keep it simple."

Another alumnus said, "I came back to see my family. This is where I got my start nineteen months ago. Acton gave me a foundation. I was so bad when I got here that I had women's pants on and didn't know it until four days later."

Mr. Clark was the last speaker. He stood confidently at the podium and expressed how proud he was of the good that Acton did, proud of the graduates, and hopeful that they would go out in the world and come back as successful alumni. "For visitors and the alumni," he said, "you are the example of the best we have. So give it up for the alumni and counselors."

At the end of the ceremony, Danika pulled her mother and stepfather toward Mr. Clark and waited amidst a knot of graduates anxious for their families to meet the Acton administrator. Afterward, she shepherded her parents toward me, introduced us, and we headed toward a picnic table, near the spot where the blue jay had shared Danika's food.

Danika started talking to her mother. "Acton has helped me get into the body, mind, and spirit thing. I realized the problem isn't drugs and alcohol. It's about changing behavior. Drugs and alcohol were just symptoms of my disease. When I was hurt or angry, I would use. I'd use manipulative behavior . . . The way I dressed . . . I was seeking validation by men. Or from other women by asking them if my outfit was cute. All those things lowered my self-worth. Drugs were to hide the pain. Now, my eyes are opened."

Her mother asked, "How long have you been here?"

"I'm only doing ninety days. I have bills and no money for one hundred and twenty. I need to get out."

Danika's mother began speaking to me. "When drugs came into her life, she completely slipped away from the family. I didn't know how or where to find her. Or if she was alive or dead. I resolved myself to assume that she was going to die. I only knew that she was in L.A. I would hear from her every two or three years and she got worse after a number of years. We had to prepare ourselves . . . No one wants to say that my toddler is going to be a prostitute and drug addict."

"They know I'm glad to have them back," Danika said to me.

I felt like an intermediary and wondered if they would be having the same conversation without the presence of a third person.

Her mother was looking at me. "We're grateful. This time she means it. This time she wants it."

The graduation had ended on a high note. Danika, like many others, had reconciled with estranged family members and was excited to move on with her new life. She once again had hope for a better life. Despite that hope, despite Danika's renewed relationship with her mother and her mother's cautious optimism, the words of the man sitting next to me echoed in my mind, that Danika's adult movie career would "haunt her for the rest of her life." I really hoped that wasn't true. I wanted to believe in Danika, in her future, and a bright future for all those graduating.

PHASE I

4

ORIENTATION

Rico stood at the blackboard, chalking the phrase, *To recover from a seemingly hopeless state of mind, body, and spirit.*

Eddie was among the first new residents to arrive at the bi-weekly orientation. As usual, he wore a Clare Foundation T-shirt, this time accompanied by sunglasses and a green baseball cap pulled tightly over his short-cropped salt-and-pepper hair. The naked women tattooed on his arms slid out of sight when he sat down and pulled his chair to the table, one of many pushed to the center of the room.

It was day three of Eddie's stay at Acton. He didn't like the center any better than he did his first day. He still missed the city. He was a smog kind of guy and nature could not compete with noise, ambulances, and cops. In fact, the emptiness of the land made him feel even lonelier.

Eddie was not new to feelings of powerlessness. Only two months previously he had experienced the same thing during a one-time lock-down at the Clare Foundation.

He had used that time to write about how his serenity had been replaced by the feeling of helplessness. He had reaffirmed to himself that being powerless over people, places, and things had to play a big part in his recovery. In fact, being locked down helped him focus more on the seriousness of his disease. Eddie knew he could not "run his show" any longer. He understood that he had to let his Higher Power illuminate his path. And he truly believed that the Twelve Steps along with God's will had to be the way to go. Eddie had thanked God for the Clare Foundation, believing that it and the Twelve Step program had given him the opportunity to get his life back together.

But that was two months ago and now where was he? The high hopes that the Clare staff had expressed for him were gone, dashed by his one-day relapse. Even though Eddie was grateful to Clare for giving him the chance to recover, he was angry that the staff had laid so much responsibility on him. He had felt burdened when he was asked to supervise his fellow residents. To Eddie, it was snitching. The others resented him for it and Eddie hated that. He yearned to be liked and could not stand being an outcast. Eddie was not exactly sure why he'd screwed up this last time, but he placed some of the blame on the pressures of excessive responsibility and expectations.

Other new residents wandered in and found seats. Although newcomers, they understood the Acton rules dictating that men and women sit on opposite sides of the room; by the time Rico finished writing, there were distinct men and women's sections.

Rico turned to the residents. "Welcome to the University of Acton. How you doing this morning?"

A few people mumbled a reply.

"Good. All right. My name is Rico and I'm going to be with you for a few minutes this morning, going over your mission, orientation, and objective to achieve a healthy body, mind, and spirit. Real briefly, let's introduce ourselves."

One by one the fourteen men and five women reeled off their first names. Rico occasionally repeated a name, trying to memorize both the face and name.

After the introductions concluded, Rico said, "I'd like to welcome you all to the University of Acton. I hope your stay here is positive, productive, and you have a lot of free time. This morning we're going to go over a few rules and regulations, policies, and procedures, a quick little overview of the Twelve Step process." With increasing speed, he said, "I'm from Spanish Harlem in New York and when I talk I talk at two speeds: fast and faster, so hold onto your seats and get ready for a ride."

The door opened and a man stepped inside, the stench of tobacco smoke preceding him.

"Just coming to a meeting of Smokers Anonymous?" Rico asked. "Come on in. How you doing this morning, sir?"

"Good."

"What's your name?"

"Tyler."

"I'm glad you're here. Can we begin now?"

"Oh, sure."

"Thank you for sharing. Keep coming back. Be on time. How many people here have been in recovery before?"

Almost everyone raised a hand.

"How many people have never, ever been exposed to the Twelve Step process in their life?"

Five hands popped in the air.

"That's not bad. For those of you who have never been in a Twelve Step program before, I'd like to welcome you to the Twelve Step process and tell you it works and it works real well. For those of you who have been fortunate enough to make it back to the Twelve Step process, I'd like to welcome you back to the Twelve Step process.

"Okay, the first thing we want to talk about is drop offs. Before you came here people told you about what to bring, what not to bring. There are no drop offs. This is a treatment center. No one can just drive up here and say Susan forgot something and I need to drop it off. If you forgot something or need to have something sent to you, you need to have it mailed up to you, shipped up to you, Pony Express, express mail, whatever kind of way you can get it up here without another body coming up here and giving it to you. There are no drop offs, all right? Most of you have been here at least twenty-four hours or more so whatever it is, you won't die without it. If it's important to you, write, call, get them to send it up here. Nobody drives up. If you get caught with an unauthorized drop off, tell them don't leave too quick 'cause you're going to need a ride out of here."

"Air mail?" asked one smart ass.

"If the plane can land here, tell them to come on down," Rico replied. "But you best let us know in advance he's coming so we can move."

Several residents laughed. Rico had their attention. The orientation wasn't just a boring rendition of the rules and Rico's energy was contagious.

Eddie, though, was immune. Laughing would reveal his missing teeth. Besides, he was serious about recovery and didn't need amusing diversions. Plus, he knew about the Twelve Steps. And no one was going to be making any drop offs for him.

"All right. Bed moves and bed changes. Ladies and gentlemen, we track you by your name and your bed number. If someone in your cabin or your dorm moves out," Rico's voice started picking up speed, "and they're either closer to the heater, away from the heater, closer to the door, away from the door, closer to your friend, further away from your friend, you want to be with your homie, your cellie, your homeboy, your homegirl, and all that other good stuff, forget it. The bed that you're in, for the most part is the bed that you're going to be in. You're not here to marry Acton. You're just passing through. This is a very short stop on your life's journey so you just want to make do. Please do not play musical beds 'cause when you play musical beds and we do our bed checks and we find out you're not there we're going to discharge you and you're going to show up at our office and say 'Why did you discharge me? I'm here.' And then we gonna discharge you again. So please stay in your bed. And your bed only."

Raucous laughter erupted.

"One of the most famous topics amongst most alcoholics and addicts—"

"Sex," said one man.

"No, not you. I said most." Laughter filled the room. "It's cash. Cash money. Everybody that's in this treatment center is not here for recovery, okay? Let me say it again: Everybody in this treatment center is not here for recovery.

I don't know what you're here for. I just met you. I don't know if you know what you're here for. The good news is it doesn't matter what you're here for. What matters is what you do while you're here. It's a program of action, not a program of thinking or a program of feeling. This is about what you do, not about what you say or your philosophical overview or where you come from or where you think you're going. This is about what you do. One day at time we try to do the right thing and we find out that over time we change.

"Be that as it may, if you still have some people out there who want to speak to you and you're lucky and they want to love you to death and want to mail you some money, tell them: do not send cash. If they want to send you money they should send it in the form of a U.S. postal money order or cashier's check. Okay? If you're really in doubt, just have all the checks mailed to me and I'll go to lunch and think about you."

Many residents laughed.

"Have most of you seen the doctor? Yes? Okay, if you have not seen the doctor, there is something in the packet that says: I understand that I am not to participate in any sports activities, baseball, weight room, tennis, horseshoes, volleyball, golf, et cetera until I have been seen by the center physician and medically cleared to participate. Okay? Make sure you see the doctor before you join Weightaholics Anonymous or Track Anonymous or whatever else you want to do. All right?

"The Antelope Valley Rehabilitation Centers used to consist of four centers: Acton, Warm Springs, Mira Loma, and High Desert. At High Desert we have an outpatient program now. Mira Loma is no longer used for treatment. The two centers left for residential programs are Acton and Warm Springs. Warm Springs is an all-male center located thirteen miles up in the hills of Castaic. It's a very beautiful, rustic area. I love Warm Springs. And personally I like working with the men 'cause when you work with the men you get right to causes and conditions. When you factor women into the equation, sometimes with you guys' ego and false pride all of a sudden you can't hear anymore. I don't know what it is. Some kind of a mystical thing must take place with you guys."

Eddie understood what Rico meant. The back of his father's hand had taught him to watch his language in front of women, but nothing had taught him how to keep his wits about the other sex. The only sustained relationship he'd had in recent years had prompted him to blow all his money on silly things—like a day at the Santa Monica pier to please his girlfriend and her young daughter. Eddie enjoyed the outing, too, since it was a chance to recapture his youth, the only happy days he remembered. But at the same time Eddie felt silly for losing his common sense, and cash, over a woman, especially since she had relapsed and dragged him down, too. In any case, Eddie wasn't looking for a relationship at Acton.

"Anyway," continued Rico, "because this is a co-ed set-up we have a Social Interaction Policy. A Social Interaction Policy is basically about balance. One thing alcoholics and addicts have the most difficult time with is balance. We either do all of this and none of that or not a bit of this and all of that. We don't know how to put balance into our lives. This whole Twelve Step process is about balance. It's about getting to that place where the perfect peace exists between the yin and the yang. It's a place in here," Rico pointed to his chest, "where perfect peace exists. No one ever gets there. But the awakening comes with the journey."

As Rico continued, he mixed street-speak with good grammar, sometimes omitting verbs and usually pronouncing "with" as "which."

"Social Interaction Policy says we want balance. If we wanted you not to talk to men and not to talk to women and not to look at each other we'd have an all-male and an all-female program. You're adults and we know you gonna do that. What we're asking you to do is put some balance on it. You know: don't make her your Higher Power. Don't make him your Higher Power.

"I would like the women not to ever be lurking around the men's dorms. I don't care if you stop for a cigarette, a light, or whatever. Your crime is location. Conversely, men do *not* be in front of the women's dorms. Don't tell me: 'I came from Alcoholics Anonymous, Cocaine Anonymous, we're talking about Welcoming Committee stuff, we're doing this, we're doing that.' I'm not interested in your business. I'm interested in where your body is located. The woman you coming to see in that cabin or dorm or whatever may be very fine with you coming to see her. There may be twenty-three other women in there who because of past experiences are not ready for men to be hovering around the dorm and women do deserve the right to recover and we gonna give them that right. Okay? So don't hang around each other's cabins. That's one of my pet peeves. Guys in front of women's dorms. It's just so tacky. Okay? Let 'em breathe, gentlemen, let 'em breathe."

Rico pointed to the blackboard. "There's our mission statement right behind us: 'To recover from a seemingly hopeless state of mind, body, and spirit.' There's people who are begging. Their mothers are calling, their fathers, their lovers, their friends, begging, 'Please let 'em in here, he's dying.' Yet you guys are out here in the circle, playing games. If you don't want to be here and you want to play, there's a lot of other things. This is for people who want recovery, all right?"

He read from one of a stack of packets in front of him, the words spilling out of his mouth faster and faster. "Physical contact or displays of affections are not allowed between any residents and will result in discharge. This includes holding hands, embracing, caressing, kissing, touching, and sexual relations. We are not here to judge you. If those are the things you want to engage in, I don't have anything against them. I just ask that you please leave, go do it somewhere else, and then let somebody else who wants recovery come in and have a crack at this thing called life. Okay?

"It's about balance, ladies and gentlemen: Social Interaction Policy. A lot of people lose their program over Social Interaction. They call it SIP. Don't lose your program over SIP."

He switched subjects. "Visitor's policy. If you're lucky enough to be here sixty days and nights, you're 'entitled' to a visit. And I say entitled in quotes because that means you're entitled to one, but that doesn't mean you're going to get one. Put in a request with your counselor and he or she will either grant you or deny you a visit. It will be based on how you've been programming up to the sixty-day point."

Rico moved on. "Locks. We asked everybody to bring a lock since not everyone is here for recovery and some people still have that stick-em on their hands. The other thing is if you loan something to an alcoholic or addict be prepared not to get it back. Don't let anybody rob you of your serenity. Alcoholics and addicts are probably the world's greatest people pleasers, they want to be loved, liked, accepted, and will go to every length to get that. If you loan somebody something let it be because you can afford to be without it. You loan somebody your jacket in the middle of the night and you wake up in the morning and find out that person's been kicked out of the program and they gone and you come crying to me." Rico switched to a whiney voice. "'Rico, they took my jacket.'" Without a pause, Rico returned to his normal intonation. "And I'll say, 'No, dude, you gave it to them.' We're not advocating don't share, but take care of yourself first.

"Review forms. Consent to be tested for substance abuse. If a staff member asks you to test, you must test. They do random tests here. They call you in and ask you to go. And you have to go within a two-hour period. That's if *they* test you. If *I* test you, you need to go within an hour. Doesn't matter if you're clean, dirty, or indifferent, you gotta test. If you don't test you have to leave the program."

Rico announced that he was not going to read the whole package of documents in front of him, just highlight some things. He explained that all residents would be provided with a photo ID that they were required to wear at all times. Weapons were banned. "Anything that's in your area that is perceived as a weapon, you'll leave this program quick, fast, and in a hurry, okay? That includes a sharpened toothbrush, broken mirror, golf club, cane, broken glass, anything. One of your commitments of living here is that you gotta keep your area neat and clean so if someone puts something in your area that doesn't belong there, you gotta go. If it's in your area, it's yours.

"Dental care. There is no dental care except emergency dental care. If you have an emergency, all they gonna do is take you to L.A. County-USC, and the only thing they're going to do there is extractions. So if you want your teeth don't go to L.A. County-USC."

Others laughed, but Eddie looked even more glum. His real teeth had been destroyed during a bad drug deal in a bar when a bullet had shattered his teeth and split his lip. He had spit four teeth and a bullet onto the bar as blood pumped out of his lip with every heartbeat. The only positive thing to come out of that incident was that it led him to the Clare Foundation where he finally kicked heroin. His recent loss of dentures pushed him away from Clare and to Acton. And more and more it was beginning to look as though Acton was not the place for him.

He was deeply disappointed about the lack of both dental and medical care. He desperately wanted a new pair of dentures and he also needed to get his foot fixed. His first foot injury had occurred during a volleyball game. He had been playing barefoot and jumped for a killer shot. When he slammed to the ground he heard his foot crack. It healed poorly, but was even more severely injured during another barroom fight. Eddie had been wasted on reds. A man called him out after they bumped shoulders. The other guy swung and missed as Eddie twisted out of the way. Eddie's ankle gave way and he fell to the ground.

His opponent took that opportunity to smash his ankle with a tire iron. Eddie had had enough stamina to drive himself to the emergency room. Doctors put pins into his foot, but somehow the ankle had not healed properly and Eddie was often in pain.

Rico was saying, "We want you to work on you. It's not that we don't trust you, it's that we don't trust you trusting you."

One person laughed, but Eddie found Rico's words too true to be funny. Eddie did not trust himself. He had lost all confidence in his ability to live without supervision. Relapse was just too easy.

At the second orientation of the week, Deborah took a seat along a side wall midway between the door and Rico. It was a strategic choice; from her vantage point she could view Rico easily, but was not in his direct line of sight. Although she was wearing what she called her "hooker skirt," Deborah's attire was subdued, almost school girlish. The pleated skirt would have allowed easy access to men if she had been back in MacArthur Park, but at Acton it and her demur accessories—white cotton shirt, white running shoes, and turned-down socks—aided her effort to blend in with the others. Deborah intended to study Acton and its inhabitants so she could learn how to fit in. To do that she thought she had to be invisible and keep her thoughts to herself, something not natural to her blunt and gregarious personality.

Rico welcomed the group and announced that two Acton residents about to complete their programs were re-visiting orientation to remember where they came from. The two men, both standing near the back of the room, quickly introduced themselves and told the new group to pay attention because Rico's words were wise.

A male resident slipped into the room and took a seat by the door, trying to avoid notice. Rico smiled at him and asked, "You plan on wearing a skirt today? No? Then that's not your seat." The man slunk to the men's side of the room.

As soon as Rico began to speak about recovery, Tex, a wild-haired man wearing a stained orange vest, piped up, saying with great disdain, "What do you know about it?" Tex stared across the table, as if it was a wide gulf, separating not just their physical selves, which appeared disparate enough since Rico was impeccably dressed, but their entire beings.

Rico did not pause. "The way I look today, nothing. The way I used to look, everything. Move those cigarettes off the table and remove those glasses, please. You're ruining my serenity."

Five of the Twin Tower women thronged into the room and perched on chairs along the windowed wall. Four of them quickly melted into the room. Marisa stood out, looking like she stepped out of a 1950s television set: she wore both the black and white clothes—a slinky white blouse, black pants, white socks, and black patent leather shoes—and a prim, self-conscious attitude. Knowing people were watching, she began peeling an orange, her eyes concentrating on the fruit, but her ears attuned to the room.

As the orange's fragrance began to permeate the air, Rico resumed his presentation. "When you finish this program—"

"Show me what finish is," Tex interrupted.

"I will when your lips stop moving," Rico replied.

"But I want to stop using and you're talking about finishing."

"Sir, I don't think you want to stop using. Your lips are saying you do. Your behavior is saying you don't. Sit up, please."

Tex reluctantly straightened his spine.

"I want to talk about balance," Rico began again.

Tex nodded. "Balance is what it is all about."

"Not *all* about. But in the beginning, balance is important."

"It's what I want," Tex said.

"That's what your lips say, but I'll be watching you."

"And I'll be watching you."

"That's a good thing."

Rico covered the same material as the previous orientation and then moved on. "For those of you who get to know me, I'll treat you with dignity and respect, too, but I'm one of the firm believers in tough love. I will tell you the truth about you, your behavior, your attitude. Generally when I bring you to that point of enlightenment, you don't like me. And I'd much rather you hate me and we come to a seemingly healthy body, mind, and spirit one day at a time than you die as a direct result of you practicing this disease. I'm interested in whether you live or whether you die. I'm not interested in whether you like me or you like what I say. Hopefully through our interactions you will be able to look at you. Hopefully our staff is a mirror because you're not going to change until you see you.

"We're going to show you how to change the problem one day at a time, if you're open-minded. Somebody showed you how to roll that joint just right so you didn't have any creases in it, showed you how to fix that pipe so it pulled the smoke up just the right way—"

Laughter rattled the room.

"—showed you how to tie that thing around your arm, fix that rig. You listened attentively and you got results. You have to do recovery the same way. You have to listen attentively, do what we do, and you gonna get results. You had sponsors before, just the wrong kind of sponsors. You want to get a different kind, the kind who will enrich the quality of your life. If you're just here not to drink and not to use, you're wasting your time. What we want to do is change our behavior one day at a time. So there's some actions you need to take."

While many of the others paid rapt attention, Deborah shrank into her chair. She didn't like Rico's challenging tone and hated the thought that he or the others at Acton would expect her to change.

Rico continued. "Statistics say that in a room this size—there's maybe twenty people here—one or two of us will be clean and sober this time next year. This time next year, one of us will be clean and sober. Maybe two. That's going to make it rough on you guys because one of them is going to be me."

Everyone became very still.

"It's not because I have more time than you or I'm any better than you. It's because I am willing to do what*ever* it takes for me to stay clean. I am willing to do whatever it takes for me never to have to live underneath that

Dumpster from whence I came. I am willing to do *whatever* it takes to go to bed tonight and not be loaded. Whatever it is. And when you get to that place you too can be clean. Now, that's what statistics say. *I say*: every man and woman in this room can be clean this time next year.

"You need to get a commitment, get a sponsor, you need to take all twelve of the steps in the order that they are written in. You need to reach back and help another individual. These steps are designed to help us. There was no way in the world for me to get from underneath a Dumpster and sit at this table without genuine love and concern from men and women that I'd never seen in my life." Rico's voice lowered; it was almost inaudible. "One day at a time.

"Nothing magical. Nothing mystical. You don't have to walk on water. You don't have to quote Genesis, Revelation, chapter and verse, backwards and forwards. You don't have to go to church every day. You don't have to go to a mountaintop and meditate thirty hours until you reach nirvana. It's real simple: take these Twelve Steps and your life will change. I've never seen anybody take these Twelve Steps and their life didn't get better.

"Some of us will have to keep having the same experience over and over again until we go to the penitentiary, die, or just keep coming back to these programs. Whatever your experience has to be, I guess it's gonna have to wake you up. But if you lived under a Dumpster as long as I did, I don't know how much more wake-up you're gonna need. The only time I got up out of that Dumpster was to rob you or shoot up."

Tex interrupted. "Were you shooting heroin?"

"No, I was shooting baby formula."

Tex adopted a wounded look. "I just want to know."

"I was shooting heroin and cocaine, if you must know."

"I just wanted to know where you're coming from."

"It doesn't matter where I'm coming from. It matters where you're coming from," Rico said.

"I just wanted to know because if you can do it, I can do it."

"Anybody can recover. If they're willing to do whatever it takes."

"My mouth says I am."

"Your mouth says a lot of things, but you still here."

"I'm trying," Tex said.

"My sponsor always says trying is lying." Rico paused, his eyes burning into Tex. "You probably going to wind up my best friend and you don't even know it."

Rico glanced at the sheaf of papers on the table. "Personal hygiene. Please take a shower every day, okay? Don't be walking around here like you're a member of Tweakers Anonymous."

Chuckles floated through the room. The new residents understood that tweakers, methamphetamine users, talked fast and obsessively, started several projects at a time but rarely finished anything.

"If you don't have clean clothes, we will give you clean clothes. They may not be Gucci or GQ, but they will be clean. Don't walk around here ungroomed, unkempt. We're in recovery. We're walking toward the light, walking away from darkness. There's no reason you can't take a shower and wear clean clothes every day."

"Or you'll look like you're still using," interjected a male resident.

"I'm glad you said that," Rico replied. "When we go into cabins and do a cabin check, make it look like there's some recovering people living there. Don't make it look like somebody's been in a rock house for two weeks and didn't find their way out—"

The residents cackled.

"—stuff thrown every which way but right. In early recovery you need discipline, systems, and direction and that's all we're here for. We're not God. We don't walk on water. We're just here to give you some grounds on which to build the foundation. You have to do the rest."

Rico turned to a new subject. "The Big Book of Alcoholics Anonymous and Narcotics Anonymous talk about a Higher Power of your understanding. The Big Book of Alcoholics Anonymous in its chapter to agnostics states that deep down inside, every man, woman, and child has a fundamental idea of God or Higher Power. It says that it may be rocked by calamity, which are problems that we all have, it may be rocked by pompousness, which is ego we all have, it may be rocked by worshiping people, places, or things. Surely we have worshiped people, places, things. *We* have worshiped crystal meth, heroin, cocaine, alcohol, sick relationships, we have worshiped all kinds of things, most of the things that block us from us. It doesn't matter what your views are, where you're coming from, where you're going, what you believe in, it doesn't matter whether you're agnostic, atheist, it doesn't matter. For this program to work, you don't have to believe in *anything*. All you need to know is that there is something out there that makes the sun rise and sun set and that something is not you. I came into this program with no Higher Power, no

God, didn't want to be bothered with God, any kind of idea
of a Higher Power—"

A loud sneeze echoed through the room.

Without pausing or noting the irony of his words, Rico
continued. "God bless you—because of the way I lived my
life, I knew He didn't want to be bothered with me so why
should I be bothered with Him? I was angry, I was hostile, and anybody even looked at me and looked like they
wanted to talk about God, I was going to hurt him. And so
I came to recovery and they told me the same thing: 'Rico,
all you need to know is that you're not the center of the
universe and there's something out there that makes that
sun rise and that sun set. Take these Twelve Steps, apply
them to your life and when you're finished, you will have
some sort of concept of a Higher Power.' And that's what
happened to me. This is a spiritual program, not a religious
program. Religion is for people who are afraid to go to hell.
Spirituality is for people who have already been there."

Many people laughed. Deborah shifted uncomfort-
ably in her seat. After a childhood of day-long Baptist services, she didn't want to hear about religion or spirituality
or a Higher Power or whatever. She dismissed religion as
bullshit and had no respect for people who succumbed to
it.

"Alcoholics and addicts," Rico continued, "have already
been to their own living hell so they don't need to worry
about going to hell. What we're talking about is: how do
I enrich the quality of my life? So don't let the God thing
turn you away from this program. I was one who got turned
off. My first meeting of Alcoholics Anonymous, a long,
long time ago, they sat around and said the Lord's Prayer

and I went out and got loaded for six more years because I thought I was in a cult. Don't let the God thing chase you away like it chased me away."

Deborah was frightened by Rico's words and intimidated by his life. She didn't want religion, recovery, AA, a Higher Power, or any of that bullshit. She had agreed to come to Acton and planned to go to an aftercare facility for one reason only: to convince the judge that she was a good girl so he would free her to return to her old life. But after listening to Rico, Deborah wasn't sure the stress of conforming for ninety days would be worth it. And she certainly didn't want Rico acting as a mirror and forcing her to look more closely at herself.

What Deborah didn't know was that Rico was a good mirror for her; they were much alike. Before descending into the world of drugs and debauchery, both had been to college; Deborah studied history and Rico had a degree in psychology. Both began, as do many addicts, by using drugs recreationally. Deborah had worked in the same engineering firm as her husband, a white Englishman who shared her enjoyment of cocaine. Every Friday night they joined four other couples in cocaine orgies and played games, the husbands against the wives, for blow jobs. Rico had used cocaine and marijuana while he was in his twenties, and later, when the stress of graduate school overwhelmed him, added Black Russians to his repertoire.

Both Deborah and Rico gave up middle-class lives for the streets. Deborah began her descent during the worst year of her life: her husband divorced her, then her father died; she wrangled with her family over her father's inheritance, spent her portion of the money, became depressed, took a medical leave from work, and lost everything when she went to jail for six months. Her jailhouse education included a course on prostitution, and after her release, Deborah plied her new profession with enthusiasm.

Rico's middle class life dwindled away piece by piece as drugs and alcohol became more important than school, women, or his job. After his connections to others were broken, he walked away from his life. Without knowing his destination, he left behind his three-bedroom house with den, furniture, and personal items. He never looked back. Instead, he began hustling drugs.

Another trait common to Rico and Deborah was their deliberate disentanglement from friends and family. Not only did Rico toss away his possessions, he also abandoned everyone he knew, vowing never to let his family see him in reduced circumstances. Deborah, who already had been disenchanted with her family, also decided to sever her ties with them.

Deborah and Rico's similarities included much time spent at MacArthur Park, a place that indirectly led both of them to Acton. Set against a brilliant Los Angeles sunrise, MacArthur Park can seem an idyllic oasis, its glittering man-made lake surrounded by greenery. But, in the unblinking harshness of midday or in the inky shadows of night, MacArthur Park is a scary place frequented by suspicious figures living on the margins of society and selling whatever they can for a few bucks or a hit of crack.

Rico used the park to buy and sell drugs, get high, and for eight months to sleep. The park became his living hell, it was where he finally hit bottom. By the time he dragged himself to a homeless shelter, his face was gray and shriveled, his hair matted after a two-year sabbatical from a comb. The homeless shelter became his springboard to Acton, where he learned the Twelve Steps and created his own future.

For Deborah, MacArthur Park was an exciting place. It was where she went to meet friends and johns. She laughingly called it "her office." The park was also the site of the arrest that had sent her to jail and eventually to Acton. Though she did not arrive at Acton looking for a change as Rico had, Deborah had come with the same skeptical wariness and fears about the program and her ability to fit in.

Deborah sat in the waiting room outside the Admissions Office. After class officially ended, she had told Rico she was intimidated by Acton and he suggested she come see him so he could "unintimidate" her. Although Deborah dutifully waited for him amidst a swirl of activity, she wasn't sure Rico could alleviate her anxiety. She found it frightening to be in a situation where she had to follow so many rules. Previously she answered to no one, which was exactly how she liked her life. As a hooker, it was good to be highly visible. At Acton, visibility would be detrimental. Previously, she had been able to flirt with anyone. But not Rico. Deborah was agitated by the thought that he would be watching her every move. She wanted to study Acton, its inhabitants, and staff members, not the reverse. She understood New Yorkers like Rico and knew he would be on her tail every minute. There was no way she could survive such close scrutiny.

She contemplated her dilemma for several minutes. Soon she began to calm down. Slowly it dawned on her that the situation at Acton couldn't be that bad. She had been through a lot in her life, and ninety days in rehab, even if it included a tough-love New Yorker, couldn't be that bad. It was simply one frustrating but necessary step between arrest and returning to her old life.

Deborah jumped to her feet.

The commotion in the Admissions Office was unceasing: people were getting their photos taken, others were trying to check in, and staffers and residents were darting from place to place. Rico was nowhere in sight. Deborah didn't care. She no longer felt the urge to speak to him, to try to win him over or, failing that, discover the secret of how to succeed at Acton without losing her self.

Deborah left the office, firmly closing the door behind her. She knew what to do. She had survived on the streets of Los Angeles. Surely she could take the pulse of Acton, learn the ways of the center, and find people to relate to. At least she knew they weren't all Twelve Step-God-will-save-you-Higher-Power freaks. In fact, she had already renewed her acquaintance with one person from the street, an ex-lawyer who had been kind enough to give her a few dollars. Based on that chance meeting, she surmised that there must be others like her, others willing to play the Acton game, but not compromise themselves. Deborah didn't have to use Rico or anyone else as a mirror, or share her feelings or any of that shit to survive. So long as she kept her feelings private and didn't challenge others when they blathered about stupid things, she would withstand whatever tortures Acton could bring. So long as she stayed far away from Rico, something she definitely intended to do.

5

STELLA

Stella, a former Acton resident and current counselor, worked the afternoon-evening shift. On a hot
Sunday afternoon in late August, she drove her old car
through the ever-open gates of the Los Angeles county facility. The faded black Camaro crawled toward a volunteer
resident standing guard near the first speed bump. The
resident recognized Stella and stepped back to allow her
onto the grounds. Stella continued down the lane, snaking
by the grassy area filled with addicts reuniting with their visiting families. She passed a cluster of small buildings. The
cabins on the right hosted residents; the house-like structures on the left contained the administrative and financial
offices. Stella parked behind rehab services, put out her
cigarette, and began her first workday of the week.

As she exited her car, shafts of light scorched Stella's
pale skin and emphasized her fatigued countenance, the
result of years of physical and mental stress, much of it
relating to drug addiction. She was forty-three, but carried

the weight of a longer lifetime of worries. Wispy blondish-brown hair, tucked behind her ears and falling to her shoulders in uneven strands, framed her pallid face. As usual, she wore faded blue jeans and a loose-fitting top.

Sunday afternoon was the time Stella elected to meet with the men she had been assigned to advise. Each counselor had approximately thirty men or women, never a mixed group, to guide through the 90-day program. Stella preferred advising men. She claimed that they didn't have the same petty issues that women had: "Someone stole my shampoo" or "She's a pig" or "She won't do her chores."

Stella strolled to the auditorium. Eleven men vying for spots in the shade were waiting for her to unlock the door. She smiled at them. "Congratulations for making it on time."

After the initial group entered, other men continued to wander in. About fifteen were seated when Stella asked, "Where is everybody else, you guys?"

"I know where I am," one resident replied.

Without waiting for her full caseload, Stella plowed forward, explaining what most had heard several times before, that the weekly "program review" was a place where they shared "thoughts, ideas, feelings, experiences . . . where I get to know you guys." Stella tried to use the hour to bond with the men on her caseload. She also hoped to get the men to bond with each other so they could provide mutual support through their journey of recovery. Other than that, the way Stella used her time with her group was varied. Sometimes she scolded. Sometimes she comforted. Before it was banned, she often took them on walks into the hills, beyond the "Out of Bounds" signs. Other days she played games with them, like the time she sent them on a treasure hunt-bingo game to find out who in their group had the highest education, who had been in prison the most, who had spent the most time in recovery, and who had the most children.

All counselors' caseloads were a rotating group of residents that entered and departed Acton at different times, so Stella wasn't surprised to spot some new faces. She asked the men who had entered Acton during the previous week to introduce themselves to the group.

One by one, the men stood.

"Chase, T-4 and an addict."

"Harold," said a small black man who had not yet settled down to his new life at the Center. As he put it, he was "discontent" about Acton. He was discontent to learn that there was no horseback riding. He was discontent that Acton no longer had a music program. He was just plain discontent.

"Bill, alcoholic," said the next man, an average-looking thirty-nine-year-old white man with a mustache and medium-length brown hair.

"Matt, and I'm an alcoholic." Matt was a skinny white man who could not stand still. His jittery movements threatened to dislodge the cigarette tucked between his left ear and shaved head.

"I'm Raymond and I'm a drug addict," announced the last newcomer.

By then, twenty men were present. Two sat at the front, serving as meeting secretaries and signing program cards so each resident could receive credit for attending. Despite the sweltering temperature, one resident wore a long-sleeved shirt over heavy jeans and had pulled a ski cap to his ears. The others were dressed in Acton summerwear: whatever they could find that was short and lightweight.

Stella turned to a group sitting near her, asking, "Did you guys get rid of the stinger? Whoever it is, you better put it away because it'll get confiscated."

"What's a stinger?" asked Chase.

"Two spoons, taped together. Plug it into a wall and it heats up so you can make your own coffee," answered a resident.

"It's a fire hazard," Stella said. "If you saw the Acton Fire Department, you would be concerned. It looks like something out of Mayberry RFD." Another resident belatedly rushed in and sat. Stella looked at him. "Good thing we made a deal I wouldn't front you off in public anymore, isn't it?"

The man looked down.

Stella changed subjects. "Those of you who are missing PE: you'll get written up. With enough absences you can be discharged."

She asked the residents how they were doing.

"I found out something about Acton," volunteered one man. "This is like a shelter for abused animals. Animals here are used to abuse and might shy away. If I hear of anybody abusing an animal, I'll snipe you from a tree. Think about adopting an animal. I adopted a cat, Sylvester."

A handful of serious-looking men clapped. They may have abused their bodies and other people while on drug-induced trips, but most residents were earnest animal lovers. The nearby pet cemetery showed how much residents cared about animals. The final resting place, which had become out of bounds in recent years, once was a well-kept garden. Its perimeter, outlined by a series of painted rocks, was anchored by a truck tire proclaiming, "Last Call." Clusters of stones rested beneath wooden crosses bearing the names Blacky and Betty and inscribed "In the memory of Michael" and "RIP Gunin." One memorial mimicked a headstone, its green and red ink stating "RIP Charlie Baby," followed by Charlie Baby's now-faded birth and death dates. Long-time staffers remembered elaborate pet funerals with processions of weepy residents accompanied by a trombone.

Stella, who adored her dog and cat and had spent numerous night times nursing baby birds back to health, understood the attachment that residents formed with the animals discarded at Acton. She and other staffers had long ago recognized the importance of pet therapy. They understood that animals were easier to relate to than most humans and offered the only unconditional love for many addicts who had been abused, abandoned, or forgotten, often before they had reached their teens.

Acknowledging the heat and the residents' short attention spans, Stella said, "I want to get out of here, too. Let's have some intelligent conversation. How many of you are working? Why?"

"Community service," reported one dutiful resident.

"Get myself prepared for when I leave here," said another.

Stella nodded. Volunteer jobs at Acton fulfilled a vital need. The underfunded center could not operate without residents who sought out assignments and applied for them, much like they would when—if—they stayed clean and returned to the outside world. The jobs also helped the residents by acclimating them to real world conditions. Residents made promises and were expected to fulfill them. The small responsibilities helped them relearn how to live by the clock, imbued them with a sense of pride, and boosted their confidence.

"I work for self-worth," a resident claimed. "My family taught me you don't just eat free meals and lay around— you help out."

A fourth man declared that he worked because "I get the inside scoop."

"When I was a resident," Stella said, "it took up my time and I did it to get a little responsibility and keep out of trouble. I tended to read my Big Book and stay in A/C."

What Stella didn't mention was that she also used her Acton time to begin a relationship with another resident. She had known it was forbidden and hadn't listened when others warned that it might retard recovery. Since then, though, she had learned how difficult it was to make and sustain a relationship while new to recovery. The man she met at Acton had become her second husband and though they were still together, life was not easy. The couple lived fifteen miles from Acton, in the Antelope Valley, a place known as the methamphetamine-producing capital of the world. Their house was not far from a scruffy area where drug dealers hung out. They had piles of bills; Stella prayed to keep her old automobile alive just so she could drive to work. On top of precarious finances and the difficulties of remaining drug-free, Stella's health was often shaky.

Stella knew that the pressures of daily life and worrying about recovery for both of them made life much harder than it might have been had she postponed a relationship until after leaving Acton. If she could do it over again, she definitely would have waited. So whenever she saw a "couple" at Acton, she pulled them aside and talked to them. She explained that the majority of addicts who hook up early do not succeed and many end up OD'ing. Stella also explained to addicts how her "picker"—and theirs—was broken; addicts don't know how to choose appropriate partners.

In class, Stella pulled out a recovery guide that explained Step One. She was one of the few counselors who emphasized the importance of starting the Step process while at Acton. She believed her primary job was to break through a substance abuser's denial and get them to meetings. Step One, admitting powerlessness and agreeing that life had become unmanageable, was a good way to begin.

While handing out copies of the recovery guide to each resident, Stella asked them to complete the short writing assignment in class. "You need to do this step one hundred percent or you'll get loaded again. Write a paragraph or two about each question. This is a lot of deep writing so have fun with it."

Heads immediately bent in concentration as the residents addressed the questions. When the residents finished writing, Stella collected the paragraphs, intending to read them before the next week's session.

Not ready to turn the residents loose, she asked about them, inquiring how one was sleeping, and dispensing advice to another, saying Tylenol was bad for Hepatitis C and suggesting that the resident not take it. Stella knew plenty about the blood-borne infection Hep C, as she and many others called it. She was not sure how she had gotten it, although she'd had many opportunities; Stella had gotten a tattoo and a transfusion and had been stuck with a methadone needle. Fortunately, she did not have HIV, but Stella considered Hep C a death sentence and treated it like AIDS, keeping people away when she bled.

For the first year after the health worker had tracked her down to tell her she was infected with the communicable disease, Stella had hidden under her bedcovers. She had been depressed and wanted to die. Finally, she had summoned the strength to contact the Centers for Disease Control to find out more about the viral disease. Most people with Hep C display no symptoms, although they can develop jaundice, abdominal pain or swelling, fatigue, loss of appetite, or nausea. Complications can arise decades after exposure and, untreated, the virus can lead to cirrhosis or liver cancer. Learning about Hep C had empowered Stella and though she still dreaded future illness, after five years of living with the infection, she had accepted her condition.

"Who's leaving Acton?" Stella asked. "Come say good-bye."

A young man walked to the front and said, "Hi, I'm Andy and I'm an addict."

"Hi, Andy," chorused the room.

"Where are you going?" Stella asked.

"Home . . . L.A. . . . to my parents' house."

"Is your mom going to kick your butt if you get out of line?" asked Stella.

"Yeah."

"Good." Stella looked earnestly at the group. "I don't care what everyone else is doing. I care about my caseload.

You guys have come into my life for some reason and you're the ones I care about."

Stella's concerns actually extended far beyond her caseload. She cared about everyone, especially the downtrodden and helpless. When new residents arrived fresh from jail with only the clothes they were wearing when arrested, Stella asked the others to watch out for them and lend them things they needed.

Once, during the winter, when residents straight from jail had landed at Acton too late on a Friday night for a trip to the shed where donated clothes awaited, Stella took matters into her own hands. Enlisting the aid of a resident, she supplied him with a huge sack and they crept in darkness toward the locked building. No one was permitted inside the tiny two-room structure without the supervision of the woman who ran housekeeping. Since she had gone home hours before, the mission seemed surreptitious, almost illegal. After sneaking around dim pools of light, trying not to be seen, they unlocked the padlock and hurried inside.

Risking discovery, they turned on the light. Without wasting any time, Stella hurried to a bin containing men's pants. Not knowing anything about the men she was scavenging for except that many were wearing shorts and would be freezing in the frigid desert night air, she extracted several pairs of pants in various sizes. She quickly gathered an assortment of T-shirts, sweatshirts, and packages of new underwear and socks.

When they were done, Stella locked up behind them and, looking somewhat like an elf leading Santa with a huge bag of goodies, guided the resident back to her office. One by one, they called the new residents to the

rehab services building and dispensed the clothing, warn-
ing each recipient that he could never tell where he had
gotten the garments.

"What clothing?" asked one man with the barest of
smiles as he hurried out of the office wearing enough layers to keep him warm for the night. The others merely
nodded. Long ago they had learned not to comment or
question.

The Sunday program review was not quite finished. A
second resident stood up and faced the counselor. "I want
to say good-bye to Stella . . . too bad she can't be my sponsor." He turned toward the residents. "If I can make it, you
can make it. I wanted to leave the first three days . . . I don't
share much . . . Keep it strong and keep it real." He sat
down.

Stella dismissed the group, saying she would see them
next week.

As the others ambled out, Harold remained seated.
"Wow!"

Stella's office adjoined the rehab reception room. She
perched in a captain's chair while staring at the new residents' charts piled on her scarred wooden desk. The gov-
ernment-issued furniture, including a wall clock and a
battered brown file cabinet, had been personalized with
memorabilia from Stella's life in recovery. A bulletin board
rested above her desk, displaying haphazardly placed items:
a headshot of a would-be actor whose career took a detour
through Acton, line drawings colored in by residents during "recreation therapy," cards of thanks sent from former

residents, poems written by residents, and a bumper sticker proclaiming, "The Big Book Says It, I Believe It, And That Settles It." Varied diplomas and certificates lined the walls, attesting to Stella's expertise in counseling substance abusers. A dream-catcher, made by a resident and presented as a gift, hung in the corner, serving as a reminder that hope for a better future was what sustained everyone who entered Acton.

The counselor grabbed the top chart and asked the receptionist to call the resident over the public address system. Soon Bill, the same average-looking Bill who had attended his first program review the day before, entered Stella's office.

She invited him to sit and explained that she needed to complete an intake interview with him. "Are you on probation or parole?"

"No. I just got lucky."

"On any medication?"

"High blood pressure."

The questions continued and Stella dutifully recorded the answers. Bill had been at Warm Springs twice, another facility once; he had detoxed three times. He used crack, popped Valium, and drank a half gallon of vodka a day.

"I'm a recovering alcoholic my own damn self," Stella said. "There's something about us. We go to vodka when we get to the end of drinking."

She delved further into Bill's drug-using habits. He reported that he began drinking when he was thirteen and first used cocaine when he was eighteen. He had used needles, but not in the last twelve months. He was not homeless.

Stella told him that she was mandated to report him if he ever abused children or old people. Letting him know that she meant business, she said, "I'd rat on your ass in a heartbeat." To mitigate the sting of her threat, she told him, "Just remember, I'd never do anything to hurt you. Unless I need to."

Gently, with obvious concern, she asked, "How are you doing?"

"I was kicking when I got in. Had two days when I came in. Cold sweats, shaking a bit. I had been drinking on this run for six hours. I had seven months clean last year. Then I moved out of sober-living."

"You convinced?" Stella asked.

"Yeah. I surrender. I been doing this too damn long."

"I liked your note you wrote in program review."

"I tried to be honest," Bill said.

"Ever been married?" Stella asked.

"No. I have one kid. A fourteen-year-old girl. She lives with my mother."

Stella knew what it was like to be apart from her children and her heart ached at the years that her daughters from her first marriage had been absent from her life. After Stella descended into the hell of addiction, her ex-husband, a navy man, had taken the girls on an overseas assignment. For years, her only connection was the dunning of her paycheck for child support. But eventually the girls became teenagers and proved difficult for Stella's ex-husband and his new wife. The girls returned to California and had been living with Stella for more than a year.

Referring to his daughter, Bill said, "I see her all the time. Her mom is a tweaker and moved away. She lives with a bunch of cooks. She's tore up." By "cooks," Bill meant people involved in the dangerous work of producing methamphetamine.

Stella empathized with Bill's daughter. She knew what it was like to have an uncaring mother. Stella claimed that her mother did the best she could, but it had been an awful performance. Her mother had not been able to protect her from a childhood of molestation by her father, a drunken pedophile, nor was she inclined to save her from drug addiction. Stella was twelve when her father died. Her alcoholic mother moved to Hollywood where she managed an apartment building. Most of her time, though, was spent in bars which meant that Stella was unsupervised. Hippies living upstairs held frequent parties and one night Stella joined them. She ingested the alcoholic punch made with wine and fruit slices and smoked hash through a hookah. Stella was addicted immediately; she loved the high.

By the time her mother came looking for her that night, Stella was giggling and had a hard time walking. As her mother tried to pilot her down the stairs, Stella kept crashing into walls. Suddenly, her mother grabbed her shoulders and spun her around so they were face to face. "If you're gonna drink," she spat out, "you've got to learn how to handle it."

That piece of advice, the only time Stella remembered counsel from her mother, was useless. Looking for a family, Stella gravitated to the motorcycle gang that lived across the street. She remembered the men treating her like a kid sister and the women letting her put on make-up. The gang members often got high, but objected when Stella joined in. Trying to scare her off drugs, they told her that they supplied dope to women so they could get them loaded and take advantage. Stella didn't listen. She liked the effects of getting high; stumbling became part of her life. She enjoyed the easy availability of massive amounts of Thai sticks and cocaine as well as Frisbees full of hash that looked like compressed manure.

"Have you ever been arrested?" Stella asked Bill.

"Four or five times. Three DUI's and failure to appear."

"Do you like recovery?"

"Yes."

"Are you ready to go to any lengths to change your life?"

"Yes, ma'am."

"'Cause it's going to take everything you've got."

"I'm ready," Bill said.

"Try not to kick yourself too hard in your butt. You know why? You'll get your foot stuck and hop around on one foot. Don't forget, but don't dwell there. I'm telling you from experience. Were you raised by your mom and dad?"

"Yes."

"Do you have any siblings?" Stella thought it helped to learn the birth order of addicts. She knew that the oldest male got lots of pressure while the youngest son of several children would be spoiled and know how to "run" women, to manipulate them into working for him.

"I have a younger sister who's a tweaker."

Next, Stella asked about his family's drinking and drug-use history. Bill said that alcoholism ran deep in his family; both grandfathers and an uncle had the disease.

Stella nodded. She knew that there was a genetic component to addiction and to many of the traits that accompanied addiction. "I have a lot of male traits," Stella confided. "Blackouts. Tendency to violence." She glanced down at Bill's chart and asked the next question on the list. "Were you working at the end?"

"I started a business last year and worked until the end of May. Drinking screwed up the partnership. Once I had it going on, had lots of money. Every bit of it is gone now. I shined my sponsor on."

Stella asked if he had any hobbies.

"Surfing. Fishing. Hiking."

"Will you need a sober-living?" Stella asked, wanting to know if he had plans after Acton.

"I'm going to Progress House. They said come back any time." Bill said he was working on Step One and was almost done.

"If you need me," Stella said, "come see me."

"I'll need to." The emotion of the moment started to affect Bill and his eyes glistened with tears.

"Normally I don't hug," Stella said. "But do you want one?"

Bill nodded.

Stella moved around her desk and opened her arms.

Some of Stella's interactions with residents nourished her soul. Others sapped her energy, such as the day Matt was accused of theft.

A short time after Matt arrived and before Stella had been able to have a private conversation with him, Matt wound up in her office, fervently denying that he was a thief.

Stella slumped at her desk. She rested her head on her left hand and held a pencil in her right hand as she stared down at a writing tablet. Cisco, a fellow counselor, stood on the other side of the desk, his short legs firmly planted, tattoos peeking out from his white T-shirt as he glared at Matt, the skinny, fidgety new resident with a shaved head. Matt squirmed, the tip of his own tattoo, a cross with an image of Christ, showing at the top of his T-shirt.

Cisco's words were accusatory as he grilled Matt about a missing twenty-five dollars. Matt had been caught looking through another man's clothes in the middle of the night and claimed that he was sleepwalking. One of his cabin mates had reported missing cash. Matt kept insisting that he didn't take the money.

"It's convenient that you claim to be a sleepwalker and then the cash is missing," Cisco declared.

"I didn't steal anything," Matt repeated.

Accusations and denials flew back and forth as both of their positions became more entrenched. The antagonism between the men was palpable. Cisco thought he had the upper hand morally; residents had stolen before and he was determined to get a confession from this new punk. Matt was more articulate than Cisco and tried to use his righteous indignation to twist the counselor's words. Stella remained silent, documenting Matt's responses.

"I don't appreciate being called a liar," Matt said, shifting in the chair.

"I wasn't calling you that."

"You're implying that either I'm a liar or a thief. And I'm neither!" Matt had once been diagnosed with attention deficit disorder and was a meth user, so throughout his stay at Acton he appeared to be in an almost constant manic state, but his jerky movements intensified even further under Cisco's contempt.

Without looking up, Stella asked, "Can anyone verify that you're a sleepwalker?"

"Yes." Matt eagerly gave her the names and phone numbers of two women that he said would confirm his condition. Stella picked up the phone and called the first woman. There was no answer. Stella called the second woman. Again, there was no answer.

"I'll call them later and let you know what I learn," Stella said, dismissing Matt.

With a nervous glance at both counselors, Matt departed quickly. His future at Acton was in jeopardy, but he was grateful for the reprieve.

Exhausted by the episode, Stella just wanted the day to end.

6

BOUNCING

Early days of sobriety are a challenge. Addicts are often anxious, unfocused, and unsettled. Their bodies and minds are off-balance. Physical symptoms can include weakness and exhaustion, shaky movements, and an inability to sit still. Mentally, a newly clean addict experiences sharp mood swings from depression to relative highs. Acton staff members call this period "bouncing."

Patty had been bouncing from her first day at Acton. By her fifth day she had experienced several peaks and valleys. She was on an upswing the morning she joined her first PE class. It was eight o'clock in the morning, an unusual time for addicts to be awake, but there were already dozens of other residents scattered near the centerfielder's position on the baseball field. The sun had barely topped the mountains, but the temperature was already rising from a low of fifty-seven to somewhere near ninety degrees.

Facing away from the baseball diamond, Patty watched as five volunteer residents geared up to lead the group in a series of calisthenics. Her T-shirt, sweat pants, and athletic shoes matched the hastily thrown-together clothing worn by the others. Patty's new-found friend, Blanca, stood nearby, her over-sized top disguising her pregnancy.

Patty was grateful to Blanca, who had offered friendship when Patty's dorm mates had ridiculed her. The women were the same age, but Blanca's acne-scarred face, rounded figure, and hard living contrasted with Patty's more youthful appearance and perpetual naiveté, allowing Blanca to use her considerable Acton experience—nine days—to guide Patty. Blanca also served as Patty's gauge, a way to measure her life. Instead of feeling sorry for herself, Patty was thankful she hadn't lost as much as her friend.

Blanca had poured out her life's history to Patty, expressing anguish that her four children, including three-year-old twins, were in foster care and she could see them only if the court ordered it—which translated to never. Blanca had been court-ordered to Acton and knew that she could lose her kids permanently if she didn't remain in rehab. Yet she feared that if she did stay she'd lose her sanity. What sustained her was the new life hidden beneath her swelling belly and her nineteen-year-old boyfriend. After nine years with a complete dog, Blanca was thrilled to be with a man who wouldn't call her a bitch or punch her. She found his way of expressing anger charming: he stomped his foot. During their first encounter, when Blanca couldn't give herself a fix, she asked him to hit her with a needle. He had blanched at the track marks on her arms which Blanca found endearing. She had immediately invited him to live with her.

The resident leader began a series of toe touches, calling out as she moved: "One." Hands on waist. "Two." Hands on knees. "Three." Hands on toes. "Four." Stand up straight.

Patty followed along, more enthusiastically than most of the others. Some residents simply bent over slightly, pretending to be involved but lacking both the motivation and energy necessary to fully participate.

Karen, the staff member in charge of recreational therapy, walked among the residents. Her curly dark blonde hair and blue eyes, accompanied by scattered freckles, lent her a friendly air as she monitored the residents' movements and tossed in the occasional reprimand: "Put your cigarette out or I'll have to hose you off because you're on fire."

"You're doing real good," boomed the resident leader. "Are you ready for thirty-five jumping jacks . . . no? . . . okay, only ten. You ready?"

Patty kept up with the leader, but some of the residents simply flapped their arms. "Discontent" Harold stood still, hands in pockets, muttering that exercise was bad for his health.

"Okay, roll out," came the order for the finale: an easy jog around the grounds.

The residents' pace varied. Most walked, some leisurely, others with a purpose. A few people leaned forward in a mock jog. Fewer still took the exercise seriously and put effort into their movement.

Patty set off as though on a mission, head high, arms pumping vigorously. She felt great. She had enjoyed jogging in the past and was determined to use the exercise to restore her health. She ran the length of the baseball diamond, past a series of buildings, through the visitor parking lot, and reached the chain-link fence ringing the center before her body forced her to slow down. Aerobic stamina and muscle strength were among the many things drugs had stripped from her.

Gasping for air, Patty slowed to a walk as the reality of her diminished strength set in. She felt deflated, somewhat like she had three days before when Owen, the resident who had dubbed her Smiley, had stolen a kiss from her next to the vending machines. The euphoria of his pursuit had evaporated immediately as her gut told her it was wrong to be alone with Owen.

Flirting had been part of her old behavior and she hadn't thought about the significance of Owen's kiss until it was over. Then her feelings had kicked in, causing her to feel what she called "poopy." She had reminded herself that God put her at Acton to do better and that, though she craved male attention, she didn't need it. She was trying to follow advice from various counselors by repeating their mantra to herself: The men at Acton are as sick as I am and I don't plan to take any of them home. Since the kiss, she tried harder to avoid being a tease, but even as she told Owen and the other men who came around that she was sick and they needed to have respect and help her, she couldn't resist responding to them.

As she reached the edge of the rehab center's three-hole golf course, Patty began jogging again, willing herself to move faster. Even her relationship with God had had its ups and downs since she arrived. The Holy Spirit had led her to Acton, but by the third day she was an emotional wreck. Thoughts of her past—the many men she had slept with, the times she allowed addicts around her children, permitting alcohol and drugs to take her away from her family, remaining with a boyfriend who beat her as their three-year-old shouted, "No, Daddy"—crowded out the image of God. Her anxiety had washed away the nickname Smiley and she had wanted to leave Acton. Patty had barely survived that wrenching day, but she had done it without turning to drugs or running away from Acton—an achievement in itself. Now she needed to concentrate on the Lord. The 6:30 A.M. Bible Study had beckoned, but her path to the early morning session had been blocked by cusswords when her roommates were awakened by the tap meant for Patty. With the words "Fuck" and "Jesus Christ!" echoing throughout the room, Patty had shrunk under the covers and prayed for her dorm mates.

She rounded the north and east sides of the golf course and turned onto the dirt road bisecting the grass. She jogged past the trees lining the road and around the first set of dorms and cabins, the backyard of the street called Skid Row. Patty again slowed to a walk.

Dorm life also affected Patty. She had found out that some of her dorm mates gossiped about her. Another resident had told those women to shut up, but to her face had called Patty "The Virgin Mary" and curtly pointed out her every misstep. Two other women had encouraged Patty to sunbathe near the Admissions Office, something that resulted in a severe tongue-lashing from Rico. For some reason, it had not occurred to Patty that lying in a swimsuit around almost 250 sex-deprived men was a terrible idea that could have gotten her kicked out.

Craziness in her dorm had erupted the previous day, culminating in the dismissal of two of Patty's cabin mates. Soon after her arrival, Patty had felt bad vibes between the women, but it wasn't until the day before that she had fully understood their animosity. She had been outside her dorm and heard angry voices. Needing to pick up her program card, she had entered the cabin. One woman was calling another a "greasy, scummy nigger." The second woman slapped the first woman. Patty immediately stumbled outside, her stomach roiling. Men from nearby cabins, leaning toward the sounds, advised her to stay out of the fight. Patty stood on the sidewalk, listening to the screaming, stomping, and what sounded like rolling on the floor. A counselor arrived and separated the combatants. They were expelled that day, but Patty still felt unsafe, like she was living on the streets.

Patty slogged by the last building on the path. As she reached the baseball diamond, she picked up speed and then broke into a run. Only two people were in front of her, both men. With renewed energy, she sped by home plate, third base, the outfield, and headed toward the bridge which marked the end of the run.

The first man to reach the bridge called out to the others, "Eat my rump!" He cockily marched across the bridge, followed by a man wearing a red plaid shirt, green night cap, and black shorts. Patty soon caught up to them and checked in at the table set up by Karen. Like unhurried ants, the other "joggers" stretched far in the distance. Patty ignored them, happy in her small triumph.

A few days later, Patty sank into a deep valley. She needed to make an important decision and disliked both choices.

The women from the adjoining V and W dorms clotted the area in front of the administration building, nervously awaiting individual interviews with the center's administrator. There had been no official word relating the reason for the meetings, but the group knew exactly what was happening: Rose had snitched. Angry women voiced their outrage that one of their own had committed the ultimate offense and snitched on Yolanda, another dorm member.

Patty hovered near the others, hugging her shoulders to keep from shaking. She didn't want the anger to poison her further. At the same time, she was afraid to stand apart from the others. She didn't want the pack to turn on her, too. She knew more about the incident than most of her dorm mates. The previous night, while most in the dorm slept, Patty had gone to use a toilet in the communal bathroom. Rose, a resident from the adjoining dorm, bolted into the bathroom, saying there was a man in her dorm having sex with Yolanda, the woman who had arrived recently from Twin Towers wearing extremely short shorts. Rose said she was afraid the man would rape her and asked Patty to peek through the curtains separating the dorms.

Her stomach had turned. She was disgusted with Yolanda's action and sickened by Rose's request. She knew neither woman well, but wanted nothing to do with them. Stuck in the middle of the situation, Patty talked Rose into going outside for a smoke. Once Rose was calm, the pair returned to Patty's dorm and Rose lay down on the extra bed there.

In the morning, Yolanda apologized to her dorm mates, saying she had made a mistake and promising not to do it again. Nevertheless, Rose told her counselor, who informed Mr. Clark, and now the dorm mates were being called to the administrator's office, one by one, to tell what they knew about the incident. Patty stood amidst her angry fellow dorm mates, deeply conflicted. She was trying to work what Acton considered an "honest program." Every day she prayed aloud to God, asking Him to give her strength to work her program to the fullest. Yet, she suspected that if she truthfully explained to Mr. Clark what happened, the others would find out and crucify her.

Before Patty was called into Mr. Clark's office, another disturbance broke out on the Acton campus. A sheriff's car rolled onto the grounds, creating a visceral chain reaction of fear and contempt among the residents. Almost everyone in Acton had been at the wrong end of a pair of handcuffs at least once in his or her life. Drawn to the cop car like maggots to a dead body, they cast distrustful glares at the uniformed man who had entered their sanctuary.

Staff members fanned out, shooing away the curious, telling them to return to their cabins and dorms. The residents retreated to porches and doorways, but many still had a good view when the deputy confronted an ex-resident who had driven drunk to the center with her young son. The drunk protested, but the deputy arrested her. The boy screamed and cried at the separation from his mother. His anguish reverberated across the campus.

No one was happy about the situation—the staff least of all. They understood the irony of asking a deputy to take an addict from a treatment center. But they also had a responsibility to protect the child and others from a drunk driver. The residents were divided in their opinion about the arrest. Many—mostly men—thought that the health of the boy was paramount and the mother should be hauled away. The women's reactions were more nuanced. They cared about the boy, too. But they were also mothers who, like Blanca, understood well the threat an arrest posed to the relationship between mother and child; once a kid got into the system, it was difficult to regain custody.

The boy's anguish cut through Patty's heart. She trembled at his predicament and prayed for him.

Finally, Patty was called into the administrator's office. She sat down, burst into tears, and told him everything.

The next day, her tenth in the program, Patty was feeling better physically and people were telling her she looked better. She believed that by the grace of God her tattling had escaped anyone's notice. Yolanda had been dismissed. Rose was shunned. But Patty was okay. She was working an honest program and things were looking up.

At two in the afternoon, there was no place to hide from the sweltering heat of a near 100-degree day at Acton. But the program continued and Patty joined a knot of residents outside the auditorium. Her white shorts and sockless white shoes were topped by a striped short-sleeved top exposing a lot of skin.

Counselor Walt led the Thursday afternoon Chemical Dependency Class. His face in an ever-present smile, as if he had a secret that he was not sure he would share, Walt watched the residents amble into the small auditorium.

The room, like most at Acton, was painted a dull white and bore the scars of numerous collisions with chairs and elbows and oily hair. There were Spartan furnishings: twenty-nine stackable plastic chairs in nearly straight rows facing the front of the room, a well-worn wooden lectern, a battered metal table, and a clock. A television-video player rested on a high shelf wedged between two of the six windows. Open windows did not mean that the air circulated; there was no escape from the brutal heat.

"I'd like everyone to take off sunglasses and head gear, please," Walt requested, still smiling faintly. "Hats off, please."

Patty and a dozen others settled into chairs. Matt, the fidgety sleepwalker, was there, too. He was still at Acton, still wondering if he was going to be kicked out. Stella had not gotten back to him to explain whether anyone had verified that he was a sleepwalker.

Walt raised his voice slightly. "I've been a counselor with the county for nine years and can't talk over a lot of noise." He announced that they would be watching a video that would explain the medical aspects of mind-altering drugs. The video, he said, would divide the subject into six categories and focus on the physical, emotional, and spiritual damage caused by mind-altering drugs. The residents, already walking encyclopedias about drugs and their interactions, adopted bored or skeptical looks.

"Forty cups of coffee is enough to put someone out," Walt stated.

"That's hard to swallow," cracked an anonymous voice.

Undeterred, Walt said, "People walk around with Big Gulps, thirty-two ounces of coffee. What is it that they have in the other hand? A cigarette? What is the number one drug-related death? Cigarettes. Almost one half a million people die significantly prematurely due to cigarettes—from strokes, heart attacks, cancer."

Walt moved toward the television. "The video is a little dated. The material is current. Pay attention. There will be questions afterward and a brief discussion."

The residents turned their chairs toward the television and slumped in their seats as the screen flashed the black-and-white title. It quickly became clear that the presentation consisted of a series of textual slides accompanied by a male voice. There would be no flashy video or sound effects. The residents resigned themselves to a tedious lecture.

A rich, deep voice announced the "drugs of entry": alcohol, marijuana, nicotine, and inhalants . . .

Even in the heat, Matt could not sit still. His left hand nervously smoothed his trim Van Dyke-style beard and then moved toward his shaved head. He leaned forward and back as his tie-dye shirt spasmed along with his body, radiating yellow, pink, turquoise, and lime green. The only thing at rest was the unlit cigarette behind his left ear.

Most of the other residents were lifeless; the heat had sapped their energy.

The video voice droned on, focusing on sedatives: alcohol, barbiturates, and tranquilizers. No one in the room was talking, no one moved. It was as though they had ingested a sedative and had escaped their imprisoned bodies. Even Matt was still for a moment, although his mind continued to race. He concentrated on the video discussion of broken sleeping patterns, believing that he now had proof that drugs could have induced his sleepwalking.

The video continued through the next categories: narcotics, inhalants, and hallucinogens.

Two residents began talking. The conversation started low and got louder and louder. Walt floated toward the back of the room and softly asked the pair to stop talking.

After the final category, stimulants, the video informed the audience that drugs affected different people in different ways and the important thing is not to start using. "If you have used," the voice told the addicts, "you need to stop. Don't worry. There is a lot of help out there."

Before the residents could start talking amongst themselves, Walt turned off the television. "Now we have a true or false exam for everyone to participate in."

Reading from a piece of paper, Walt shot a question to each person. "The brain can shrink, true or false?" he asked, looking at Matt.

"True," replied Matt eagerly.

"From what?"

"Don't tell me . . . shit . . . marijuana?"

"Right," said Walt. He turned to Patty and asked, "Marijuana enhances sexual performance, true or false?"

"False."

As soon as Walt moved onto the next person, Patty slipped out the back door, heading toward the nearby restroom. Patty liked Walt, but found his class difficult to sit through. The previous day had rocked her, and though she was doing better, stress without resorting to drugs was still difficult.

In the auditorium, Walt posed a question to José, who said he spoke no English. Matt, the only perky person in the entire room, offered to translate. The question was an easy one—"Is it okay to have one drink?"—but the correct answer ("no") was impressive anyway considering that José had sat through a twenty minute video without understanding a word.

"Right," Walt said. "We can't use Nytol or near beer because we'd be off to the races. It's a disease. A real disease. It's genetic. Just like cancer. If we have a disease we need to treat the disease. Nobody here is responsible for having a disease, but once you find out about it then you are responsible, right?"

It was 2:48. People were beginning to shift in their seats. Everyone knew they got to leave soon. Patty returned from the restroom.

"Drugs can produce mental illness?" Walt asked.

"True," answered the next resident.

"Absolutely. About half of addicts also have a mental illness."

"It's called dual diagnosis," Patty said. She had been in the program long enough to know that many of the women in her cabin had been diagnosed with a mental illness.

"Alcohol is not a drug, true or false," Walt asked the next person.

"True . . . oh, false."

"Right," Walt said. "It is a drug. A legal drug. Supposedly some people drink a few and stop."

Laughter filled the room.

"That ever happen to you?" Walt asked.

Everyone laughed again. "Never happened to me," Walt said.

A huge dragonfly zoomed through the room. Matt popped to his feet.

Walt was nearing the end of his list of questions. He had asked everyone in the room and started again with Patty. "Does PCP suppress pain?"

"True," Patty said.

"I was reading about body piercing and the newest thing is branding," Walt said.

"I grew up on a ranch and the only thing I branded was cattle," Patty replied.

Many others in the room were getting restless. One man in a not too quiet voice said, "Since you talking about bullshit, can we leave?"

Matt didn't wait for an answer. He bolted through the back door.

Walt calmly said, "You've been a good group here, and I think you've gotten a lot out of it. You have and I have."

The residents clapped. Patty joined the others as they moved faster than they had all day, rushing toward the front, crowding around the table so they could get their signed program cards which would prove that they had completed the class. Patty bounced her way out of the room, having taken one more step on her road to recovery—or at least toward completion of the program.

7

TO STAY OR NOT TO STAY

The first month at Acton is the most perilous. Not everyone survives. If residents decide to leave or are discharged for breaking rules, it often occurs during the first weeks. Most people are scared when they come in and have misgivings about everything. They doubt whether they should be at Acton. They aren't sure how—or if—they'll be able to fit in. They don't even know if it's worth the effort to try. Plus, there is the lure of the outside world. The "war stories" they tell each other or themselves make their drug-addicted lives appear exciting. Acton is dull in comparison. Attending classes and meetings is too sedate, too boring. It allows too much time for introspection, something not always welcomed by people who have purposely anesthetized their feelings. So the questions that new residents need to answer are: Should I stay? If so, how can I fit in?

Deborah had already made the decision to stay, but it took a few days to work out how to behave. Her evolving strategy involved avoidance and invisibility. She tried to avoid staff members and when that wasn't possible, she aimed for invisibility.

One afternoon, Deborah donned jeans shorts, white socks, and two-inch heels. She followed the concrete path from her dorm to the canteen classroom, a space once used to sell snacks and personal items. Several residents had already congregated there. Deborah chose a seat in the middle of the women's section, positioning herself in an unobtrusive spot behind two women she could use as shields against the instructor.

A counselor strolled into the room and to the front. He welcomed the residents.

Deborah opened a romance novel that she had acquired from the Acton library, balanced it on her knee, and tuned out. She still felt completely blackmailed into going to rehab and resented being there. Nevertheless, she was tired of going to jail and admitted that "every date I went on was a chance I took with my life, my health, and my freedom, so I only took a chance when I absolutely had no choice." She felt that the continual fight to maintain her drug habit was no longer worth it. She hated the rehab system and didn't want recovery, but she knew that she needed to change. So she planned to grit out her time in rehab and then go to a sober-living facility where she would play their game. She'd get a job doing something, even cleaning houses if necessary, until she was back on her feet.

For the duration of the class, though, she happily escaped into the love life of a fictional woman.

—•—

My first extended meeting with Tiffany was on a hot, windless afternoon. We sat at a picnic table under a tree in the grassy area. Her gray eyes, embellished with thick blue eye shadow and heavy mascara, gazed at me through large purple-and-blue-framed glasses. The base of her brown hair was shaved upward about two inches. The unshaved portion was bound into a ponytail.

Tiffany's acquired Hispanic accent was heavy, so I had to concentrate to understand her. "I was born in Albuquerque to a well-off family, had lots of money, a car. I went to a rich high school. I wanted to be accepted. But I was overweight, insecure. I was a fat bitch, a fat cow, hung with the marijuana 'weed' crew, bagging it for all of them. My father caught on when I had the munchies at his store. By then I was a hard, rude teenager and simply asked him, 'What the fuck you looking at?'

"I was kicked out of high school and went to an alternative school. Juiced it for a while. It was lax. Did a half-ass job.

"I started working, moved out of my parents' house, bouncing here and there. Dad took my car. I was still smoking a little weed, drinking Coors every day. Lived with my friend's mom. She wasn't wrapped tight. I had a taste of the ghetto, started snorting coke. I had a yuppie girlfriend who was a straight cokehead and moved with her to a hick town."

Tiffany's accented voice picked up speed; tinged with bitterness it cut through the still, dry air. "I found what I thought was love, but Homeboy was married. I moved back to Albuquerque for a minute. At a softball game I dislocated my knee. The hospital called my parents. I got a shot of morphine. All I wanted was my dad's love, all I could get is anger. Dad was pissed, mad. He said, 'Look at what the fuck you're doing.' My parents left me outside, waiting for my own fucking ride."

A lone leaf silently fell to the worn table between us. Tiffany continued, "I got money to go back to the small town. I was a city girl in a one-horse town and I was cool, drank every night. I didn't use crutches so the other leg got dislocated. I called my parents. I was crippled, knew Homegirl couldn't help, wouldn't let me order her around when I couldn't whoop her ass. I was forced to stay with my family and take their shit."

Tiffany was in a wheelchair for six months. Her father made her go back to school. She completed in eight months and graduated. Her parents were so happy that they gave her a car and money. She was excited to have the positive reinforcement, but, Tiffany explained, "I went to fucking town and ran amok.

"I got pregnant and quit using cold-turkey. I went to school to become a phlebotomist. I had a daughter, got a job, and was down for the cause for a minute."

The job had too much structure and Tiffany was too immature for the responsibility of raising a child. She began selling speed, moved in with a crack dealer, got hooked on crack, and lost custody of her daughter. After two years with the dealer, she tired of his abuse and left him.

"I had a dope dealer bitch's habit and was living with a pregnant hooker and her mother. Then I bolted, was walking down Central, 66, in Albuquerque with two grocery bags, talking to myself. I went to a motel, was going to use a phone. There were some Cubans. They were brand new to Albuquerque. They gave me two pieces of crack worth forty dollars for a bag of fruit worth two or three dollars."

Tiffany laughed at the absurdity of the transaction. Her accent became more pronounced as she described her new-found friends. "There were about thirty fucking Cubans and all had dope. A GQ fucking Rolex guy took me into his fucking room and gave me everything I wanted as a dopehead. He was the head of the fucking gang and had a bodyguard with a gun. I didn't speak Spanish, they spoke almost no English. We partied. They fed my addiction. I got anything I wanted. Homeboy was fine. He was treated like a king, I was treated like a queen.

"One day he smacked me for smoking up his dope. I took one thousand dollars' worth of dope and moved to a crack house where I ultimately sold my ass for five bucks a trick. I don't cheat, lie, or steal, but was okay trading ass for dope. I didn't get it in a good way, but got it in an honest way."

Tiffany didn't seem to notice her contradictory statements.

"I ran around with other Cubans. I knew that when Homeboy found me, he was going to kill me. Fuck it. I'd seen a hooker killed for five dollars. I moved to the 'hood, wouldn't have a pimp. I was the only white girl who could hang. There were drive-bys all day, every day. A year after I left Homeboy, I went to a motel for fifty dollars. I'd sold my ass in truck stops from Albuquerque to L.A. to Albuquerque.

"Inside the room, I saw a bed and four or five guns. Then I heard Homeboy say, 'Close the fucking door. Tiffany sit down here.' Homeboy made everyone leave and then said, 'Son of a fucking bitch. I've been looking for you fucking everywhere. I wasn't looking for you to kill you. I was looking for you *por qué* I love you.' He said, 'You like fucking crack too much,' but he gave me lots of money and dope. I took a hit and let Homeboy's bodyguard talk me into staying.

"I finally lost weight and looked thinner. I found that I had a body. I taught the Cubans how to sell dope properly, taught them how to dress, fed them out of my motel room, cleaned for them, made their beds, and washed their clothes. They called me *la dueña*, boss. We sold dope day and night, sixty Cubans and me."

A horn squawked, loud and obnoxious, breaking the afternoon peacefulness. Tiffany jumped up from the picnic bench, knowing it was a fire alarm, but not certain if it was a drill or if a real fire threatened Acton. Either way, she realized that she was supposed to do something, go somewhere. Despite her excess weight, Tiffany moved quickly, instinctively gravitating to the baseball field where others were gathering.

A few days later, I met Tiffany again and asked how she ended up in California.

She told me that she left the Cubans and went to Las Vegas. "In Albuquerque I gave blow jobs for twenty bucks. In Vegas I got one hundred and fifty dollars for a hand job. So I got a room and hooked up with a stripper. I did steroids to get firm. I was thin, but not firm. I started stripping and made lots of money.

"Then I ran into one of my old truck driver clients and left with him. I had a thousand dollars on me at the time and ended up in Palmdale, California, when the truck broke down. I soon ran out of dope. I thought, 'Every fucking town in America has dope. I'm going to get some.' Then I looked one way and saw desert. And the other way was only McDonald's. I asked where the ghetto was and got blank looks. Finally I found a guy with some dope, but he thought I was a cop and wouldn't sell me anything."

Tiffany traveled fourteen miles north to Lancaster, the closest town. "I found Big Baller in a garage. He said, 'Goddamn, you're fine. Come to Lancaster. There's more money here.' I caught a two-hundred-dollar trick, but there wasn't enough dope in Lancaster. I ran into a big guy who gave me a big piece. I started cooking dope for him and was catching smoking tricks in Lancaster. Then Big Baller's homeboy, Hit Man, was paroled from prison and I was selling four thousand dollars of dope a day for the dude. One day Big Baller sent me to L.A. with Hit Man. He gave me two bags of dope. We took the beater car. I was smoking crack the whole time. The car broke down in Long Beach and I ran out of dope again.

"We were staying right on crack alley. A girl came and asked if I had a pipe for sale. The girl took me to a junkyard, a big, huge dope stop. We had dope for days. I got hooked up to the main connection, Kilo guy. I cooked up kilos and smoked, but shit was going down. Some guy came up and killed Kilo while we were in the car."

Kilo's death scared Tiffany and she sank further into her addiction, almost wishing that someone would kill her to put her out of her misery. Soon she was busted on a possession warrant and sent to prison. Kilo's killer was then picked up and the district attorney assured Tiffany that her parole would be transferred back to New Mexico if she testified.

The first trial resulted in a hung jury. During the second trial, the killer got sixty-eight years to life. Tiffany was paroled to New Mexico two weeks later. She immediately got high. Soon she was back in California, where she was picked up on a warrant for parole violation and court-ordered to Acton.

Tiffany's arrival at the rehab center heralded the first time she had been out of prison without immediately getting high. She was confused, stressed, and overwhelmed. Furthermore, she had ballooned from a size eleven to a size sixteen. Teenage insecurity flooded back. But her home-girl accent and her outwardly brash attitude carried her through the first rough days. Then she decided to throw herself into recovery by doing what she knew best: running everything.

At the beginning of his second week in the program, twitchy Jason made a major decision. He told me, "After twenty-seven years of being an addict and shit, that's not what I want today and I've made a lifetime commitment. I'm never going to use."

The NA meetings and classes had helped him focus on important thoughts. Sometimes they brought up his insecurities, like when a woman told a story that aroused his guilt about being broke. But more often they prompted deeper thinking on his part. He considered his life and his prospects and realized he had to change. He finally understood an essential truth: after years of looking for someone to stay clean for, he knew he had to do it for himself.

He had been especially interested in the Chemical Dependency class that helped him understand what alcoholism does to a person's body. Jason was both relieved and dismayed to learn that chemical dependency was genetic. He was relieved because it explained his situation: as the son of alcoholic parents, he was prone to addiction. But at the same time, the knowledge made Jason afraid to have kids. He got emotional just thinking about the genetic thing. He knew it was tough enough for a non-addict to bring children into this cruel world and would be even more difficult for an addict, but he really wanted to have a kid, to experience being a father, to cuddle an infant.

The class had taught Jason that it was possible to break the cycle of addiction and that he did not have to pass such a legacy on to his child. Yet he understood that it would be difficult to erase the addictive and abusive behavior that he had learned from his parents. His father, often drunk, had beaten him severely; Jason still had a belt buckle mark on his face from the time he got home five minutes late. His mother was only a social drinker, but she yelled at him and had thrown glass ash trays and shoes and whatever else she could find.

Believing he was the black sheep of the family, Jason had begun using drugs in an effort to numb himself from his parents and other abusive adults, like his mean first-grade teacher who flunked him, and the male teacher who often smashed his ring against Jason's head. He started with weed in fifth or sixth grade, about the same time he got expelled for fighting. By the time he was eleven, he was using cocaine, speed, and PCP. Alcohol and heroin eventually became part of his arsenal against frustration and anger.

Now, though, Jason felt that he could leave behind his lifetime of addictions. Maybe he would even be able to live more like a normal person and could start a relationship with a woman. One of his biggest disappointments was never having a girlfriend. He almost had one in high school. There was a girl who did drugs and ditched school with him. But he was arrested and thrown in jail before he had a chance to tell her he liked her.

Jason's wistful memory of a first love did not extend to the first time he had sex. Not long before he dropped out of high school, his cousin bought him a hooker for his birthday. Jason and the hooker smoked some sherm, a joint dipped in liquid PCP, and had sex. He was too ashamed to tell her it was his first time and later regretted not mentioning it. Maybe if she had known, it would have been a better experience. All his other sexual encounters occurred when he could afford a motel room and a woman with fishnet stockings and high heels. He wanted something more than those quick encounters. He wanted a relationship.

Jason had grandiose dreams. He wanted to start a burger place with a digital menu and video games for kids. He also had a fantastic idea for what he called "a tattoo attention-getter," something so wonderful that tears came to his eyes when he thought his dream might not be realized, something so great that he made me promise not to laugh or reveal his invention to others.

Jason admitted that he was scared about the rest of his life, but wanted so many things that he knew he couldn't have while continuing to use. So, no more drugs. Never again. Definitely. At least not while he was alive. It would be okay to have something pumped into his body after he died, but not before. In fact, he welcomed drugs after death, hoping to preserve his body. He had read an article about cryonics and was convinced that such a procedure would be best for him; maybe after dying and being brought back to life he would better know how to live. In the meantime, he believed, "Until the day I die I'm never going to use."

8

RELAPSE AND RECOVERY

Eddie sat on a worn plaid couch in his counselor's office. He was still shaky about being at Acton and, during his first one-on-one meeting with Jeff, he had mentioned his guilt about relapsing. Now that his counselor was also focused on the topic, Eddie leaned forward, somberly soaking in every word Jeff spoke.

"Relapse isn't always bad," Jeff said. He had turned his chair away from his desk, toward Eddie, and gently rocked. The constant motion could be mesmerizing or annoying, but Eddie seemed immune to the movement. His eyes remained on Jeff's face as if memorizing the blue eyes, straight nose, and brown hair, each strand combed straight back and blow-dried into place.

"Relapse is almost part of the process," Jeff continued. "It becomes part of someone's history that eventually gets them to the place where they're ready to surrender. I remember my last treatment program, when they told me that relapse was an important part of the process, and they were right. Addicts have a moment of clarity where they are ready to go to any lengths. You can be in bed, rolling around, and get that moment of clarity. It took me fourteen years in and out of treatment programs—that's the wreckage of the past. AA says we don't wish to dwell on it, but don't wish to shut the door on it."

Jeff stopped rocking, turned toward his desk, and opened a manila file folder containing Eddie's rehab history. Reading from the file, Jeff noted that Eddie had been to Warm Springs in 1994, was at Acton for the first time, and had attended one other treatment program—Clare. Jeff asked, "Can you give me a summary of the main event that led to your coming here? You were in Clare for nine months and then relapsed?"

Eddie leaned forward, his shoulders hunched. "When I went to Clare to detox I had been shooting one and a half grams of heroin for nine months, facing a third strike for boosting. I stole liquor to turn it for money. An ex-junkie gave me a card for detox. I did the program at Clare, then worked for Clare. I had a caseload. After eighteen months I relapsed with a woman who had a year cake. I got caught up in affection and didn't want to lose it. I thought it was working—living in recovery and not working the program.

"I detoxed in Clare, the men's center. Did nine months and then relapsed again. On liquor." Eddie's second relapse was prompted by following what AA deemed "old behavior." He had returned to a familiar neighborhood and ventured into a bar, triggering the need for a drink. He also forgot the AA saying "One drink is too many and a thousand is not enough."

Jeff listened in silence as Eddie continued. "Some counselors and people there suggested Acton. An Acton alumni told me to come here to get my head together. Get serenity. I used to apply the first three steps daily if I could. I need to get back, focused. If I do complete here, I'll go to sober-living because I do have a job."

Jeff asked the next question on the social history worksheet that he was required to complete for each resident on his case load. "When did you start using?"

"I began alcohol at around fourteen, experimented with marijuana about fifteen, but didn't like it. I took Seconal plus a couple of beers at around sixteen, seventeen, eighteen. Too many beers and I'd pass out or get sick. Used it off and on. It made me feel comfortable in my own skin. I could talk to people—girls—dance at parties. I was kind of an athlete but couldn't function well on drugs. I gave up sports for drugs."

The alcohol and marijuana meant nothing to him. Eddie's drug of choice was heroin. His love affair with that drug began in prison. He didn't like needles and turned away when a helpful cellmate injected him, but the momentary discomfort was worth the result: a wonderful out of body experience. Heroin killed all his pains, physical and psychological, and mentally transported him from a cell to a beach in Acapulco. But after three decades of injecting heroin, Eddie's body was torn up. Since detoxing off heroin, he had not touched the drug.

"What about drug use in your family?" Jeff asked.

"My dad was a functioning alcoholic and workaholic. He held a job until the day he died. As soon as I knew what

I was, I knew what he was. Both my father and his father drank. My mom never touched a drop that I know of."

"Brothers and sisters?" Jeff asked.

"I have an older brother, he's a normie, and a younger sister. She doesn't use."

"Relationship with your brother and sister?"

"I haven't seen my brother in ten years. The last time I saw my sister, there was a big argument with her and her new husband. She told me to stay away." And Eddie planned to do that until he felt comfortable and could make amends.

"How much education?" Jeff asked.

"Twelve years." Eddie didn't mention that he'd barely made it through high school. It was the '60s; he partied all night on acid and there were lots of girls. Sports, even his beloved baseball, became less important than hanging out and having fun.

"Any military history?"

Eddie shook his head, hiding from Jeff what he hid from the world and desperately tried to forget himself: he had been a soldier in Vietnam.

"During the last twelve months what has been the source of your support?"

"GR." General Relief. The state supported him.

"What about medical history? History of hospitalization, meds?"

"I had an operation on my left ankle. It has pins in it. The ankle was broken with a tire iron in a bar-alley fight. I also had an abscess from heroin use—the needle." Eddie didn't tell Jeff that he sorely needed a new set of choppers.

"Any psych history or treatment?" Jeff asked.

"No, sir."

"Ever married?"

"I was married six years. Divorced when in prison. It was a long time ago."

"Any other significant relationships as long or longer?" Jeff asked.

"No."

"Do you have a history of domestic violence?"

"What's that?" Eddie asked.

"Violent behavior in a marital or significant relationship?"

"No."

"Arrest history," Jeff stated, moving onto a new topic. "Are you currently on probation or parole?"

"No."

"Give me a brief arrest history," Jeff said.

"Most of it is drug related." Eddie started with his most recent arrest, explaining that in 1995 he had spent a year in the county jail for being under the influence. In the early 1990s he was in and out of jail for the same thing— for six months, four months, thirty days. Eddie said that from 1983 to 1989 he had what he called a dry spell; he hadn't stopped using drugs, he just hadn't gotten caught. Prior to that, he did two prison stretches for possession and sales.

"What about social skills, recreational skills, hobbies?" Jeff wanted to know.

"I played ball before I messed up the foot. Softball, slow-pitch, handball. I like working with wood." Eddie did not mention how important baseball once was to him or that he had tried out for the California Angels. He believed that his chance of success had been good until he sabotaged himself by getting loaded the night before.

Jeff asked about a tentative discharge plan.

"I'm going back to Clare. I plan to get involved in a fellowship in the community. I still have people back there who care about me and want to see me do good. I want to go back to the west area. Good people, good meetings."

"Any questions?" Jeff asked.

"I been hearing that for some people this program is ninety days and some it's one-twenty. What is it for me?"

"You're a self-referral. You stay ninety days. If you need more time, you can get another month."

Eddie nodded. Jeff continued rocking. After a few seconds, Eddie spoke again. "I'm getting along, meeting people. A couple of days ago I went to the hospital, they took blood. I missed two NA meetings and did CA instead." Eddie didn't care if he attended Narcotics Anonymous or Cocaine Anonymous meetings. He said, "As long as there's one, I'll go."

"I claim NA as my fellowship," Jeff said. "And have gone to many AA and CA meetings. But I've only given myself of service to NA. An old guy named Pepe said you can't serve two masters. But I've gone to other meetings. I've gone just to go and look at the girls. The first six years I was learning the service structure of NA."

"Went to other meetings, but only took a commitment to NA," Eddie repeated. "Maybe I should do that."

Jeff said, "NA doesn't have as rigorous guidelines and structure as AA."

Eddie's brain shifted gears and he said, "I got along with the service provider at Warm Springs. He was rigid, but as long as you stayed out of the mix, he was okay."

Jeff ignored the nudge to tell Eddie anything more about himself. Eddie could observe, though, that Jeff's office was as fastidious as his appearance. His desk held a variety of office supplies, all in their own spot and accompanied by a well-tended ficus tree in a gray-striped clay pot. There were very few personal touches. A stuffed monkey looked down from an orange shelf above the mini-blinded window. Next to the animal were six strategically placed note cards and an NA plaque.

"AA," Jeff said, "is a training ground. Boot camp. They can get you involved in recovery, change behavior. They stress action, action, and more action. You practice behavior to develop a program of self-management. Go to meetings, raise your hand, offer to help, serve. You can practice Step Twelve in the first meeting, if you have a mind to. When you go to a meeting, you don't need to listen to what they are saying. Instead, I watch behavior. Look at people who look like they belong and try to be like that."

"When you do that, you get out of yourself," Eddie replied. "That's why I tried to stay busy."

Jeff agreed. "Action, action, and more action. That's what it's all about. Later, you can start dragging out all the demons."

"Now I just need to get over the hump. The more I'm uncomfortable, the better I feel. I want to be shaky, stick in my craw. When I'm comfortable, I screw up."

"Pain is a great motivator."

On his tenth day at Acton, Eddie along with eleven other heat-addled men, slumped in classroom seats, waiting for the Post-Acute Withdrawal Class to begin. After his first tentative days, Eddie felt as though he was getting over the hump. He no longer dwelled on the negative. Instead, he concentrated on the recovery process.

Counselor Jeff took his place at the front of the room, but before he could begin, one man asked, "Is this going to be painless?"

"I don't know. I don't know what your threshold is." Jeff turned to the others. "My name is Jeff. I'm a counselor here. Welcome to Acton. I'm also a recovering drug addict. Because you guys are new, use this as a chance to meet me and get to know me."

"Do you mind telling us your drug of choice?" Tex, the man who had irked Rico during the orientation, posed the same question to Jeff.

"Heroin and alcohol, but I used lots of other drugs," Jeff replied.

"I just want to know how to relate to you," Tex said.

Jeff ignored Tex and launched into a recovery autobiography. He related that he had gone to AA meetings beginning four years before enrolling in his first treatment program. After that, he was in and out of treatment programs for almost a decade. Eventually, he became a resident at Acton, though he had departed Acton without finishing the program. He explained that he had needed to experience all those programs and return to drugs several times in order to understand that he couldn't use drugs like other people.

"I can't use at all," Jeff said.

Eddie was beginning to understand exactly what Jeff meant. He finally comprehended that part of recovery was to go out and test the waters and come back and make a deal for life. Finally, he felt ready to make that deal.

"The people that are here that don't want to be here, that's part of their process," Jeff said. "Maybe the next time they'll be ready. Maybe next time they'll start to be ready. Maybe they'll get clean when they reach thirty-five. Or fifty."

"Or die," added a resident.

"Or die," Jeff repeated. Death was a big part of Jeff's life. He believed that before he could come to terms with life he had to come to terms with death. He owned several death-themed books like *Tuesdays with Morrie*, containing the wisdom of a dying man, and well-thumbed and marked-up copies of M. Scott Peck's missives about death. Life and death were so entwined in Jeff's mind that he had temporarily stored a somber photo of himself at age three in the Peck book. Jeff's attempt to understand death was not an abstract notion; he had Hepatitis C and knew the deadly ramifications of that disease. Plus, he had had personal encounters with death. At age twelve, the same year he began using illegal chemicals, Jeff witnessed his father's ghastly death from cancer. Much later, while shooting crank and drinking, Jeff was mugged and seriously injured by three men who left him in an abandoned building. Those experiences gave him a greater appreciation for life; he was happy just to be alive and lived each day in deliberate awareness.

Jeff declared that some people were just not ready for treatment. "They're in 'pre-treatment.' But that is the overall process. Realizing that makes it a little easier for me to deal with people not ready for recovery. It's that way in any treatment program, but it seems worse at Acton. It seems like there are so many more people in pre-treatment than who actually want recovery because it's the largest treatment program in the West."

After giving his introductory remarks, Jeff announced that the class was about the management of withdrawal. Claiming that he still experienced difficulty with symptoms of post-acute withdrawal, Jeff passed out a sheet of paper headed, "SIX SYMPTOMS OF P.A.W."

Jeff read aloud: "Number one: 'Inability to think clearly.' Number two: 'Memory problems.' Doubt. Confusion. Number three: 'Emotional overreactions or numbness.' That's if you're easily upset. Or feeling nothing at all. Number four: 'Sleep disturbances.' Too much or too little sleep."

"What's sleep?" Tex asked.

"Number five: 'Sensitivity to Stress.' For most of twenty-two years, I used every day I possibly could. When I took drugs away, I had big time stress. Number six: 'Coordination problems.'"

Tex walked out of the room and lit a cigarette.

Jeff explained that when he got stressed, he got headaches, backaches, and constipation. "If I don't do something, I wouldn't be able to get out of bed. But if we manage post-acute withdrawal we will feel better." Jeff offered one solution: writing. "Just writing relieves stress and makes you aware of where you're at and that you need to deal with this stuff. Feeling unpleasant will lead people to relapse. But if you're feeling good, enjoying life, why are you going to use drugs? That doesn't make sense."

He turned to the next portion of the handout, labeled "HOW CAN WE MANAGE STRESS?" and announced that the residents' behavior needed to adapt so that they could manage stress. He elaborated on each of the listed points, saying that a "Twelve Step involvement" is a must. Twelve Step programs provided recovering addicts with a sense of belonging, a way to relieve stress. They aided in behavior control and cognitive changes. "Daily affirmations" stopped negative self-talk. "People like us have a history of saying negative things about ourselves," Jeff said. He pointed out that addicts would say things like "I don't give a damn" or call themselves an asshole because they did something stupid, or call themselves names they wouldn't call anyone else they genuinely cared about.

Other ways to manage stress included talking to a counselor, taking a walk to change a negative frame of mind, or relaxing and meditating. Jeff said that when he first got to a program at age twenty-one he thought slogans were lame, but, at age forty-nine, he understood that slogans brought him back to reality. "'Easy Does It' or 'One Day at a Time' can calm people down, otherwise the slogan becomes 'Crash and Burn.'"

Exercise was also important, Jeff continued. "Even after all these years being clean and sober, stress nails me if I don't get enough exercise. Another stress reducer is prayer. If you aren't atheists or too much of an agnostic, you should try prayer. I do, every day. Another important path to managing stress is sharing with other addicts and alcoholics." Jeff emphasized sharing with one or two people who genuinely cared about them. His additional tips included developing regular sleep habits, attending two or three Twelve Step meetings a week, following Step Ten and taking a daily inventory, eating properly, and taking vitamins.

Referring to the food at Acton, Jeff said, "You get good nutrition here. It might not taste that good, but it has everything you need to beef up, pork up."

"It has lots of fat," criticized a physically fit soccer player-coach. "Lots of fat."

Several men disagreed.

"I'm grateful for the food."

"I've gained weight."

"I've lost weight."

"It is healthy," Jeff said. "And I've heard people say that they love the food."

"Not everyone is the same," the soccer guy argued.

"It all depends on your perspective," Jeff said. "You're capable of changing your perspective and thinking the food is good."

"Better than on the streets," one man said.

"Some people say they don't like the program," another resident said. "I like the program."

"I like the program here," the soccer player said, his face flushing. "But I don't like the food. I think it's terrible. It tastes like shit. I wouldn't give it to my dog. Just because I used drugs doesn't mean I didn't think about food."

Eddie didn't care about the food or the disagreement about it. He already knew what he had to do and was ready to get more involved in his own recovery. He had tried to go to NA meetings, as Jeff suggested during his intake interview, but the people in NA weren't serious enough for him. Instead, Eddie had begun concentrating on AA. Though he wasn't entirely comfortable at meetings and didn't usually talk, he had recently spilled his guts at the podium. That was a beginning. Now, he needed to get back to the basics, to begin with Step One. Again.

9

BUGS

One morning after breakfast I observed Uta, one of the Twin Towers women, as she tried to locate her cabin. She was still wearing her shapeless shift and continued to appear drugged, disoriented. She trundled up the three concrete steps of a wooden cabin in a long row of identical buildings, opened the door, peeked inside, and shut the door. She turned around, lumbered to the next cabin, and repeated the process.

If Uta had examined the areas surrounding each cabin, she would have had an easier time finding hers. While most cabins were uniform, the residents, charged with keeping their dirt "yards" clean, expressed creativity in unique rock formations or other signatures of individuality. Some rock arrangements spelled out aspirations or Twelve Step platitudes such as "Recovery" or "One Day at a Time." Others shouted their address: "S" or "T." One yard sported a colony of tiny, people-like figures consisting of three or four fist-sized rocks perched on top of each other. Another cabin featured a heart-shaped group of pebbles surrounding clumps of grass soon to decay into lifeless brown strips. Some residents shunned rocks in favor of creating intriguing designs in the dirt, often spending hours clearing away stray pebbles and raking the dry soil to perfection before leaving their imprint.

Yet Uta seemed to notice none of those distinctive displays as she methodically made her way down the paved sidewalk, testing each cabin, her expression never changing. Oddly, no curses or yelps of surprise greeted her intrusions.

Uta ended her mission at the end of the row, finally reaching the largest building, the twenty-four bed women's cabin.

According to the counselors, Uta was one of the many "dually diagnosed" people who cycled through Acton. Those residents were among the almost nine million people in the U.S. who had both mental and substance use disorders. Since the defunding and closure of state mental institutions in California during the 1980s, the severely mentally disturbed had no defined place in society. Many became homeless. When they ran afoul of the law, often through illegal drug use, they got trapped in "The System." Their first stop was the county jail. Often, their next stop was Acton, another county institution. Acton accepted the dually diagnosed but could not aid addicts suffering from extreme forms of mental illness or those too violent to control. The center's only option in those cases was to transfer the individual to the mental ward of a county hospital. Frequently, the dually diagnosed had a short hospital stay because hospitals were required to release non-violent patients who didn't want to remain. Soon the dually diagnosed person departed the hospital and returned to the streets to begin the cycle again.

I later learned that Acton staff members had concluded within a few days of Uta's arrival that she needed more help than the center could provide, so she was discharged and transported to a county hospital.

Neil, another dually diagnosed resident—or "bug," as at least one Acton counselor called them—was different from Uta. While Uta's brain appeared numbed, Neil couldn't shut off his thoughts.

I met Neil when I exited the administration building and saw him standing alone in the middle of the lane, his six-foot frame hunched, his right index finger pressed against his jaw, making him look like a mahogany cane.

He said, "I have a toothache and the nurse won't give me anything for the pain."

I was tempted to ignore him, but he looked forlorn and I didn't have anywhere else I needed to go, so I invited him to sit and talk to me. I quickly learned that he was forty-one, had been at Acton for almost a month, and had a torrent of thoughts that didn't always make sense.

To try to focus our conversation, I asked Neil to tell me about his experience at Acton.

"This place gives me a conscience," he said. "It has helped me regain myself without alcohol and drugs—and that's a phenomenon. There is a psychic change when people give you the best gift they've got and that's time from their heart. Most people have motives, but people here say hello from the motive of the heart.

"There was a kid with a white power symbol tattooed on his stomach. I said hi to him. It fucked my mind up when the guy responded." Neil was astonished that an Aryan-type man would be civil to him, a black man.

"My mind healed and my heart healed," he said. "The streets raised me. Now, I'm getting re-raised here.

"Deep down inside every man, there is a great deep reality: God. That's how I'm growing. Here, I'm away from high drama, parents, girlfriend, media. I've always been somewhat positive. When people open up now, it's a reflection; I see something in the other person that's in me but I can't articulate.

"I can't be isolated at Acton."

Neil's thoughtful expression disappeared, replaced by an agitated intensity as his eyes narrowed and locked onto mine.

"That man, Jesus Christ, was sold out. Now He needs to help out.

"I came up here real angry, scared, not knowing what it would be like. Some other guy told me there would be horseback riding. I love canoeing. It was a good lie.

"I tried to commit suicide. My mother has a Ph.D. She's a neuro-surgeon. She wouldn't give me three hundred dollars. I spent one hundred dollars on alcohol, speed, and cocaine. I went to sleep on Saturday and woke up on Thursday. I was in a semi-coma. I had hit my head. If my mother gave me money she would have been aiding me."

He briefly looked up to the sky, as if remembering something. His dark eyes then bore into me as he resumed speaking, this time at a faster pace.

"Before coming here, I would give someone a drink of acid if I didn't like him.

"I've been sprinkled, dipped, dunked, and prayed over, and sang in a choir and still found myself reaching into a truck and getting a beer. The church allowed me to pray over what I had done. But I had to keep it inside. I couldn't release the stuff that's been keeping me drunk.

"Now I go to AA and NA.

"I went to my counselor's class and he kicked me out. Maybe he thought I was a clown. I wasn't. He has difficulty with people skills. He yelled: 'Go to the office!' I didn't like his attitude and was getting ready to hurt that man. Then, I bit my tongue so hard it bled. All I could see was a policeman putting me in cuffs and a morgue taking him away. So, instead, I went to his supervisor and my counselor apologized and said he was glad that I dealt with the situation the way that I did."

He glanced away and began talking more slowly.

"This program works. Talk about taking an inventory. My old code, taught to me by the system, was: you hurt me, I hurt you back.

"A guy gave me a penny. Heads it's your way. Tails it's the other way. God's got the edge.

"I could have hit the man, played nuts or crazy."

His gaze began jumping around, almost as if he was watching a movie and couldn't focus on only one section of the screen. Once again, his speech sped up.

"I was age eight when I suffered from seeing my mother get raped, jumped on by my stepfather. Another guy she married, and is now divorced from, jumped on her, shot her six times. Now he's trying to make amends by fixing up the house and not charging her. He's trying to make amends to both my mother and to me. I'm trying to accept it. If a program helped my mother's ex-husband then maybe it could help me.

"I love to drink. I put a hose line through the steering column, using the container of windshield washer fluid to funnel alcohol directly to my mouth.

"I've been told that I have the type of mind that could plan a gang rape and keep the woman happy. Now, instead of thinking how to hurt people, I'm thinking how to help people.

"I got up this morning and thought about going to the security guard and beating his ass, seeing how martial arts works. I was angry that someone woke me up. Then I realized that the guard was worried about me because I had been rolled up in a ball.

"Acton is the first time anybody cared about me. Down in L.A. they only care about what you brought to drink.

"I've killed some beer. I would kill a twelve pack before breakfast. My specialty is Grand Marnier. I drank a full fifth at a time. At first I'm feeling good when drinking. By the middle I'm crying, sad. By the end I'm mad.

"This place," he said, referring to Acton, "is God's operating room. God couldn't deal with me anywhere else so he put me in this nice place.

"I often say to myself, 'I have victory in all things and in two weeks I will not be defeated. Victory will be complete.'"

———

The next day, Neil strolled into the canteen classroom. As he settled into a chair, Counselor Suzanne, lean and angular, strode to the lectern. She said, "Welcome to Winner's Circle."

Using the obvious bruise on her face as an attention-getter, Suzanne said, "A love seat attacked me. I didn't get it from a barroom brawl. I told my husband that he best be nice to me because I'll get some mileage out of it . . . How many people have been in treatment before?"

Six hands shot up.

"How many have never been in treatment?"

Neil and five others raised their hands.

Glancing at the eight people who didn't bother to reply to either question, Suzanne asked, "You couldn't care less and don't like stupid questions in the morning?"

She then leaped into the subject of the Winner's Circle class: recovery. Like the other counselors, Suzanne used her class time as a way to educate residents about the disease of addiction, and to serve as an example of someone in recovery. Speaking louder and faster, she explained that she had not just gone into a Twelve Step program and said, "Hallelujah." She had to do much more "research," implying that she continued drinking while deciding whether or not to make recovery a full-time pursuit. "It was the third step that tripped me up. Turning my will and life over to a Higher Power bothered me. I needed to barter with my Higher Power which led me to get clean temporarily, relapse, and then come back. I thought I understood the program, but hadn't given up *all* my life to the third step. One thing that really helped was understanding this graph."

Suzanne drew a horizontal line on the blackboard. On the far left she marked a small bisecting line and labeled it PAIN. On the far right she placed a notch and wrote EUPHORIA. She tagged the middle as NORMAL. The graph was a rough representation of an addict's pendulum-like experience on drugs. Normal was the resting point. When using drugs, the pendulum swung toward euphoria but inevitably swerved back, past normal, and to pain. When an addict continued to use drugs, the euphoria lessened and the pain increased.

"Normal," Suzanne explained, "is arbitrary. When I was a kid I looked forward to handouts because I enjoyed inhaling the fumes."

The residents laughed, probably remembering their own attempts to get high from the blue-inked mimeograph paper or other sources.

"Do you think everyone did that?" Suzanne asked. "No. Some got headaches. But I'd ask for more. I wouldn't really get loaded. I was nauseous and it was cool."

Neil and many others nodded.

Suzanne told about spinning when she was little. "The future normie kids said it made them dizzy. Us budding alkie addicts would spin and spin and fall over and go 'Ahhhh' and then do it again. We're always looking for more mind-altering stuff.

"I remember going to Grandma's and purposely coughing so I could get a great concoction of honey and alcohol. Sniffing gas was a biggie. I've never been normal in my life, but I was still taking care of business and sort of normal. The key is that when you come down, you come back to an arbitrary normal."

Suzanne paused. "You guys look tired. You look all flat."

She became more animated in an attempt to pull the residents out of their lethargic state. She explained that drinking and using to feel better works—but only for a short time. "If you're honest, you can count the really good times on one hand. Every time you get high the pendulum swings a little less forcefully toward euphoria and then goes back a little less than normal. We think the problem is that people are cutting drugs, watering down vodka, or whatever. We also think that when we don't have chemicals in us, we're uncomfortable. So we drink to be normal, to get through the day, to get rid of pain. But we're way away from euphoria."

Several of the residents, including Neil, nodded. Others agreed with a "Hmmm, hmmm."

"Then, at the left end we're doing whatever is necessary to get drugs." She indicated the spot with the word PAIN. "We drink, use, and feel worse. Didn't you hate when that happened? I was ticked."

More nodding and "Hmmm, hmmm."

Suzanne explained that addicts have an incredible way of forgetting the bad and remembering the good. "I would claim that I wasn't going to use anymore, but would have just one. Then I got high, but the high led quickly back to pain, bypassing normal. I'd never get euphoria. Pain is where I spent the majority of my dope career.

"Users need to reprogram ourselves. Once, when I was at an airport, I had an hour-and-a-half wait. The airport noise was muted, but the bar noise kept getting louder and louder." Laughing at her own craziness, Suzanne said, "I swore I heard the bar calling to me, saying, 'Pssst, Suzanne, come on in.' I knew I shouldn't follow my feet, but I didn't have time to call my sponsor. Soon I found myself sitting, shaking, drooling, and holding tightly to the chair. At that moment, I thought someone was coming for me with a butterfly net. Suddenly, I realized where I was and raced out of there. The bar noise receded. Now I know that airports are a trigger for me.

"Are there any roach smokers?" Suzanne asked.

Six people raised their hands.

"Pretend I have three rocks," Suzanne said. "Nickel rocks. They aren't much." She pointed to a man near her. "He's got a pipe and he's going to smoke it."

She pantomimed giving him a rock. He pantomimed smoking it.

Neil moved forward, pretending to take one of the rocks.

"Neil," Suzanne said, "get out of his high."

Neil sat down.

Suzanne turned to the smoking resident and asked where he was on the chart, "assuming you started at normal." He indicated that he was half way between NORMAL and EUPHORIA.

"Do you want me to hold onto the other rocks?" Suzanne asked.

He shook his head, still pretending to smoke.

"Now he's starting to tweak," Suzanne said, laughing. "But he insists on smoking his last. Then he ends up here." She pointed to a spot to the left of NORMAL, near PAIN. "Did you at any point see him die and go to heaven?"

Residents shook their heads.

"Lots of you were uncomfortable for him. Some of you were salivating. If we don't reprogram the tapes in our head, we'll end up back in the pain arena.

"How many of you have had drinking and using dreams?" Suzanne asked.

Neil raised his hand, as did several others.

"A big part of addiction is to the drama around using; we glamorize things like uncorking the bottle or the places where we used. I once thought bars were romantic. They reminded me of Bogie and Bacall. But the smell of dives and shooting galleries and places that seal out light is awful. Those places are filled with urine, feces, old Burger King wrappers, people slamming and smoking. They smell of stale sweat, cigarettes, vomit, and urine. I spent a lot of time hugging porcelain. How romantic and glamorous was that?"

One man said, "Trust me, it's true."

There were several audible yawns. One woman, not understanding the point of Suzanne's description of the hell she experienced, decided to tell a "war story," explaining how she had faced down three Rottweilers and had gotten away. "It was so cool," she finished.

War stories as told by residents and other addicts usually ended with a semi-heroic or, at least, lucky escape from a dangerous, drug-ridden situation. Acton residents delighted in one-upping other addicts, trying to prove their bravery or luck and claiming that they had hit a deeper "bottom" than anyone else. Those stories sometimes involved some sheepishness at the stupidity of their past, but more often a certain awe at their own miraculous escape from the depths of hell. Many people new to recovery exhibited pride in such an accomplishment. Others repeated war stories as both a reminder of their own mortality and as a life-affirming moment from their past.

Suzanne was trying to convince the residents that using was not glamorous and that war stories weren't something to glorify. She didn't want them to dwell in a mythical past; she wanted them to remember the pathetic and disgusting aspects of drugs so they would never again use. She didn't believe that war stories described a romantic or exciting event. Or that addicts were heroic.

"This," Suzanne said, pointing to the PAIN end of the continuum on the board, "is where I spent most of my drinking career." She explained that residents must replay the tape of their binges all the way through so that they don't mistakenly stop at the falsely romantic part and think that was reality. Instead, they must remember that the haze of feeling good quickly disappears, plunging them to the bottom where they dwell in agony.

"If you reprogram yourself," Suzanne continued, "a fancy drink will look like a skull and crossbones."

Neil looked thoughtful, as though he were contemplating every concept. He leaned forward and asked Suzanne, "What do you think about the reptiles telling you to go and have a beer?"

Suzanne ignored Neil and said, "You can't continue to do the old things that got you in trouble. Don't return to the site of your drinking or using. Don't go to the liquor store to get cigarettes. Don't return to your old neighborhood."

"I have victory in all things," Neil said. "I will not be defeated. Victory will be complete."

VALERY GARRETT

A few days later, Stella was in her office when a group of residents from Neil's dorm burst into the room and dropped a butter knife onto her desk, claiming that Neil had stolen it from the kitchen.

Stella blasted into action. A knife, any kind of knife, was a potential weapon and forbidden by Acton.

She raced to her supervisor's office, told him the situation, and then sprinted toward Neil's dorm. Stella's supervisor followed her onto the street, but, according to Stella, feared for his safety and quickly retreated to his office.

Frustrated that she had been abandoned, Stella dashed to the Admissions Office and enlisted Rico's help. Stella and Rico found Neil in his cabin, pacing.

When Stella asked him about the knife, Neil began shouting, "Goddamn mother-fucking bastards."

Angry at the men who had taken the knife and ratted him out to Stella, he continued to spout obscenities. Yet, when Rico demanded that Neil accompany him to the administrator's office, he did not resist.

Within hours, Neil was discharged. Victory was not his that day.

10

ENDINGS

The end of Phase One was approaching. Jason and Eddie had finished most of the required classes and meetings for the first phase and were almost ready to turn in their completed program cards proving that they had attended the proper courses. Eddie's last hurdle was writing an essay about AA's Step One, something his counselor did not require but Eddie found important. "Psycho" Jason's last obstacle was to stay out of trouble long enough to make it through the last week of the month.

Two weeks after Jason made his lifetime commitment to sobriety, he and another man ran naked through the women's dorm at 2:00 A.M. Two female residents reported the incident and an Acton staff member confronted him. Jason denied it. Another staff member searched Jason's cabin locker and found an illicit tattooing instrument. Jason admitted that the tattooing equipment was his and that he had used it while at Acton.

Both the dorm episode and possession of the tattooing equipment were infractions serious enough for discharge, so Jason's last view of Acton was through the window of the county van as it escorted him off the property the next morning.

One day at the end of September, Eddie retreated to his cramped cabin to write his Step One essay. He sat at the tiny table, surrounded by four iron-framed beds, lockers, and bedside tables. He began the essay by copying Step One: "We admitted that we were Powerless over addiction, that our lives had become unmanageable."

His thoughts tumbled forward as he wrote:

> . . . *for a longtime in my life I realy thought that I had a handle on getting loaded and being able to maintain a good life stile. it took me meny hard years to secome to the fact that I dident have a pot to piss in. This last relapse convenced me that I had to truly surrender to this desease or I was going to either die or go to prison for the rest of my life. by writing my admittence on paper and explanning the things that led me to being powerless over my addiction is pure honesty for me. you see haroin brought me to my knees. and I never wont to forget that feeling comming into recovery and how sick I was for 9 months I shot a gram of dope every day. you see I had to steel or do what ever I had to do to acheve that amont to survive. every day. so kicking cold turkey was pure hell. it took me 17 days and nights to sleep. my body was so fucked up that I couldn't even control my body parts.*

He clearly, painfully, remembered how sick he had been and how he had stayed at the Clare Foundation only because the people there told him he'd be a punk if he left. That pissed him off so much that he was determined to gut it out and show them exactly how tough he was. Even at his sickest, though, Eddie still planned to go back to using. He thought he could get clean and then use on weekends. His gut-wrenching physical withdrawal took seventeen days. He vomited everywhere, every day. For seventeen days. His only detox companion was a mop; the Clare staff forced him to carry the mop everywhere so he could clean up after himself. Finally, on the seventeenth day, Eddie's stomach began to settle down and he got some sleep. But he still had to carry that damn mop for another two weeks. At that point, the mop was more punishment, or a reminder of where he came from, than necessity.

Eddie didn't know what most affected him—the seventeen miserable days, the mop, or the people at Clare— but something prompted a desire to stay clean. The Clare Foundation brought out the best in him and helped him gain confidence in his ability to live clean. Finally, he felt that he belonged somewhere. He never wanted to return to heroin, and clung to the memory of those seventeen days to ensure that he'd never again go down that path.

He continued writing:

In my early life I had meny jobs that pade pretty well, and I fucked them up getting high or drinking. See for me being a party person was the way I grew up. they say that I enharited my addicted persinality from my parents – but the funny thing is that my father never used drugs. but he drank beer and wine every day I can remember. he was what you would call a fuctionning alcohalic. he always managed to go to work sick or not. the difference between us was he fuctioned and I wouldn't. I would call in sick on monday and I lost meny a good job doing just that. back in the early 60's there were pleanty of jobs to go around so I realy didn't give a fuck if I got fired because I could stop getting loaded for awile and clean up my act and get a nother. it was just that semple back in thoughos days. but that was when I didn't relize that I had a problem. after a while I just dident care about making it to work atall. I started hanging with the Gangs. being part of a Gang that time was greate because when ever we robbed some-body or pulled a burglare we all got a peace of the action. money, dope, or women. using became a real problem when I needed to fuction in every day living. addicted on haroin was my down fall because I would do everything to get it. rob, cheat, or steel. even from famley. and that realy hurt me the most – but that dident start until later in my addic-tion – wanting to be a part of was my whole exestence. I just want to fit in some where.

Much of Eddie's life had been a quest to fit in. His childhood was fun. He loved playing with other kids and having his family around. But childhood for him was short-lived. His parents settled into a newly developed suburb, a former farm, after his father was discharged from the army at the end of World War II. At first, life seemed idyllic. But the promise of the suburbs didn't pan out for Eddie, just as it didn't for many people. Those who didn't adhere to the dream of a white picket fence, three point one white children, a station wagon, a stable, working father, and a cookie-baking mother were made to feel as though they didn't fit in. In the suburbs, the misfits often were hidden, insecurities glossed over with attempts to keep up with the neighbors. Dreams of anything outside the pale of what passed for normality in the 1950s was squelched. Everyone pretended to be living and loving a "Leave It to Beaver" existence.

Eddie's "problem," though, was not one of his own making, nor one that he could hide: he came from a Hispanic family. His parents had been born in the United States and only spoke Spanish to keep secrets from the children, but Eddie was dubbed a "Mexican." He had white friends and didn't know the difference until junior high school. There weren't many non-whites in his neighborhood, so to be branded a "Mexican" was to be cast out of the group. He was different and the suburbs couldn't tolerate difference. The racial slurs snowballed and he increasingly felt as though he didn't belong. Even when playing baseball, where he got the most home runs and had the highest batting average, he never felt that it was a group effort. All those purposeful exclusions prompted Eddie to join the only team that welcomed him without reservation: a gang. It made him feel as though he belonged.

When Eddie was young he had seen his brother chased home by a gang. Telling himself that he didn't want that to happen to him, Eddie became quick to hit back. He was an average-size kid, but gained a reputation before he joined the gang. That reputation aided his easy acceptance by the gang, and there he found a home, a place where he fit in.

He started getting in trouble at age thirteen. All the kids did, but he got caught. Eddie felt his father's disappointment, but since the old man wasn't around much he continued doing what he wanted. His gang was violent. They robbed and split the spoils. They used weed and acid, and later he graduated to PCP and heroin, the drug that provided him with his favorite out-of-body experience. For Eddie, heroin worked as either a stimulant or a relaxant, whatever he needed at the time. Then heroin began using him.

Eddie concluded his essay:

Today I know I'm powerless over my addiction. and that my life is unmanagible. One thing I dident relize the last time I did the steps was that I completely surendered this time. and that I truly belive in my higher power. for me, I have to use a lot of diciplen in my program. I never wont to get to comfortible in my life. when I stop doing what I'm supposed to do like talking to my Sponser, going to meetings, and not wrighting I simply don't have a program. Looking back on my past relapesess I know now that I dident truly surender to my higher power. I thank God that he has giving me the opprotunity to go on with this thing called subrity.

PHASE II

11

WORKING THE PROGRAM

By the beginning of the second month, most remaining residents have detoxed and returned to reality or "landed." Their mood swings have stabilized and they obtain adequate rest, food, and physical exercise. Those residents who want recovery have begun working on themselves, learning how to resolve personal issues through classes and introspection, and they faithfully attend Twelve Step meetings. In recovery language, they are working the program.

Deborah's way of working the program was different from residents who sincerely concentrated on recovery. She did the minimum required and tried to be inconspicuous to the counselors and staff. She still claimed that the Anonymous meetings and the Twelve Steps were bullshit and that she didn't need recovery. Even so, Acton was beginning to have a positive effect on her. She had decided to quit both prostitution and drugs permanently. She recognized that her profession had been taking a toll on her health, that it didn't pay well, and often led to jail. At age forty-six, it was time to do something else.

Although Deborah knew that drugs were not good for her, she still believed that when she had used recreationally the high was exciting and energizing. She didn't change personalities, she simply became more . . . Deborah. But she also realized that when she used, her manic energy impelled her to start a million projects that she never finished. She remembered once taking apart a VCR, popping a cake into the oven, and then losing interest in both.

Deborah admitted that using drugs to get through bad situations had never worked. The first time she had used drugs as a crutch was three years previously. She had broken up with a boyfriend and was jailed for driving without a license. She was so depressed that she called her sister. Instead of offering help or sympathy, her sister bitched at her. Deborah hung up and turned to cocaine for solace. But the drug didn't erase her pain. The only thing Deborah gained from that episode was a firm resolve to never contact her family again. They weren't there when she needed them so she had no need of them. Besides, if she did talk to them, what would she say? That she'd spent the last years living on the streets, that she was a homeless prostitute? No. She didn't need their middle-class sneers.

Not believing that Acton was in any way responsible for her changed attitude, Deborah tried to maintain a façade of invulnerability. She knew that she came across as arrogant and perhaps she also knew that her attitude was an attempt to mask self-loathing. Outwardly, though, she pretended that she needed no one, that she didn't require help of any kind, that she could do everything on her own through willpower. Yet, occasionally she revealed glimpses of self-doubt, a desire to learn how to live better, and a yearning for the key to happiness.

Deborah had returned to her dorm after the morning class. She lifted a romance novel from her unmade bed and after pulling up the sheet and blanket, hefted her thickening body onto the still-wrinkled linens.

Before opening the paperback, she grabbed the water bottle from the nightstand littered with used Styrofoam coffee cups, a plastic Coca-Cola cup, and various toiletries that wouldn't fit onto the window ledge crammed with books, tea bags, and hoarded food. The nightstand drawer, filled with candy, remained partially open, as if mocking the rules prohibiting personal stashes of edible goodies. Sugary scents wafted throughout the area.

Deborah sipped water, secure in the tiny world she created with the aid of care packages from Ralph, her ex-john and current boyfriend. Food and clothes and clutter now served as substitutes for the drugs and constant male attention she once sought in frantic attempts to fill her soul. During her six weeks at Acton she had added another ten pounds to the thirty gained during her jail time. Long gone were the days when she had to wear two pairs of jeans to be a size five. At 170 pounds, it was difficult to feel attractive, but her current lovers—a carton of Tootsie Roll Pops and other sweets—ignored her weight.

She surveyed her area, the corner of a once-sterile cubicle containing four iron beds, four nightstands, four cabinets, each with its own lock, and scant space between the furniture. Deborah's cubicle was at the end of a line of five additional cubicles, all alike except for individual touches added by residents.

Others had brought or collected a few items that livened up the dorm, but Deborah won the quantity contest. She had scrounged or traded for so many clothes that her cabinet appeared to be the locus of an explosion. Sweaters, blouses, and pants competed for space inside the locker and threatened to topple out of the half-opened door, while hangers filled with silk skirts and fancy dresses rested on the outside of the cabinet and along the low wall above Deborah's bed. Gone were the hooker boots, traded for a red-white-and-blue sweater. Now she mostly owned sensible pants and cotton blouses, clothing that complemented her new girth and aided the shedding of her hooker persona. The multitude of fashion choices allowed Deborah to change outfits often, providing her with a self-induced therapy which kept her from telling herself, "Deborah, you're a bitch."

During her weeks at Acton, Deborah had gained more than weight and clothes; she also added a consonant to her name. A needlepoint nameplate that she made during recreation class proclaimed her new moniker in shades of purple and blue: Deborahh. Other residents displayed similar signs saying "Jesus," but Deborahh put her faith in herself. No longer was she Deborah, the hooker and drug user. Now she was Deborahh, an exciting new incarnation.

Deborahh settled back onto the bed and opened the book, losing herself in a world where the hero was tall and strong and white and would rescue her from the uncertainties of her future.

The luxury of relaxing in bed at 11:00 A.M. aided Deborahh's ability to make peace with Acton. Learning more about her new home had also stemmed her apprehension. Her preconceived ideas about the mandatory this and that had evaporated once she understood that Acton was like college: pick your classes and go, do your electives and you're done. There was no heavy-ass control. After realizing that, Deborahh had calmed down and tried to minimize what she called her hooker-tease impulses, knowing that if she got her ass rolled out of Acton, she'd have to do a program twice as hard.

She tried to be both relaxed and vigilant. She knew the rules and how to bend or break them without getting caught. She attended classes but continued to carry a book and read whenever she could do so undetected by the instructor. Some rules—like the prohibition on food in the dorms—were not enforced regularly, so she ignored them. If the most trouble she could get into was a "write-up," basically a scolding, she ignored the rule.

The one thing that continued to concern Deborahh was the Social Interaction Policy that Rico had outlined. She thought Acton went overboard on the prohibition against male-female contact. The way she looked at it, most residents had few social skills and the only way to improve was to practice on each other. Deborahh wanted to learn how to relate better to men—and she missed sex. At the beginning of her Acton stay, she had flirted and even playfully grabbed a few guys. But after realizing that the staff was scrutinizing her actions, she heeded Rico's warnings and quit flirting—at least that's what Deborahh hoped the staff would believe. In truth, Deborahh's attentions were now focused on one man, Pete, who was exactly what she wanted: white, tall, and good-looking. So far, their flirtation was platonic, but they were beginning to do things that Deborahh knew could result in her expulsion. They had flouted Acton rules by sitting together in the canteen during the nightly movies and twice Deborahh flashed him when he peeked through her dorm window.

Other rules were easy to skirt without much danger. The requirement that she go to Twelve Step meetings was something she followed haphazardly; most of her meetings were "drive-bys"—she left her program card at the beginning of the meeting and picked it up when the meeting ended. Occasionally, she attended daytime meetings if coffee was provided. If possible, she avoided going to NA meetings. They seemed too much like a religious revival, and she believed the Acton joke that all the women in NA had only one set of teeth among them. Deborahh especially loathed the "sharing" part of meetings. She thought that the residents were bullshitting each other with admissions of guilt and professions of redemption. The only time Deborahh shared was in the weekly women's meeting, though she was careful about what she revealed. Her sole reason for participating was so that news of her good behavior would reach her counselor.

Deborahh still thought the Twelve Steps made no sense. She had reluctantly finished the first step by admitting that she was an addict and saying that her life was unmanageable, but she didn't believe it. She had dutifully completed the worksheet that her counselor, Alicia, provided. She spent an hour hunkered over the questions, writing whatever she thought Alicia would believe, and was dismayed when the counselor told her she had finished the assignment too quickly. Fuck it. She was trying to give them what they wanted, but she wasn't going to abide by stupid rules.

Yet Deborahh knew enough not to argue with Alicia. The counselor might not be the greatest, but she was the best for her. According to Deborahh, the counselors fell into two groups: the textbook type and those who had lived hard lives of drug abuse. Alicia was textbook; she hadn't been a drug abuser, didn't know what it felt like to need a hit, and would get her ass kicked if she was on the street. But, if Deborahh had been assigned to a street-smart counselor, she wouldn't have gotten away with so much bullshit. Like the time Alicia asked her to be a tutor. Deborahh had gotten a 98 percent on her literacy test, qualifying her to help the residents who couldn't read.

Thinking fast, Deborahh had told Alicia, "It would take the focus off my program." Deborahh was too selfish to give up her time. And why meet someone stupid?

"I can see that you have a tendency to lose focus," Alicia had said. "But we all know that you can accomplish whatever you want."

Deborahh had been stunned by what she saw as Alicia's keen insight. With confirmation of her aptitude from Alicia, Deborahh felt as though the future was hers to shape. More than ever, she became determined to finish Acton—on her own terms—and go to a sober-living house and get free of judicial entanglements. Then she would find a new career. She was uncertain what path to follow, though. She wouldn't boost or jack. Her strong sense of right and wrong would prevent her from hurting other people. Likewise, she thought it was wrong to play someone, set them up, and steal. She wasn't fearful of the police but quaked at the thought of karma kicking her ass.

The dorm door opened, bringing with it loud voices, and then banged shut. Deborahh's dorm mate silently sank onto a bed.

Deborahh glanced at her watch. Time for lunch. She slammed her book down and bounced up, weighing the choices for a lunchtime outfit.

One chilly morning, Deborahh entered the Recovery House. She wore a short white skirt and a blue-and-white striped long-sleeve top, accessorized by matching white pumps, dangly earrings, and a white ribbon in her pony tail. The classroom was rectangular, but there was a small addition, almost forming an L, which held four chairs crammed together. Deborahh gravitated toward the small space, away from the direct gaze of the instructor. She did not glance at the off-white walls or the windows which over-looked eucalyptus trees, a few small buildings, and, in the distance, the golf course.

The weather, so oppressively hot when she arrived at Acton, was changing; the autumn afternoons were still warm, but the nights were cold. Most of the residents entering the female-only class dressed in a hodgepodge of clothing styles in an attempt to stay warm during the crisp morning yet remain prepared for the afternoon heat. Patty, sporting a cardigan sweater over a patterned skirt and skimpy blue tube top, took a seat near the instructor's spot. Her pregnant friend Blanca sat nearby as did Marissa. Marissa's heavily powdered face and thick red lipstick contrasted with her little girl hair, divided into uneven clumps clipped together by orange, blue, or green plastic butterflies.

Alicia entered the room. Her cheerful countenance brought immediate energy to the lethargic atmosphere.

"Are there any questions about last week?" Alicia asked.

"Yeah, last week was a really good class and I want to know the rest of it," said one woman.

Deborahh chuckled. She couldn't believe that these women seriously listened to Alicia's lessons about men. The two-part class was called Achieving Intimacy, but Deborahh had heard nothing realistic about intimate relations in the first class and expected nothing useful in this week's lesson either.

Alicia drew a ladder on the board. Next to the lowest rung, she wrote: Acquaintance. "We're on a ladder and moving up. The first step, the first rung is a little package." She drew a square with a ribbon on it. "It's the gift of attraction. For a long time when I saw someone I was attracted to I would say, 'Uhmmmm hmm,' and he would say the same and that was as much conversation as we had and we'd plunge into sexual stuff. What would we be thinking of at that point?"

"Hormones" and "Heat," offered different women.

"Right. Those are physical attributes," Alicia replied. "But, I want you to learn to think broader, to look at attractiveness in terms of character."

"Friendly."

"Rescuer."

"If I had a history of sexual abuse," Alicia said, "then I would only relate on a physical level. The message that abuse teaches is that unless I look a certain way, I'll be alone."

"Attracting the wrong people?" asked one resident.

"Not so much attracting the wrong people," Alicia said. "But choosing to let them into your lives."

Patty leaned forward. "This is the first time I've been in an environment where I hug people I don't know and it's not sexual, but it throws me off. Somebody'll be really hanging onto me and I wonder if they like me."

"Assume nothing," Alicia replied. "Your primary relationship is you to you. Invest in yourselves. Sometimes I think I'd like to take three months off in life to get to know myself. This is your time to get to know you."

Deborahh rolled her eyes. There it was again: the message to get to know herself. From Rico to Alicia, the staffers at Acton were a broken record. Deborahh didn't need that advice. She knew herself. And after forty-four days in the program, she knew that there was nothing she could learn from the counselors. In fact, Deborahh felt she could get more valuable information on the street. Even so, she found Alicia entertaining in her naive, ignorant manner. So she listened.

Alicia turned to the second rung on the ladder and labeled it Casual. "You're not going to find someone issue-free, but at least find someone you can be friends with. What is a casual friendship? With men?"

"Say hi."

"Lunch."

"Nothing real deep. Not even having lunch," Alicia said. "Anyone see themselves as having a casual relationship with me?"

Marissa raised her hand.

"Very good. We've passed by each other. Marissa is always bustling around. I know she works in rehab and I know her name, but that's it. We have only a casual friendship. And that's where you need to spend time." Alicia pointed to the third rung from the bottom. "On the next rung, we might have lunch. What will we discuss?"

"Hopes, aspirations."

"Past relationships," Deborahh said sarcastically.

"General stuff, but don't get in too deep," Alicia replied. "What if you go into past sexual abuse, say you've been raped, spent time on the street as a prostitute? Check, please! What would that be a sign of?"

"Low self-esteem," Deborahh said. Although she knew the answer to the question, Deborahh didn't know how to resolve the bigger problem: What *should* she talk about to a casual friend? Ignoring the past ten years was impossible. So was keeping her mouth shut. Besides, she was what she had become. She couldn't hide the fact that she was a prostitute. Moreover, she refused to hide her profession. She told herself that it wasn't like there was anything immoral about offering men what they wanted in exchange for something she wanted. There should be no shame involved. Prostitution was no different from being a housewife.

"We pick people based on self-esteem," Alicia said. "If we're feeling down on ourselves we go into a party and we know the guy to pick."

"An alcoholic asshole," said someone, knowing the answer too well.

Alicia nodded and continued, "The next rung in the friendship category, the Close stage, is building trust in a friendship. If we follow what the program teaches, we're taking a year to do this, right?"

"It sounds like work," Patty said. "I'm tired of investigating myself, tired of digging in."

"The idea is to spend time with yourself. Either you want to learn to trust or you don't. If you don't do it right, you'll end up isolated and then come back here in six months. You can't go through your first year superficially. You can't think everything is fine or you'll end up back here."

Alicia's words made no sense to Deborahh. She didn't need a drawing of a ladder and facile explanations. She knew more about men than Alicia ever would. Her awareness of men and her powers over them had come early in life. Deborahh's mother attempted to guard her three girls from predatory men as the family followed the father from one army post to the next, but Deborahh often escaped her mother's protective eyes and found her way to the single men's barracks. As soon as the soldiers learned who her father was, they backed off. But Deborahh, who was well-developed by age thirteen, honed her flirting skills on military men, conning them into buying candy and comic books. She claimed that at college she had charmed her professors without sleeping with them and earned a bachelor's degree while expending most of her energies on the social circuit. Now, she had an ex-john sending her money and candy while Pete, her Acton boyfriend, provided excitement.

Unlike Deborahh, Patty was trying hard to work her program.

She listened closely to Alicia's advice about spending time with herself but wasn't sure how to put it into practice.

Echoing Patty's earlier words, Marissa said, "I'm thinking it's a lot of work. I have a relationship on hold. Is it possible that you'll choose someone who has dealt with issues more than you or do you always choose those as sick as you?"

"It's an individual thing based on your self-esteem. If you think about it, you'll know the answer," Alicia said.

Marissa's perplexed look disappeared.

"You're looking more like lights are going on. Generally speaking, people choose based on self-esteem. If I'm needy I might choose someone who knows how to take care of me. But I also run the risk of rejection. You guys have the power to choose who can come into your life." Alicia threw her chest forward and teasingly twirled her hair in a parody of sensuality.

"I do that so good," Marissa said.

Everyone laughed. One woman leaned toward Marissa and said, "I immediately thought of you."

"I do it all the time," Marissa said.

"I don't even want a relationship now," Patty said. Not only was she tired of investigating herself, but it was also difficult to remain free of relationships while at Acton. It would be even more challenging when she departed.

At Acton, it had been hard for Patty to stay away from Owen. Her flirtation with him began when she was still doing cartwheels in her excitement about getting into Acton. She had mellowed since that time and tried to avoid him. He still flirted with her, but she ignored it as much as possible, preferring to think of him as a friend.

Patty had also found it a challenge to deal with Marissa. Her dorm mate was bisexual and had made several advances to her. Patty found it disgusting, insisting to Marissa that she wasn't "like that," yet Marissa continued to tell her that she had a sexy, edible body.

Even with the Acton problems, Patty knew that her biggest challenge would be when she left the center. Ben, the father of her baby, was pressuring her to live with him when she left Acton, but she wasn't sure she wanted to do that. Ben had been there when she got baptized. He had stood with her kids, mother, and grandmother and witnessed her commitment to God. Plus, he was getting close to God himself. That should count for a lot. But did it mean she should live with him?

"Jumping into a relationship without having worked on yourself is risking relapse," Alicia stated. "I have a rule of thumb that, if anyone asks you your name, say it's Recovery."

Patty was still puzzled about the timing on relationships and asked Alicia, "You're talking about one year not to get involved? The father of my baby wants me to be with him when I get out. What should I do?"

"This is a safe place to be." Alicia pointed at the friendship level. "If he is serious, he'll be happy with this. Take it one day at a time."

"So me getting my own place with my daughter is the right thing?" Patty asked.

"Whatever your counselor says. It sounds like you already sort of know where you're going, you just want verification."

"But when he's in front of me, I say, 'Oh, Honey, whatever you want,' and all this talk is meaningless."

"I know. I changed guys like underwear." Alicia moved on, pointing to the next rung on the ladder: Multiple Groups (no pairing). "This is the next step, after spending time with yourself. You might find friends who want to go further, but tell them this is where you're at."

Noticing Marissa's look of skepticism, Alicia cheerfully turned to her. "Marissa, I wish I had some snapshots of your face." Her gaze returned to the entire group. "What do we have to gain by going up the ladder?"

"Learning how to interact with others," someone replied, summing up the entire class.

"Boy howdy, don't you learn a lot of stuff here?" Alicia said.

Chairs scraped against the linoleum floor as most of the women stood up, knowing they had been dismissed and eager to depart. Deborahh was one of the first out the door, soon followed by Marissa.

Patty and pregnant Blanca remained for the next class. They were soon joined by a dozen men.

Alicia also stayed. After waiting for everyone to settle down, she addressed them. "Anger Management is not a mandatory class. If you're here because you saw it on your program card and thought you had to be here, you don't. If your counselor said to be here or if you came on your own, then stay."

No one moved. "If you're going to comment, that's fine, but make comments to me, not to someone else in the class, because the things we discuss are sensitive. If you have something to contribute, say it to me because I can handle it. Tell me, what did you get out of last week's Arrested Development lecture?"

"That we stay immature emotionally if we had abuse," someone offered.

"Remember the equation?" Alicia asked.

"Rejection plus abuse equals arrested character development plus two years."

"Exactly. If you were abused when you were five, then growth stops and you don't get emotionally older than a seven-year-old which means you can have a thirty-six-year-old who acts like a seven-year-old emotionally. And that's what I was for a long time."

Alicia drew a triangle on the dry-erase board. She labeled the lower left point Phase I, the top Phase II, and the lower right Phase III, explaining that the beginning of Phase I was an irritant and the line leading up to the top was the build-up phase. The point at the top, Phase II, was the volcano, an explosion, when a person lost control. The line sliding down was the angry, 911 phase. Phase III, the horizontal line, was the honeymoon, damage control, when the angered person attempted to rectify the blow-up.

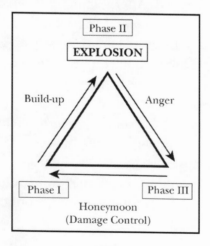

"Usually it takes about twenty minutes to go from zero to an explosion, but for some it takes only five minutes," Alicia said. "What are some of the things you feel physically, within your body, when you're in the build-up phase?"

"I shake," Patty said.

"Your adrenaline is pumping," Alicia said. "What else?"

Class members offered a variety of symptoms: tightened stomach, clammy hands, sweats, gritted teeth, flushed face, eyebrow spasms, headache, foot-tapping, clenched fists, and twitching arms.

"My lips flap," Patty said. "I go off and don't know what I'm saying."

"And you get louder?" Alicia asked.

"Yes. That's an uncomfortable feeling."

"So are you responsible?"

No one answered.

"You know the signs of anger, "Alicia said. "You need to take responsibility for them. I know it's going to set some of you on end, but here's a flash: these irritants are part of life and they're not going away. You can either keep doing what you're doing or you can change. What happens when a seven-year-old gets angry?"

"Stomps."

"Destroys things."

"Beats brother up."

"What about a thirty-six-year-old seven-year-old?" asked Alicia.

"Crashes cars."

"Saws cars in half."

"Brakes on the freeway."

"Shoots dope."

Patty slipped out of the room, heading toward the nearest restroom. Even through Marissa was no longer in the class, Patty's mind kept returning to her. Attempting to manage her anger was not helping. Patty was angry at Marissa and was not ready to forget or forgive. Patty wasn't irate about Marissa's sexual advances to her. Those episodes were upsetting, but nothing like Marissa's recent actions.

On the previous Sunday morning, Patty and a few of her dorm mates were in the common room between the sleeping compartments getting ready for church. One woman had beckoned Patty to the curtain separating the common area from one of the sleeping quarters. "Patty, look at what Marissa's doing."

Thinking that Marissa, the dorm comedian, was doing something silly, Patty had opened the curtain and peered in. The room was dim. Two women were still in bed. Marissa was on her knees. A man stood facing her.

"My gosh, Marissa, what are you doing?" Patty had said.

She had turned away, sickened that Marissa was giving a blow job to a man. In the dorm. On a Sunday. Before church.

Patty wasn't totally free of guilt herself. One morning, soon after she entered Acton, Owen had walked into the dorm and given her a kiss. But she had told him never to do that again. Marissa, on the other hand, had welcomed her boyfriend into the dorm and had sex within a few feet of two sleeping residents. And had then gone to church!

Later, Patty had asked, "Marissa, where are your morals?"

Marissa had claimed that sex and God had nothing to do with each other, but Patty couldn't understand that attitude and was angry at Marissa's disregard for God.

Patty was also angry at Marissa for putting her in an awkward position. Once again, a resident had invited Patty to witness the sexual act of another resident. Once again, she was in the wrong place at the wrong time. She only hoped she wouldn't have to talk about Marissa to the staff or anyone else.

Patty tried to shake off negative thoughts and returned to the classroom where the residents were sharing stories of anger.

"I remember when my significant other beat me and then wanted to go to bed with me," recalled one woman. "But I'd put up a wall and refused to talk to him. Later, we'd make up. But if he thought I was getting ready to leave him, he'd beat me up, tear up all my clothes, and lock me in. I'd go to bed and pray."

"For me," Blanca said, "there would be a brief time out between damage control and sex. He'd leave me alone for a while and then have sex."

"I never hurt the lady," declared one man, "but I'd smash the hell out of things. Tore up my own stuff and it only hurt me. I'd get angry and explode and think I had a right to sex."

"I don't destroy property," said another man, "because I learned long ago that I have to replace things. I don't hurt people because I'm afraid of being hurt. But I did Phase I and II over a cat. I went to Phase II because I wanted a cat in my cabin and someone else didn't."

"There are two ways to stop this," Alicia said. "When you get good enough, get to know yourself in Phase I and recognize the physical stress symptoms. Take a time out. At least thirty minutes. No drugs. No alcohol."

"No smoking," said Blanca.

"Right, Blanca. No caffeine. And no leaving unless your life is threatened. Think about your behavior. When this happens, and it will probably happen today, think about it. The other thing you can do is create a visual."

"When I get angry," said a small black man, "I don't hit women because I'm not supposed to. Instead, I wish I were a woman so I could kick her ass. I can see myself as a big-ass woman, twisting her head off . . . is that a visual?"

"Yes," Alicia replied. "Next week, we'll talk more about how to resolve this problem. Most people come in here desperately wanting to break this cycle and you can break it. You don't have to go to prison behind this stuff."

A white man was frantically writing on his hand, copying words from the board, as if in an effort to capture the key to life.

Patty, apparently oblivious to Alicia's attempt to end the class, said, "I used to think that because I cut my blow-up phase from ten to twenty minutes down to five, that I was doing better. But after coming to the first class I know I shouldn't have that blow-up."

"Blow-ups will come if you don't have self-control or self-respect."

"My whole thing would be erupting for a long time," Patty said. "Now I don't do it for as long." And she hadn't blown up at Marissa, though she was angry at her for disrupting Patty's attempt to work the program.

"The question is: What are you going to do about it?" Alicia asked. "No one is responsible for any abuse except the perpetrator."

———

That afternoon, Patty was summoned to Alicia's office. As soon as she entered the room, she knew that her day would get worse.

The room itself was peaceful. Heart-shaped rugs rested on the floor, their pastel pink and blue hues creating a home-like atmosphere. The microwave and stereo system added to that feeling as did the dream-catcher and bulletin board crammed with photographs. A luscious array of plants completed the picture.

But Patty wasn't feeling the warmth of the room that day. She warily sat on the couch, her back to the lone window.

Alicia faced her. "Mr. Clark, the Acton administrator, wants you to finish your conversation about Marissa and Alan."

Patty shrank back, trying to disappear into the small brown-and-white pattern on the couch. She whispered, "I never talked to Mr. Clark about Marissa."

Her mind was racing. She had feared a staff inquiry and had hoped it wouldn't happen, but the center had been buzzing about the incident all day. Every resident seemed to know about it—just like every resident knew that Marissa had sex with Alan in various spots around the center. Marissa had bragged about "doing it" on the golf course, she had asked her dorm mates to act as look outs while she and Alan used the dorm bathroom, and there were reports that she had gotten scratched from sneaking under the fence and huddling in the bushes outside the compound. There were even rumors that the pair was into kinky sex acts, giving each other whippings with tree branches.

Everyone knew these things. But Patty had not talked to anyone about them. She could draw only one conclusion: someone had used her name.

"Do you know anything?" Alicia asked.

Patty pondered the question, knowing full well that her honesty was being tested. It was one thing to keep quiet about sinful things happening in the dorm. It was another to lie. She didn't have a choice: it was either throw her program out the door and save somebody's butt or continue to work an honest program.

Feeling fully the mantle of being a woman of God, Patty spilled her guts.

12

DROPPING BURDENS

Patty retreated to her bed immediately after her conversation with Alicia. She felt ill and didn't want to talk to anyone. Even though she believed she was right to tell what she knew about Marissa and Alan, she understood that there would be repercussions. By closing her eyes, she hoped to shut out everything.

The news that the Acton staff now knew about Marissa and Alan spread throughout the center. Residents learned that Alicia had interviewed Alan and everyone from Patty's dorm. By dinnertime, the campus was abuzz with speculation about what would happen to the pair.

The suspense didn't last long. After dinner, Marissa exited her dorm, lugging several garbage bags full of clothes. As she carried her personal possessions toward the Admissions Office, one resident wag announced from her dorm porch, "The wheels of justice are rolling."

By the time Marissa reached the office, a knot of women greeted her. They hugged her and offered both sincere and guilty good luck.

Stella leaned out the office door and shooed away the small circle of well-wishers. She had known about Marissa and Alan's relationship for days. The pair had gotten write-ups for spending time together, but the incidents weren't deemed big enough to discharge them.

Stella ushered Marissa into the inner room where Lynne sat, filling out the discharge paperwork. The assistant administrator had been involved in Marissa's discharge for most of the afternoon. At one point, there were several people willing to make a statement, but by the end of the day many had backed out. An hour previously, Lynne had been subjected to a harangue by one of Marissa's dorm mates who, to avert any blame for Marissa's demise and avoid being labeled a snitch, had stood outside Lynne's office, shouting, "I didn't see nothin'. I didn't say nothin' and you can't say I did." Throughout the afternoon, Marissa had continued to deny the incident, but with the original eyewitness's account and Patty's corroboration, the Acton staff had decided that the story was credible.

As soon as Marissa stopped fiddling with her garbage bags, Lynne got her attention. "Take this experience and learn from it. You don't have to drink and use behind it. Get into another program before the court gets to you. Don't wait for the court to contact you. Call them and tell them you're no longer at Acton, but are at a new place. Let them know that you were not discharged for drinking or using. Tell them you just broke a rule. I remember you when you first came in. You were really serious. You came in here all gung-ho and then strayed the last few weeks. Maybe this is the best thing that ever happened. You can get back on the right path."

Marissa nodded, the butterfly clips in her hair bobbing up and down.

Stella offered her own advice. "If you call the Council on Alcoholism in the area that you're going to, they can tell you what's going on." Stella handed Marissa a list of major facilities. "Call those places and if they don't have openings, ask for referrals."

Within minutes, Marissa, her list, and her garbage bags were in the county van. Alan, who had been discharged by other staff members, rode in the same vehicle, heading toward downtown Los Angeles where they would be dropped off.

The next day, Patty tried to concentrate on her program. She put at the back of her mind the fact that her dorm mates suspected she had tattled on Marissa and that the self-appointed dorm leader had called her a snitch. Along with other residents, she crowded into the old chapel. So many people eagerly filled the chairless space that it looked more like a social gathering than a class. Patty, jittery Matt, and at least two dozen others stood waiting for the instructor.

Counselor Mike, a solid-looking man wearing wire-rimmed glasses, entered the room. A troublemaker during his youth, he had used drugs for several years and spent time in prison, yet he had never completed a drug treatment program. After prison, he turned to AA and got clean. As a counselor, he favored an edgier, confrontational method of treatment, and believing that Acton often became "Jurassic Park after dark," he never hesitated to point out unacceptable behavior.

Mike's thick, multi-colored moustache moved as he announced, "This class is Drop Your Burdens. What does the title mean to you?"

"Spilling your guts out."

"Stopping old behavior."

"Relationships."

Mike gave his own answer. "Mop up the stuff that's been camping with you for a while. 'Letting go and letting God' doesn't mean much unless you understand what letting go means to you. About half of you were here last week. I want those people on that side of the room and the other half here."

After dividing the people, Mike said, "You guys who have seen Magical Michael before, your job is to observe the others. You guys who haven't seen Magical Michael, tell me what you see when he's done. Look with more than just your eyeballs."

Mike placed a nine-inch stuffed gorilla on the floor. The animal, clothed and sporting a banana earring, immediately somersaulted, its yellow-and-black tank top clinging to its black fur. It rolled forward and then backward, forward and backward. Next, it began rocking from side to side, banging its head against the ground. During its frenetic motions, the toy emitted panicky, frightened sounds. Finally, it came to an abrupt halt.

"The gorilla was acting silly," one woman said.

"It was doing front somersaults and back somersaults and squeaked eleven times," Matt said with careful precision. "The squeaking was unintelligible. Its hands were doing something."

"Where'd he get to?" Mike asked.

Patty continued to lean forward, her eyes squinched in concentration.

"That's what *we* are," said Matt in a hushed tone. "We keep doing the same thing over again and getting nowhere, squeaking about nothing."

"Yeah," Patty said.

"I seen the monkey in myself, doing crank," said one resident, using one of the many nicknames for crystalline methamphetamine.

"What does it have to do with dropping your burden?" Mike asked.

"I always considered disease a burden, like a monkey on our back," Matt said.

Many residents considered their addiction to be a monkey on their back, though they probably didn't realize that in Spanish *tener un mono*, literally to hold a monkey, means to be addicted.

Matt continued, "I saw myself going in circles, bumping my head and squeaking but saying nothing."

"'Letting go and letting God' is your primary treatment," Mike said. "Hopefully some of you have detoxed already and the fog is starting to lift. I ask you to pay attention, not necessarily to me, but to you. As a newcomer, you don't have a lot of resources. You need to get the tools. One tool is paying attention, to yourself, your thought processes, your immediate environment. Some of you caught it right away, saw the monkey going nowhere. The single most important resource for you as a newcomer is the art—not science—of letting go. That simply, that quickly. It takes a long time to work on that. Turn it over to God. Let go. Drop your burdens. Whatever you want to call it."

Mike turned to one man. "You paying rent?"

"Yes."

"What happens if you lose your place?"

The man didn't answer so Mike did. "You forget about it and move on, right? Here's an opportunity to let go. I'm not saying ignore or bury your problem, but let go. Use your resources wisely. What if you have five dollars, but need to get across town to pick up money for smokes? What do you do?"

Matt spoke up, giving an involved explanation, based on priorities and decision-making, of how he would get a friend to take him part of the way, then would walk part way, and use some of the money to get back home, but would still end up with most of his five dollars, along with cigarettes.

"You're a methamphetamine addict, right?" Mike asked.

The class laughed. Matt nodded and grinned. "I'm a junkie."

"Ladies and gentlemen," Mike said, "it depends on your values. You need to have a plan. If you think you can get a ride, go get your smokes. But budget wisely. You can burn up all your resources just to make it to chow without socking someone. Every time you turn around, there's something here at Camp Snoopy that can make you crazy. Think about it: how important is a pair of shower shoes?"

"Very important," one man said. "You could get athlete's foot."

"So what do you do?"

"Ask housekeeping."

"Borrow from someone leaving."

"The idea," Mike said, "is to budget what we have and treat it like a value. What happens if you run into trouble? Where can you look for help?"

"Big Book."

"Counselors, teachers."

"Peers."

"It takes years and years to get what you're looking for in other people," Mike said. "Basically, when we observe, we have the tendency to judge and project our tendencies onto other people. What happens when we make a mistake? What happens when we run up against brick walls, and there's confusion, depression, et cetera, and we're not okay with ourselves?"

"We need to figure out a way to do something different."

"Get a jackhammer and bust through the wall."

"Go to a meeting and share with fellowship."

"You just said a mouthful," Mike said, referring to the last comment. "A whole treatment program in one sentence."

He pointed to a broken piece of furniture. "How many legs on this table?"

"One."

"Do you think if I lean on it, it's going to tip? But if I sit on a table with several legs, I'm spreading the burden around. What do we do when we spread the burden? We increase our resources. Letting go and letting God. We're not going to think our way out of this disease. Self-knowledge alone will not save your ass. The idea is to expand resources any way we can. You need a plan. So think about it and be a problem solver . . . So what's your plan?"

"I'm going to deal with life on life's terms," volunteered one resident. "One day at a time, using my Higher Power."

"I'm just trying not to forget that I'm an addict," said a second person.

"Thank you for bringing that up. If you're an addict, you have an instant 'forgetter.' You get comfortable and stop going to meetings because, guess what, *Law and Order* is on. Use your resources and problem-solving strategies so there isn't a conflict about watching TV. Or a conflict about going to a meeting . . . Why is letting go an art form and not a science?"

Mike paused before answering his own question. "We are constantly perfecting our own life, never to be perfect, but constantly working to let us be more effective. But no matter how much we study, if we don't put it into practice, we'll continue to do the same stuff. Just like the monkey."

Patty, like the rest of the class, was paying close attention to Mike's words. What he was saying clicked with her. It was a simple idea: if things bothered her and she had no control and couldn't deal with the situation, then she should put aside those problems. Let them go. She really liked the concept.

"Principles," Mike continued, "are like a cement floor: unmoving. Bedrock. Not elastic. Truth *is*. There's no middle ground. Addicts take truth, call it honest, and bend it to fit ourselves. That doesn't work.

"Has anyone seen my office door? It has the twelve principles. It comes from steps from NA, where I hang my hat. What your roadmap is, I don't care. But the more beliefs you pump into a balloon, it expands. To expand your balloon you might have to let some of the old beliefs out, but you also need to let new ones in.

"Years ago I had to have one thousand dollars in my pocket at all times in case I got busted so I could make bail before they called my parole officer. Now I get more value out of that thousand dollars than I ever did as bail. I didn't understand that until I was about six years clean. Things change. You change."

Mike surveyed the room, concluding with "Things can change . . ."

After dinner, Patty attended a mandatory dorm meeting.

The women gathered in the sitting room between the two dorms—the place Patty had been when spying Marissa's knee-dance. Patty sat at the end of the couch, trying to appear inconspicuous.

Lynne, who had called the meeting, introduced herself as the assistant administrator and said that she wanted to talk about any issues that they might have.

There was complete silence. Patty and the others looked blankly at Lynne. Patty was remembering what a self-righteous dorm member had said earlier: "I think people should keep their mouths shut, especially if they're as guilty as the next."

Finally, one woman mentioned a problem with the trash cans, saying they were dirty and had flies.

"I'm not here for trash cans," Lynne said. "I want to talk about guys in the dorm."

Every mouth tightened and every pair of eyes looked anywhere but at Lynne.

"Okay," Lynne said. "I want to talk about recent events. I won't act on anything anyone says tonight. I just need to understand your point of view and I'll tell you my point of view and maybe we'll have a consensus. First, I can't break confidences, but I want you to know that several people, people outside this dorm, saw Alan go in and out."

Patty clutched a couch cushion, holding onto it in the same way that she might a life preserver. As the silence lengthened, Patty held the pillow even tighter. Her hand squeezed something metallic and she pulled out a rusty razor blade.

"Look at this," Patty said, wondering which nutty person had left behind the old thing. After everyone had exclaimed in surprise, Patty asked, "Can I keep it?"

"I'll put your name on it and you can have it when you leave," Lynne said as she took the blade.

Silence reigned again.

Finally, Lynne spoke. "I would hope that no one would engage in any sexual act at Acton. Maybe it's naive on my part, but if one person brought someone into the dorm, all eleven others should jump up in unison and tell them to take it outside. Otherwise, staff is going to get wind of these things and then, when you're asked, you'll be caught in a lie or have to tell the truth about your roommate. It's a horrible situation that you were put in. Don't let it happen again. Don't let them bring it inside. Make people find their own love nests. Maybe then they'll be the only ones paying the price."

Patty and a few others nodded.

"I heard that Alan was married," said one woman.

"That snake!"

Most of the women gaped at the informer.

"If Marissa thinks he's going to take care of her, she has a long wait," Lynne said. "I've seen it happen hundreds of times. Guys promise all kinds of things and girls believe it. I've seen couples get discharged and the man's wife will come to pick him up. The girl will come trundling up with her clothes, planning to leave with her new boyfriend, and he will tell her to get lost. The guys will tell you anything but reality."

"That's true," said one woman. Many of the others nodded in agreement. Suddenly they all had something in common: they knew that men at Acton were liars. The strain began to dissipate. Even Patty relaxed a bit.

"Remember," Lynne said, "that you were really close to each other and then all this stuff happened with Marissa. Maybe now that she's gone, things will go back to how they were."

Patty didn't believe it. And even if things did go back to how they were, she hadn't felt especially comfortable then, either. The self-proclaimed dorm leader had mocked her for trying to be a woman of God, had picked on her for insignificant things, and had made it clear that she thought Patty was an idiot.

That evening was especially trying. When Patty attended her usual NA meeting, she was greeted with comments like, "I heard you dropped the dime on Marissa."

Patty's first inclination was to yell at them. After all, this was *her* fellowship, too. It was chip night, when those in recovery were given awards for staying sober, and she always enjoyed the ceremony. Sure, Alan had been the NA secretary, but it wasn't her fault that he had gotten kicked out; she wasn't the one doing nasty things in the dorm. All she did was tell the truth.

She could feel the anger welling up inside her. But she suppressed a shout of "Fuck you all," telling herself that was the old Patty. The new Patty decided to heed the lesson from Alicia's Anger Management class and take a time-out.

She raced from the room.

Patty strode around the campus until her mind calmed and she developed another perspective, thinking that the others might be angry with themselves for lying to Alicia and, feeling stupid about their own behavior, turned their hostility toward Patty. She didn't like the way they were treating her, but she couldn't run away. That would have been behavior from the old Patty. Instead, she needed to remain at Acton and uphold her dignity.

After deciding to stay, Patty needed to vent to someone. There was no one at Acton she could talk to so she called her mother. Patty usually insulated her mother from the ragged side of life in rehab, not wanting to drag her in, but that night she didn't know where else to turn. Patty told her mother that she *felt* like leaving, but wouldn't. She didn't mention details but said there was too much sinful stuff going on in the dorm.

Suddenly, she was both crying and shaking. She said that she just wanted her mother to know the situation. Secretly, though, she hoped that her mother would tell her to come home. Patty tried to convince herself that a few weeks of sobriety was enough. Maybe she was cured. After all, she had been praying continuously that her cravings would disappear. And they seem to have abated. Her sobbing increased, but she didn't get a summons to come home.

After Patty hung up, she composed herself and started toward her dorm when she was stopped by Mike. Patty tensed, wondering if he was going to reprimand her for an SIP infraction, knowing that he had seen her flirt with men at the center. Instead, the counselor asked if she was okay and then told her that he had seen her change from her first days at Acton. *Wow*, she thought, someone noticed her efforts to better herself. She savored that brief encounter and returned to her dorm believing, at least for the moment, that she could make it through her troubles.

The next day, Patty attended Walt's class on social skills. She sat close to the counselor and tried to lose herself in the discussion about assertive behavior.

After a few minutes, Walt moved to a new topic. "Let's talk about a sticky issue: are we our brother's keeper? If someone is using, are we a snitch if we turn them in? No. We should be responsible citizens in recovery. If we let counselors know what is going on, it is not being a snitch. You need willingness. Open-mindedness. What's the other one?"

"Honesty," Patty added. She knew the answer; this was *her* area.

Walt nodded. "We're not like the average person. So we need to live by a high standard, but not an unrealistic one."

"Is that what license is?" asked someone.

"No. License would be stomping on others toes. Not having respect. Playing the radio too loud. I can think of a more graphic answer from the other day, but I'll move along."

Patty giggled. So did most of the other women. They knew Walt was referring to Marissa.

Her mind wandered briefly. When she refocused on Walt, he was saying, "We aren't trying to get even. We're trying to teach, to share info so we can grow in recovery. When you share at a meeting, what step are you doing? . . . Step Five. We are standing up for ourselves. Letting ourselves be known to others."

Suddenly, everything clicked into place for Patty and with that indirect encouragement from Walt, she knew how she would handle the NA situation: she would stand up for herself at the next meeting.

That evening, Patty attended NA, the same meeting she had bolted from the previous evening. Summoning as much dignity as possible, she stood before her peers and declared, "You know what? My honesty was tested two days ago and I had to think about how seriously I wanted this program. It was either throw the program out the door and save somebody's butt or continue working an honest program. I was honest. And that affected the others around me.

"I could have followed the old ways, the street ways, and refuse to be what some people call a snitch, but the old ways didn't get me nowhere. So I had to be honest. If people want to call me a snitch, they can call me a snitch. But people shouldn't have put me in the situation where I had to do that. Some people, they agree . . . other people look at me like I'm selfish and self-centered. But it's not like I go out of my way to find people doing something wrong and then tell Alicia. I'm not that kind of snitch. I'm just a woman of God, trying to work an honest program. That's just how I feel."

For the next few days, Patty felt enormously relieved. She was happy that she had spoken up for herself. She thought that if people knew that she was working an honest program they might hide their sinful behavior and she wouldn't be put in a similar situation again.

Oddly, Patty missed Marissa. She had been one of the few people who could almost always make the dorm erupt in laughter. But life was much calmer in her absence. A few of the others quietly admitted to Patty that that they felt the same way. Calm was good. Patty was thankful that she could again concentrate on her program. Sure, she had little intrusions on her tranquility—her drug-addicted sister relapsed and called, crying out for help; Owen continued to annoy her with his attentions; her baby's father kept pressuring her to commit to living with him when she finished Acton; and her oldest daughter was begging her to leave Acton early so she could be home for Thanksgiving— but for the most part she was content.

Patty had dropped her burdens.

13

WORKING THE PROGRAM EXUBERANTLY

Tiffany was working her program with an intensity rarely matched at Acton. She took to heart the AA concept that service to others was an important part of recovery. She was treasurer of Cocaine Anonymous and chair of ACRC, the Acton Center Residents' Committee. She attended numerous anonymous meetings each week, including the daily meeting in Spanish, helped Rico with orientations, gave tours, and met with panels of people from the recovery community outside of Acton. She was even taking extra classes in her zeal to stay busy, which meant that she was already working on the third phase of the program while those who entered at the same time were still on Phase II.

She was so busy that I had a hard time pinning her down to a meeting. I finally corralled her one Sunday. We met on the lawn and again sat at a picnic table, but this time, visiting day, other residents and their families were gathered at nearby tables. Tiffany still favored bright blue eye shadow and had a cigarette tucked over her ear, but I was immediately struck by a dramatic change: she had lost her acquired Hispanic accent. Additionally, she no longer referred to Homeboy this or Homegirl that. It was almost as if she had become a different person, someone who knew that she had a lot to overcome and was willing to do, in Rico's words, *whatever* it took to stay clean and work toward recovery.

I asked about her first impression of Acton.

"I liked it. It was so friendly. Just coming straight out of prison, I was coming from a black hole and then all of a sudden I'm in all this light . . ."

Although Sunday was the one day of relaxation for Tiffany, she still talked fast, as though she needed to hurry so she could make it to another appointment. "I'd been clean for four months before I got here. Plus I was in prison and bored so coming here was like: What can I do? What can I keep busy with? . . . I needed to take on a commitment. I've been really good with my word. That's the thing that shocked me the most. On the streets and throughout my using, I'd always say, 'I'll be there. I'll be back,' but it never meant anything because I'd never show up. But now, every time I take a commitment, I'll be there. And that's one of the things that makes me feel the best. My word is finally worth something.

"This is it. I don't think I'll ever use again. I finally found some place I belong."

The strong aroma of barbecuing meat floated toward us, enveloping our table.

Tiffany continued, talking about how she was taking full advantage of her classes and learning more about inter-personal relationships. The Achieving Intimacy class had taught her "a lot about my father, understanding what kind of person he is. He's a controller. I learned a lot about parents. When you're young, up to eight years old, as a girl you look up to your mother. And then when you hit a certain age you need reinforcement from the male. And as Alicia said, most men, what they do is they get jealous that the daughter is growing and they can't control her as much. She's not their little girl and she needs to grow yet a lot of men turn their back on their daughters.

"That's what my dad did. Instead of giving me that male figure, male role model, he turned his back on me because I wasn't doing what he thought was right. That's when I started drinking and using because I couldn't get any attention from him except when I ticked him off."

A group of people began setting up their own picnic area under a nearby tree, shaking out a blanket, noisily dropping paper bags to the ground, and pulling out pre-made food.

"Now my father's really cool," Tiffany said. "I talk to him on the phone all the time. He is so understanding. He even sent me money . . . I've got a good relationship with my family now."

Although the class helped her understand her relationship with her father, she was having problems with men at Acton. One male friend got jealous when she started spending time with a second man. Tiffany hadn't intended to start anything with the second man—and nothing sexual had transpired—but the first guy was making her life difficult, constantly taking pot shots at her.

"I was at the point where I was thinking I should drop everything," Tiffany said. "But then if I drop everything, I'm letting him control my recovery and that's crazy. He had a big ol' fit today because one of the Mexican guys, I'm really close with all the Mexicans, called me over to his table because his mom and his wife and his uncle and all them were there and they gave me a bowl of *potzole* and I sat down and ate it. And this guy wanted to throw a fit because I sat down at a table with men and ate soup."

Tiffany rested her hands on the picnic table, displaying a fistful of silver jewelry, sporting rings on her fingers and both thumbs.

"I was going to cause a big old argument, my old behavior, but I decided that tomorrow at our weekly meeting, I'm going to say first thing that it's been brought to my attention that some people were offended because I sat down to this table with men and ate soup and I apologize to those I've offended. I didn't mean to and I'll do better to change. And I'll just leave it at that. I'm not saying I'm going to change, but just to shut him up I decided that's the best way to deal with it . . . instead of letting him rent space in my head."

Tiffany explained her relationship with the guy she liked, saying that they wanted to build a friendship before they built anything else. She was awed that he had claimed to have too much respect for her to start something sexual while at Acton. "I thought, 'Wow, imagine that.'" She paused. "I'm fresh out of prison, a hormone waiting to happen and I know that."

At the end of our conversation, I asked Tiffany what she thought the future held for her.

Her reply was clear, unaccented, and strong. "I think I'm gonna go back to school and be a drug counselor."

"And come back here?" I asked.

Tiffany exploded with laughter.

Matt was another resident who tried to stay busy by helping others. He had told Stella that he found it fulfilling to be of service in NA and he enjoyed listening to people. Now he was planning a new endeavor: tutoring.

He bounded into the Learning Center, where he was scheduled to meet Frankie, a resident matched to him for math tutoring. After a quick introduction, the pair sat down. Matt had gained almost ten pounds since his arrival at Acton and his hair had grown one half an inch, along with a newly sprouted goatee. But he remained jittery as he set to work refining Frankie's arithmetic skills, starting his new pupil on a set of simple multiplication problems to see how he fared.

Frankie took the task seriously, his corn-rowed head bent in concentration. He talked to himself as he worked, ignoring the noises and activity surrounding him: one of the two computers was in use and the keyboard clicked loudly, another set of men was working together in the back, two women sat nearby, and a coordinator wandered the room.

Although he had been at Acton only a week, he was ready to get serious about recovery. He was forty-three, had four grown children and a wife, and was tired of using. He came to Acton on his own, looking forward to help in getting his life on the right track. Brushing up on arithmetic skills was part of his plan.

While Frankie worked, Matt continued to squirm. The schoolroom chair with its attached writing surface could barely contain him. It reminded him of high school. Those classrooms couldn't contain him either and he had dropped out after tenth grade, long before he had been diagnosed with attention deficit disorder. Learning the cause of his nervousness might have helped before he dropped out, but now he was dedicated to not taking medication, preferring to live with his symptoms.

After racing through the first test, Frankie handed the results to Matt who quickly scanned the paper and pronounced, "Beautiful." Matt then showed Frankie a few tricks for adding two-digit numbers. Frankie caught on immediately and when he completed his first problem the new way, Matt beamed with pride. "Beautiful. Kick ass."

Matt quickly made up a sheet of new equations, his entire body working in jerky motions, causing the tattooed cross with the image of Christ to rise and fall from beneath the top of his white T-shirt. Frankie eagerly completed the problems as Matt peered over his shoulder, offering constant encouragement. "You're kicking ass and taking names."

"Is this right?" Frankie asked.

"Yeah, man. You're tripping out. Beautiful. Add 'em up, that's okay, there you go, atta boy . . . see, you remembered."

Frankie stayed focused, earnestly concentrating, occasionally laughing at Matt's comments and smiling at his own successes. Fifty minutes passed quickly. The room coordinator announced that it was seven-thirty and told the person at the computer, "See you tomorrow." He glanced at Matt, saying that he could hang out another half hour.

Grabbing some blank sheets of paper, Matt began making columns of arithmetic problems, telling Frankie that he was giving him homework. Frankie smiled. He liked Matt and his frenetic energy. He liked this new arrangement. They seemed a perfect match.

Matt, too, was elated with the session. He reflected that he could have gotten someone dumb or really slow and that would have frustrated him. Instead, he thoroughly enjoyed the time spent aiding Frankie. Matt couldn't help noting the irony of the situation; he had been a white supremacist before arriving at Acton and now he was making friends with a "brother."

Before they parted, Matt told Frankie, "I'm gonna be in Acton a long time and I got a lot of time. More than it's helping you, it's helping me 'cause I get bored by myself."

Some residents who focused heavily on their program moved beyond the assigned classes and attended elective workshops. One of the campus favorites was the Reading, Writing, and Recovery course. Late Sunday afternoon, eleven men and six women awaited the instructor in the conference room.

Curtis was one of the first to arrive. In his short time at Acton he had become very serious about recovery. In fact, his chocolate-skinned face exhibited his earnestness about life itself; Curtis was weary of the drug life and ready to change. His short, scraggly hair and moustache framed a pair of solemn red-rimmed eyes, eyes that had witnessed too much grief, most of it self-imposed. He had a tattoo on every finger, one for each year of prison. When he had run out of fingers he refused to mark his toes, so though his years of confinement continued well beyond a decade, they remained a memory without a permanent physical brand.

He hadn't arrived at Acton wanting recovery. He had only come because his girlfriend, his sole support, begged him to detox and stay off drugs. Curtis wanted to keep her happy so she would continue to facilitate his drug use once he left the rehab center, but after a week of sobriety, it occurred to him that he didn't have to be an addict. He was tired, he had pains, and it was time to quit.

Not knowing what else to do, he doubled the number of meetings required by his counselor. He wasn't trying to impress anyone. He genuinely wanted to go. And he made it a point to get up and share at least once every other meeting. After attending a month's worth of meetings in less than two weeks, Curtis achieved a moment of clarity: if the counselors could get clean and stay clean, it gave him and other heroin addicts lots of hope.

By the end of his first thirty days at Acton, Curtis had labored through the first three steps. Now he was on Step Four which required him to make a "fearless moral inventory" of himself. He had sent a letter to his mother, admitting his sins and telling her how much he loved her. He knew that she prayed for him continuously, and Curtis was optimistic that they could build a new relationship when he left Acton.

He also had recounted his relationships with women. He began his confession by writing, "Guilt: Over the years my pattern has been to develop relationships with women who could support my drug habit. I went into these relationships professing love in order to obtain money." Curtis then enumerated his trespasses against every woman he could remember.

After recounting the wrongs he imposed upon the women in his life, Curtis was free to turn his attention to the Big Lie.

For years he had lived off of his reputation as a killer. He told people that he went to Soledad prison at a young age—which was true—and while in prison killed another man—which was *not* true—who had made sexual advances toward him. What really happened was that while at Soledad, there was a fight in the dining room. Curtis got hurt badly. He was given an institutional write-up, got more time tacked onto his sentence, and was shipped to San Quentin prison.

Whenever anyone, prisoner or civilian, asked why he spent almost eighteen years in prison, Curtis told them that he had committed murder while protecting himself. He employed that lie frequently, getting lots of mileage out of portraying himself as a victim turned hero. The truth was much more mundane; he had been imprisoned because he was a petty ass drug addict.

Counselor David entered the classroom and waited for everyone to settle down. His dark eyes looked out over high cheekbones that tapered to his chin, his pointy ears framing his mischievous face. For residents new to his class, he quickly explained that it was a place "where you can express yourself freely, talk about any subject, all subjects."

There was no grading. "The bottom line is, if you do this work, you'll learn."

David turned to Curtis and asked him to read aloud his essay assignment, an examination of his feelings about "Bill's Story" from the Big Book.

Using both hands, Curtis held a piece of notebook paper closer to his eyes. "After reading Bill's Story I took a look at the differences in our lives before noticing the similarities. I started drinking and using drugs when I was about fifteen years old, and due to this behavior I entered the criminal justice system as a juvenile offender. At age eighteen I had a felony case pending and Uncle Sam didn't want the likes of me in his army. Bill got to go Over There and I got to go to jail."

All eyes were focused on Curtis, all ears attentive to his words as he continued the comparison between himself and Bill Wilson, commonly known as Bill W., one of the AA founders.

"I had ambitions like Bill to be somebody; he played Wall Street and hit it big and I played Hip, Slick, and Kool and ended up in prison. Bill drank to the tune of millions in his early days and I drank to the tune of handcuffs and leg chains. Bill made the following statement on page two: 'Out of this alloy of drink and speculation, I commenced to forge the weapon that one day would turn in its flight like a boomerang and all but cut me to ribbons.' I, on the other hand, had forged a weapon that shot in a straight path, carrying destruction and me every inch of the way.

"Bill realized after a while that he was doomed where alcohol was concerned; I too was doomed and I knew it early on! My drinking always took me to one of two places."

Curtis set down the page and picked up a second piece of paper before continuing.

"Hospitals or prison. After my first prison term I remember telling myself that I wasn't going to drink or use drugs ever again; and like Bill, I meant what I said. Why I was only out a few hours before I picked up the first drink is beyond me. I knew that drinking and drugging would always take me back to those places that I didn't want to go, but I couldn't stop, just like Bill! I also knew (just like Bill) that I was hurting the people who loved me but I couldn't stop!

"Bill's wife went through a lot over the years that he drank and I spent so much time in prison that I couldn't get a wife. The differences between Bill's life and mine are so similar that I can't help identifying with him. Bill drank even when he didn't want to and so did I."

The room was silent except for Curtis's soft, clear voice.

"When Bill was in the hospital again after his last drink he had a spiritual awakening and knew that the only way he could stay sober was to help another alcoholic get freed from alcohol, hence, the birth of Alcoholics Anonymous. I truly believe that I too can stay sober by helping others to recover from their addictions. I will trudge this road to recovery and know that God is with me all the way. Thank you, God, for people like Bill W. and Dr. Bob."

The class burst into applause.

David nodded. "The same behavior goes into drug addicts as alcoholics. The same signs and symptoms. One is denial, the second is repressed feeling and compensating behavior. Then there's low self-esteem, medical problems, and spiritual problems. The more you write about your own behavior, the clearer the picture becomes. I've been in and out of institutions, shot, rolled out of cars, had affiliations with people who used me, never had a quality relationship, never had an identity. We get in where we can fit. But the most devastating thing is not drugs, it's behavior."

"What was most clear for me," Curtis said, "is that there is lots of esteem for the medical profession. They put people back together with pins and steel. The medical profession awes me. But it couldn't cure alcoholism. Even though they were skeptical about Bill W., the doctors were amazed. I realized doctors aren't gods. Bill W. and Dr. Bob aren't either. I'm grateful that somebody wanted to get sober bad enough to get God's help and give it to me."

David nodded again. "The doctors had to question their own adequacy because they couldn't cure alcoholism. Look at it from the global picture: there's no other cure unless you work together. And that's beautiful."

"Before I got here, I was a quitter," Curtis said. "I got discouraged real quick. Bill W. saw all these alcoholics come to his door and they never got sober. I'da thrown in the towel a long time ago."

"Bill W. did think of throwing in the towel," David replied. "He said to his wife, 'Nobody's getting sober.' She said, 'That's not true. You are.' The Big Book gives you a practical program of action that will allow you to go one day at a time. There's not much about alcohol after page forty-three. It's about a new way of behavior. If it was just alcohol, we wouldn't be here. But we need new beliefs. In the past, I used on a daily basis, went to jail, had near death experiences, but I'm still going to do it right next time? That's insane. To get sober we have to do things we never wanted to do. The entire chapter talks about working with others so that must be an important part of your program. Nothing will insure immunity as much as working with another addict.

"There are two aspects you can recover from, a hopeless state of mind and body. We need to see words and put them in action. Peeling back layers of denial and recovery is possible. I say over and over: 'The recovery process is a lot simpler than what you were doing.' It's just that simple. An easier and softer way is to blame others. To stop blaming others, you need to write, to see your past. After all the blame is gone, you can't blame anybody else."

Curtis knew David was right; it had been his choice to hurt and betray and steal from every woman he met. It had been his choice to tell the Big Lie. Writing it all down was a start, but he had a long way to go. His newly acquired sponsor recently confirmed that by telling Curtis that he wasn't finished with Step Four—he hadn't mentioned his resentments or all the people he harmed. The sponsor, who had ten years of sobriety and was an Acton alumnus, wanted him to remember everyone he stole from—which Curtis thought was unrealistic since he didn't make notes about the people or things he boosted while trying to support his drug habit.

"The first time I drank," David said, "I was in the garage, sneaking a drink. I was nine or ten years old. I fell asleep and woke up with ants all over me. Anybody in their right mind would have quit right then. But I wanted to do it again. That's twisted. Take a heroin addict. The first time you slam, you puke all over yourself. But you say, 'Damn, that's fun. When can we do it again?'"

David paused to let his words sink in. "Until we realize the problem, there is no reason to fix it. Once you realize there's a problem, you can look for a solution. I don't care what your spiritual experience, this program works. I didn't care what color your skin was or what your church affiliation was when I needed a 'rock.' None of us did. So when we come into recovery why should it matter?

"You're the most inventive, creative people the world has known. That's why you're here. We're too smart for our own good. Work is necessary. That's why I tell you to get a sponsor that's going to make you work. Don't live in L.A. with a sponsor in L.A. without a car. Some of you will do this purposely, but you need an accessible sponsor. Find a group home. If you go to different meetings no one gets a chance to know you—or call you on your shit."

"That's old behavior," offered a class member.

"Yes it is."

"How do you deal with old anger?" asked one man. "My mom said I was a piece of shit."

"I still get angry," David admitted.

"What about crying?" asked another man. "I quit writing when I cried."

"One of the biggest myths is that men don't cry," David said. "If you need to cry, come into my office and I'll cry with you. There are days when I go into my office and cry. We've been through the same thing, we just did it different places, with different people, in different abandoned buildings. We're all the same. We need to share."

David's words gave Curtis hope for his future. If David could do it, he could do it. David clearly knew the path and Curtis planned to follow it closely.

14

BAD DIRECTIONS

Stella was scowling when she returned to Acton after a morning in court at "discontent" Harold's request. Nothing in her life seemed to be going well. Although she claimed not to be drinking or using drugs, many people around her knew that she was having difficulties and heading toward relapse if she couldn't get her life under control.

Her biggest problem was her husband. Finances, ever a precarious problem, had appeared almost manageable a few weeks earlier when she and Zach pulled two thousand dollars out of their retirement plan to pay off bills, but within a week, the money was gone. Stella said she submerged her old m.o.—fuck responsibility and run—and hung onto her relationship with her husband, playing the martyr even though she knew it was over, but her husband soon asked for a divorce. Stella agreed, as long as there wasn't anyone else. He said there wasn't.

Later, Stella heard a rumor about Zach, so one night while at work, she called him and badgered him into admitting that there was another woman. She then slammed the phone down and raced home.

Her husband was sitting on the tailgate of his El Camino with phone in hand when she advanced on him, Chuck Norris-style. She was smiling as she punched and kicked him. He blocked well, but she was a whirlwind of aggression and wouldn't give up. She knew that she was going to explode at some point and felt the release and relief of her anger in the dark dance around the yard.

She thought that Zach was chickenshit for having the phone nearby and calling the police—on her!—but Zach had a lot at stake: he had served time for two infractions and with California's three-strike rule, he could have been sentenced to life for hitting Stella while defending himself.

Stella and her teenaged daughters moved out after the attack. Since leaving Zach's house, they had lived in several cheap motels, migrating whenever they got tired of the current cramped space or the bill got too high or the manager decided that three women and assorted friends were too much for the tiny room. Most of their belongings were stuffed into garbage bags, heaped to the ceiling of a storage unit.

Living in chaos was a strain on her daughters, but Stella seemed to thrive on the challenge. She missed her dog but was determined not to relocate permanently until she found the perfect place. She didn't want an apartment; she had to have a house. Not only that, she had to buy the house. Her husband was a homeowner and she wanted to prove that she could do just as well on her own. It didn't matter that her friends were advising her to find an apartment, that her daughters merely wanted stability. Stella could forgo the swimming pools and clubhouses that came with most apartment complexes; she needed her animals nearby and a place to call her own.

Stella was upbeat about the places she viewed, seeing possibilities where others found disasters. Two days before her court appearance, Stella had dragged Lynne to view an affordable house in Quartz Hill, a quaint one-street town where the horses outnumbered the traffic signals. The house was a half-hour drive from Acton, deeper in the desert, near Lynne's house. But while Lynne's house was a comfortable three-bedroom dwelling with a large fenced yard for her numerous animals, the place Stella examined was uninhabitable. It lay on a quarter of an acre that was big enough for her animals, but the lack of fences and the heavily trafficked road would put her cat and dog at risk.

Worse yet was the inside; the claustrophobic rooms contained worn and stained indoor-outdoor carpet and most windows had been smashed by incoming rocks. The bathroom was open; there was no door and a paneless window overlooked a utility room. A used shower-bath unit had been shoved near the corner, but it was not sealed in place. The sink was missing, exposing rusted pipes, and the filthy toilet had neither lid nor seat. The floor was littered with rubble.

As Stella examined the house, she kept up a running commentary about who could fix the broken drywall in the kitchen, the lock on the flimsy front door, et cetera. Lynne pointed out the extensive work that would need to be done and wondered aloud how much Stella could depend on the Acton family for yet another move and all the necessary renovations.

Later, with a bit of perspective, Stella decided to keep looking. She wasn't going to back off from her idea of a house, and buying was still a necessity, but she would find something that needed less "fixing up."

Stella's emotional tailspin made working that much more difficult. On top of dealing with problems of home and family while trying to remain sober, Stella had a caseload of addicts to worry about. Her maternal nature and the deep caring she had for every resident who crossed her path weren't diminished by her own problems, but her energy reserve was low and it wasn't easy helping people who were supposed to be learning recovery.

Two men in particular were taxing Stella's patience. One was Robert. The wiry, white-haired man was missing two teeth and looked like he had seen much during thirty years in prison. When Stella asked him to sit down in her office, he submitted easily to her authority.

Stella wearily intoned a list of grievances against him: smoking in his cabin, waking up and saying he could use a hit, taking coffee and juice without going to meetings. Robert's behavior was exactly why Stella objected to the increasing numbers of ex-cons at Acton. She felt that Robert and the others were tossed into the center because the county didn't know what else to do with them, but that didn't mean they belonged there. The ex-cons weren't there for recovery and disrupted those who were.

"How do you plead?" Stella asked.

"Not guilty."

"I'm only dealing with the info I've got. I think it's a little chickenshit. I know you're joking. I've heard you screwing around and joking and I've told you to knock it off."

Robert admitted that he used vulgar language but claimed it was the social norm in the cabin. "How can someone come over here and say that when they do the same thing?"

"I know you're hurt, but do the right thing and quietly watch them screw up. That will give you satisfaction. I know you're here doing your time. I don't really care. I just hope you make it through and maybe even learn something. You know how to do time, do it. I'm going to write it up as easy as possible. I could write you up on four to six violations, but I'll combine it into one. I'm writing that the client is counseled and encouraged to follow all of the rules of the program. It doesn't get any simpler than that."

"I don't want to get booted outta here over no bullshit."

"I'm trying to keep it light for you. I'm going to add this one on here to cover my ass." Stella began reading, "Further violation of rules may or may not result in discharge."

Robert nodded and exited.

The ex-con was easy compared to Harold, the man responsible for making Stella pull her nice clothes out of storage, stand in front of a parole board, and testify against her will. Harold's poor attitude had been evident since Stella met him. She had encouraged him to get involved by applying for a volunteer position at the switchboard. He preferred to complain. One day, during a particularly annoying episode with Harold, Stella warned him to stop trying to manipulate counselors and instead follow staff instructions.

That night, Harold took out his anger by waking a cabin mate and calling him a fat faggot. The cabin mate dressed and headed outside, where he ran into a friend whom he told about the situation. The friend got into a shouting match with Harold who then pushed, slapped, and spit at him. The friend reported the violence to a counselor. Harold claimed that he had only pushed the guy in self-defense, but the man's scratched neck seemed to prove otherwise, so Harold had been discharged.

Once back on the streets, Harold was arrested for violating parole. Believing that Stella was his savior, he had asked the court to subpoena her to speak on his behalf at a hearing to revoke his parole.

Stella had gone to the hearing annoyed that Harold was still hanging onto his old behavior, thinking that someone else would bail him out of trouble. She was also upset that she had to testify to something that was bound to harm Harold's cause. She didn't like the man, but she didn't get into counseling to hurt people. She had done her best to discourage Harold from calling on her, telling the hearing agent that she was willing to appear, but that her testimony would not benefit Harold. When she arrived in court, she again tried to thwart her testimony, saying she couldn't speak without a consent form. Harold said he would sign, even when Stella cautioned him by shaking her head and saying it would not be in his best interest because it would allow her to read letters from people who witnessed the behavior that prompted his discharge. Harold ignored her warnings and signed the consent.

As Stella testified, she wondered what the fuck she was doing in that place. In addition to not wanting to hurt Harold, she hated the fact that she had become part of the system. Somehow she, a rebel from an early age, had been forced to stand on the wrong side of the fence. Stella left the court knowing that Harold's own idiocy had returned him to prison, but hating her tiny role in the affair.

Her mood darkened more when she returned to Acton and learned that Matt was leaving the center. She saw him with two other residents near the administration building.

Matt's Keds-clad feet danced on the pavement as he penned his name and address in another resident's Big Book. A half-smoked cigarette, parked behind his ear, bobbed as words streamed out of him. "I'm collecting phone numbers and addresses . . . in a year I'm going to call you all up to come to my pad and have a Sober Party."

Stella approached Matt, asking, "Is it true that you're leaving?'

He nodded and hugged her. "I love you."

As soon as Matt released her, Stella said, "Give me another hug."

During the embrace, Matt looked at the two men who had been talking to him and said, "See, Stella's okay with it." They and others, including Eddie, had tried to talk him out of leaving, but Matt couldn't stand the confinement one more day. Despite his recent promise to stay awhile and help Frankie, he claimed he had to leave. That day he had received an SDI, state disability, check and, seeing other uses for the money, refused to sign it over to Acton. Instead, he was taking the cash and escaping.

A pickup truck rolled toward Matt. He jumped in the air, both feet wiggling in joy, as he recognized his sponsor behind the wheel.

Stella turned and walked away.

———

Two days later it was the eighth anniversary of Stella's first day of sobriety. Anonymous groups usually celebrate by having a cake in honor of all anniversaries, but Stella was in no mood to accept one. She knew she was spiraling downward but seemed helpless to stop. She claimed that when she felt unsafe she would go to the store and head for the drinks, but instead of choosing liquor, she brought and glugged a tea blend. She said that the AA philosophy continued to sustain her, but she seemed to be heading toward relapse.

Deborahh was also exhibiting behavior that could lead her in a bad direction. Sometime after beginning her flirtation with Pete, Deborahh invented Step Thirteen: Sex. Mocking both Acton and AA's Twelve Steps, she decided that Step Thirteen was the only step that she would complete.

She claimed that the excitement of flirting with Pete had diminished slightly when she discovered that he was dumb. She tried playing a word game with him, but he was so bad they had to quit. Deborahh had bitten her tongue to keep from calling him stupid. She had to remind herself that there was a certain charm to dumb beefy men; when they were in bed they weren't distracted by extraneous thoughts. So her solution was to continue flirting and avoid playing games. It was the best way to escape the tedium of recovery.

One day, during the quiet time after lunch and before mandatory afternoon classes, Deborahh was sitting on her bed. There was a knock at the window, a knock that prompted her heart to race.

She glanced toward the sunlit pink mini-blinds. A shadow, indicating a familiar hulk, confirmed that it was Pete.

"Let's go get a Snickers," Pete said.

Deborahh hopped up. Going for a Snickers meant that Pete was hungry and knew that Deborahh would buy him candy and a Coke. She didn't mind. She was grateful for any attention Pete gave her. In return, she happily paid for his snacks and did his laundry. He had become her "Acton husband."

During the past few days, Deborahh and Pete had found several places where they could express their desire. They had begun with hugs and kisses. Deborahh found those encounters both exciting and scary. The possibility of getting caught, and the enormous consequences on her life, underlay every move Deborahh made. Even so, she had been amused to find that Pete appeared to be more concerned than she. In the middle of their first lingering kiss, Deborahh had glanced at him only to discover that he had not closed his eyes.

"How come your eyes are open?" she had asked.

"One of us has to watch," he declared. She chose to view the situation romantically by believing that Pete was concerned about her getting caught. It thrilled her to think that she had plotted and planned, and chased and captured, this 6'3" hunk of a man and had bound him up so tightly that he was thinking of her welfare.

Kisses soon progressed to a blow job in the bushes. It had been dark. They stood near the exit gate, shielded by a gasoline shack. They were necking, their kisses becoming more and more demanding, when Pete spotted a chair. He pulled it into a tall hedge. She sat while he unzipped his pants. Deborahh claimed that she really got into the act, only later thinking about the strangeness of love and that by participating in such an experience she was risking a return to jail.

Since that time, Pete had begged her to meet him in private places. He asked her to be at the golf course at six in the morning and in the Hill House bathroom during the nightly meeting. Deborahh had agreed, but had not shown up; she just couldn't do the prearranged meetings, even though her absence annoyed Pete.

But she could buy him a Snickers bar, so she grabbed some money and hurried to the canteen. Pete was waiting inside. The small room was empty except for three vending machines, stocked with sodas, candy, and sandwiches. As Deborahh moved to the last machine, the one farthest from the door, Pete wrapped his arms around her. She returned the hug and they began kissing. As their kisses became increasingly fervent, Pete pulled her deeper into the corner, near an unused office door, assuring her that he had cased the place and no one could see through the reflective window.

Their lips and hands searched each other's bodies with increasing urgency.

Deborahh became so excited that she didn't care where they were. After all, she had had sex in many more open places when she worked the streets.

After weeks of playing and teasing, Deborahh was ready when Pete lifted her skirt. He entered her from behind.

The actual act was quick. Pete did nothing for her enjoyment, but in her mind, the moment was terrific; it was the culmination of all the fantasies she had envisioned since beginning their flirtation.

As soon as Pete finished, he mumbled something about taking a shower and rushed from the room.

Deborahh was pissed.

15

Closed Mouth, Open Mind, Open Heart

It was barely 9:00 A.M. and the cold morning was already giving way to warmer currents. Wavy brush strokes of clouds filled the sky. A mild breeze fluttered tree branches.

A crowd stood outside Hill House. Counselor David approached the building, a fistful of keys in his hand. Acton residents who got to know David looked up to him and trusted him. That confidence would have surprised his mother who told him that she didn't trust him when he was a baby. She later told him that he didn't cry and looked like he was plotting from his crib. He still had a secret and impish side. He liked to keep people off-balance; one minute he'd declare himself a Republican and the next he would rail against the conservatives and the prison-industrial complex that systematically swept young black men into prison for petty offenses to control and enslave them. David loved his job, claiming that it was often entertaining. He said, "All I gotta do is come to work and watch them show up."

David opened the door and thirty-five people filed inside the one-room structure for the required Big Book class. Deborahh, Patty, and Eddie were among the crowd. Eddie silently took a seat as those around him chatted.

Upon reaching the podium, David stood for a moment, smiling, and asked, "Can anyone tell me where we left off last week?"

The room went silent.

"How many were here last week?"

Several people raised their hands. David surveyed them. "I must not have done a good job."

"We talked about the Big Book and read some passages," volunteered one resident.

"About working with others," added a second resident.

"Yeah, services, meetings," said a third resident.

"I heard someone say that your restoration of memory is not part of your promises," another resident offered as an excuse for not remembering the previous week's discussion.

"Let's say I was a layman," David replied. "I might buy that. But you didn't forget where the dope house was, did you? Or the difference between a half pint and a pint? Yeah, one aspect of this disease is forgetfulness. That's why we need to study the Big Book. It's a textbook. It's important to know exactly what you're reading. It's important to have a sponsor take you through the readings.

"You're sharp, capable, qualified. People don't do the things we did with the people we did them with and stay alive if they're stupid. So we have the ability to stay clean.

Treat your life as if it is at stake. Because it is. How many of you really have tried to get clean on your own?"

Almost all hands stretched into the air. David asked, "What happened?"

"I went back to the same spots."

"I thought I could sell dope without using it."

"Just quitting didn't work. I needed more in my life."

"The fact that I was able to quit made me think I had power."

"Stress. Anxiety."

"Boredom."

"Getting comfortable."

"The truth is," David said, "most people can't give you a really good reason why. It's like blank spots in the rearview mirror. We have mental blank spots. That's why we'll get out of jail for drunk driving and immediately go back to the same liquor store to buy the same thing that got us to jail. I remember being shot in Pasadena and nine days later I was standing on the same spot. To show you how sickening our disease is, I just moved over ten feet and thought I was safe."

The room erupted in laughter.

"We need rigorous honesty. We need to know that we don't have immunity. The truth is a very startling thing. It can be painful, too. If you've been using mind-altering substances, then you don't have a whole mind."

On the board, David wrote: Mind, Body, Emotion and Spirit. "These are the things you have to get honest about. Spirit is not what we do in the company of our fellow addicts and alcoholics. It's when we go home.

"Why did you come here? To get back what was lost. You've tried everything else. I know you did. Nobody takes a wrong turn off the freeway and comes by here and decides it's a nice place to stay for ninety days. Something intervened for a reason. I know. I did it, too." He paused, looking around the room. "You don't think I just make up all this shit, do you?

"While you're here, share in a general way . . . what we used to be like, what happened, and what we are now," David paraphrased from the Big Book. "Stick to this and you'll be okay. Some of us want to glamorize our past, pretend that we were bigger than life."

Six years earlier, David had been a homeless drug addict. He lived behind a Dumpster and stole pizzas to survive. One morning he found himself crying over a bowl of oatmeal at a shelter, thinking "I'm not a dummy. Why am I here? My parents didn't raise me this way." When someone offered to send him to the Acton Rehabilitation Center, he jumped at the chance even though he had never heard of the place. The only thing he knew was that anything had to be better than his current existence. He had gladly left L.A., learned how to crawl away from the drug life. With lots of help, he cleaned up, learned recovery, went back to college, and then became a counselor at Acton. Every day thereafter he tried inspiring other drug addicts.

"There was a story I wouldn't tell when I first got to Acton because I wanted people to think I was a gangster . . . I almost got killed by the pizza man."

Eddie was sitting upright, but loose, shoulders slouched, taking in David's words. David told the pizza man story often, but even residents who had heard it before listened closely. Deborahh, too, was paying attention. Her right leg, crossed over her left knee, jiggled, and she smiled as she leaned forward.

"I was a wanna-be gangster, almost killed by a pizza man," David said. "I phoned the pizza place and ordered what I wanted and then waited in the back for him to come out and throw the pizza away when no one showed. I was out there, staring. Waiting. Finally, he came out and smoked a cigarette. While I was waiting for *my* pizza. Then he went back in and got on the phone."

"Did you get the pizza?" one woman asked, unable to wait for the story to unfold.

"I sure did. I went in and grabbed that pizza off the shelf and ran out the door. I heard a shot, but I didn't stop. I thought it was a really greasy pizza because I felt hot liquid pouring down my arm. Turns out the shot hit a trash can and ricocheted into my arm. I know it's kinda ridiculous to get killed over a pizza, but I was more than willing to take the chance."

He paused, letting the thought sink in and then continued. "That story is a good example of why I listen to very little of what newly recovered people tell me. If I really want to know what they're about, I watch their actions." What David didn't mention was one of his recent actions: he had ordered a custom-made knife crafted with a pearl handle modeled after his favorite handgun. He was no longer glamorizing his past, but he was trying to bring what he called style to his present.

"This is a spiritual program," David said.

"Yup," Patty agreed. She nodded as she tapped a yellow highlighter against her cheek.

"What do you see when you see a tree?" David asked.

"Growth."

"Life."

"Shade."

"Color."

"Oxygen."

"You need to start being able to look at a tree and see it in a spiritual way as well as a natural way. We're all connected. She's a recovering person. I'm a recovering person. There's strength in numbers. No doubt about it. There were days out there when you were alone. Now you're not alone because we are everywhere. Business. Law enforcement. They might not be advertising, but we're everywhere. It's the darnest thing I ever saw. The worse your story gets, the more they love you when you get clean. This recovery process will allow you to get along out there."

Eddie had nothing glamorous to talk about in David's classes or in other settings. Giving up baseball ambitions for drugs wasn't glamorous. Spending time in prison wasn't glamorous. Allowing a prison cellie to practice the art of tattooing on him wasn't glamorous. Nor was the manner in which the "artist" built a tattooing device using an eight-track tape player, a windshield wiper motor, and India ink. The result, naked women scrawled across his body, wasn't glamorous either. Carrying a mop to clean up his puke for seventeen days while he detoxed wasn't remotely glamorous.

At Acton, Eddie didn't share these stories. In fact, he rarely shared anything while at the center. He didn't like speaking in front of groups and always seized the chance to pass—even if it only involved reading a Big Book passage. He did the same thing in AA meetings, avoiding talking as much as possible, believing that if he opened up it would just give others a chance to hurt him. He knew that attitude was left over from prison, but couldn't shake it. The need to protect himself was too strong.

In his weeks at Acton, Eddie had only stood at the AA podium a handful of times despite pressures from others who spilled their guts every day. He listened to others' stories and sometimes related to them, but he discounted the many people who believed that they had mastered recovery. He knew it wasn't so simple. Until they left Acton, he believed, their real program had not even begun. There was no way he could stand up and sound like he knew it all. The only thing he really knew was that he didn't know much.

Eddie had been thinking about life after Acton ever since he arrived. His dream hadn't deviated. He was still plotting to return to the Clare Foundation. Eddie was grateful for Acton; the center had given him another chance. When he came in he was confused and felt he had let himself down. If Acton hadn't sheltered and prodded him, he might have given up, might have gone back to his hometown. He still knew people there, the ones who weren't currently in prison, and would have been welcomed by his old gang. That option would have led him down the wrong path, so he was grateful that Acton saved him from such a life.

But Acton wasn't home. Clare was. That was the place he felt comfortable. The people there didn't co-sign his shit, which was good, and he liked the meetings. In fact,

Clare was the one place he had learned to open up a bit. During the few times that he stood at the podium and spoke, he felt as though he was babbling and was amazed when people came up afterward and thanked him. That made him feel good.

Clare had supported Eddie when he started working with neighborhood gangbangers. Eddie and his sponsor spent time in the nearby park talking to kids who, like him, got caught up in a gang and didn't know how to get out of it. At first the youths looked at him as a rat, a cop, a snitch. But Eddie was proud that he gained their trust, and they came and shared with him. He let them know that there was a path out of the gang and its emphasis on drugs: recovery.

To Eddie, it seemed that Clare was his one chance to both redeem himself and help others; it was his best shot at creating a decent future.

Eddie had already jumped through the hoops required to go to Clare. At Jeff's suggestion, he had talked to Suzanne, the counselor in charge of the Clare list. He had lied to her with ease, saying that he had only been to Clare once, hoping that would increase his chance of acceptance.

Now, he was heading toward rehab services so he could ask Jeff about his application's progress.

Jeff invited him into his office and Eddie sat on the couch, trying not to roll to its sagging middle. Eddie asked about Clare. Jeff didn't have an answer but suggested that Eddie have a backup plan.

"Why do I need one?" Eddie asked, leaning forward. He didn't want a backup plan. He was going to Clare and that's all there was to it.

"Suzanne handles the Clare list. They take a certain amount of people from Acton each month, but not everyone on the list gets in. If you can't get into Clare from here, you need to go to another program. If you go there and still want Clare, you can call them. Your situation would be different then."

Eddie explained that he didn't know the Lancaster or Palmdale area and didn't know what to do about a backup plan. What he didn't say was that he hated the desert. It was either too hot or too cold. He wanted out. And he wanted to go to Clare.

"Do you have any funds for sober-living?" Jeff asked. Many people tried to go to sober-living homes. The ideal place offered an inexpensive room in a house with a nurturing environment that allowed people in recovery to find jobs and become more financially stable. Finding a home was a challenge in Los Angeles County; there simply weren't enough spots and often the conditions weren't supportive or sanitary. The atmosphere of each home varied, often changing with the individual residents. Acton residents sometimes tried to enter sober-living homes with newly made friends, hoping to find comfort in familiar faces. Others ferreted around for the best they could get with little money or information.

Eddie, however, didn't want to go to a sober-living place. He wouldn't have a problem getting a job. All he had to do was check out any building supply store. But he felt he needed a rehab program, a place that would force him to continue examining himself, not abandon him to his own thoughts. He also needed somewhere he could use as a base while he obtained new dentures and got his foot fixed. Besides, Eddie felt he needed more practice at recovery. He had never done anything right unless he practiced.

In addition to needing the safety and practice of a program, Eddie didn't have the money to go to a sober-living home. He had never handled money well. Even when he wasn't using, he bought stupid things that made him feel good for a brief time. He'd go on shopping binges and buy shit he didn't need, like two pairs of shoes, because they were on sale. One time, he was on his way to get a burrito when he decided he had to have an earring with the NA symbol. The next day he lost the thirty-dollar piece of jewelry.

"I'm on SDI," Eddie told Jeff. "I signed over one check. I'll leave with approximately $380. That's my only funds. And I ain't relying on that, either. I could go to a shelter. San Rochelle. If I can't get into Clare, I ain't just going to the streets. I can't function from the streets. I won't work, won't go to meetings."

The drug rehab after-care system in Los Angeles County was difficult for addicts to navigate. Finding a sober-living home with some money was hard enough, but seeking a place to stay without funds was almost impossible. Eddie was right: it was either another program, one that would delay payment, or a shelter. Very few people had other resources. Few addicts had maintained civil communications with family or friends. And family members, after years of watching erratic and often criminal behavior, were not willing to offer a second or, as often the case, a one hundred and second chance.

Eddie had burned bridges to the two family members still living, his brother and sister. His older brother had pushed Eddie out of his life ten years ago. Eddie thought his brother was probably an alcoholic, although he never messed with drugs, but he had a steady, responsible job, a wife, two kids, and no room for Eddie's shenanigans. Eddie had seen his sister three years previously, before he found Clare, and got into a spat with her new husband. Eddie knew she had immediately "writ him off." And he hadn't had the inclination to seek her out since. Disappointed about not knowing whether the Clare Foundation would take him back, he left Jeff's office.

Eddie wasn't thrilled to tell me about his life, but he never refused to talk. He was embarrassed about his missing teeth and barely opened his mouth to speak, but he didn't shy away from any subject. Until Vietnam.

Eddie had told his counselor that he had not been in the military and I would not have known any different if I hadn't read Eddie's essay about Step Two.

He had written:

Step 2: Came to believe that a Power greater than ourselves could restore us to sanity. This step I have always knew to be that there is a God. but being a catholic I thot that my God was a punnishing God. and if I went realy over the line that I would Burn in hell. I used to pray for him to get me out of jams in jail or when I was realy scared of something like in Vietnam going out on patroll that He give me just one more chance and I would do the wright thing. but as soon as that was over, I would go back to ether getting high or that same fuck-up behavior.

When I asked him about Vietnam, Eddie said, "I never talk about that." His jaw appeared more tightly clenched than usual.

I immediately wondered how I was going to overcome Eddie's stubborn refusal. At Acton, I often had people clamoring to tell me the story of their life. It wasn't unusual for me to tell two or three people a day that I wished I had time to listen to them, but that I was focusing on a few individuals. I'm sure some people in recovery had embellished their life histories or even lied to me, but Eddie was the first to decline to talk about a topic.

After a measured moment of silence, I asked, "Why won't you talk about it?"

Those words opened the floodgate as he explained, "Vietnam was a bad time in my life. My parents had hoped I would change and I didn't. It wasn't a war. It was a police action. I got drafted out of youth authority. There was so much negativity. It happened a long time ago. I didn't connect with the army. I was a grunt. Taught to kill. I saw burnt babies, women, villagers. I learned to use heroin and opiates. My father saw terrible stuff in World War II and he was okay. When he got out there were parades. When I returned, I came back in 1968, there were protests. Everything went downhill for me after that. Finding jobs was tough. I wouldn't check the vet box because people would look at me strange . . ."

Eddie didn't blame everything on Vietnam, but he knew that the war had helped push him into an insane world. And at some point he came to believe, as he wrote in his Step Two essay, that God:

. . . *could restore my sanity and fucked thinking back to normal. the first time I read this step I couldent belive that I was insane. but when I think about it, I was, when I was loaded or drunk. I did thing realy bad to loved ones. hurting people seemed to always happen when I got loaded. there is something that I learned about myself this time around. it wasent the drugs and alcohal that had me fucked up. plan and semple, it was me. I know that I have to change me. and by doing this I wouldent need something in my sistem to funtion. sometimes the program comes harder to those who have lost or rejected faith than to those who never had my fath at all. I have had fath but rejected it to do my crazy life. and never realy belived untell I got in the program. I know that its an inside job. just saying it doent work. I truly have to turn things over to my higher power. and when I do this, things just seem to go away. my anger. and my trust issues, so now I know what it means when I reed restore me to sanity. through my higher power. one of the big reasens I wonted to stick around was so I could get a little peece of mind. to feel comfortible in my own skin. I know by working these steps I can achieve this and more. Last time I worked the steps without meaning. this time I want to feel each step as I do them inside! today my thinking is vary positive along the lines of doing these steps. in the past nothing else worked for me. so I am going to do these steps the way the book suggests. with an open mind, and hart.*

PHASE III

16

ESCAPE FOR A DAY

R esidents earned twenty-four-hour passes after sixty days of good behavior if they stayed out of trouble, followed their program schedule, and attended Twelve Step meetings. They were encouraged to use the time to visit aftercare facilities—private or non-profit sober-living homes—but few people chose that option. Instead, most chose to reconnect with the outside world.

Eddie, though, decided to skip his pass entirely. He didn't think he would survive on his own, even for a day. He still planned to return to the Clare Foundation, so he didn't want to investigate other treatment programs or sober-living homes, especially not ones in the desert. Even if he could have gotten a ride to Los Angeles, to civilization, there was no one that Eddie wanted to see and no place that he wanted to visit. He knew that a day without plans would only lead to trouble.

Patty elected to spend the day with her children. She was planning to return to her mother's home after completing the program so she wasn't interested in aftercare, either. Instead, she visited with her daughters, who had been happy to see their mother clean and sober. The day went so well that the teenagers had asked Patty to return home by Thanksgiving. Patty liked the idea and decided to work toward achieving that goal even though her 90-day program didn't end until early December. She returned to Acton with more energy, but also with a longing to spend more time with her family.

Even though Tiffany had an ideal day with her family, she came away from the experience with a different attitude than Patty. Tiffany's parents and daughter had driven from New Mexico, picked her up at Acton, and then traveled to Disneyland. Tiffany was relieved that her parents didn't bring up the past. She knew she had fucked up many times and was touched that her parents still had faith in her. The hardest thing she had to do was to stop cursing in front of her family. The rest was easy. Her daughter appeared enchanted with her, saying, "My Mama Tiffany is *so* pretty." All the child wanted to do was sit with Mama Tiffany on the rides. Tiffany was equally in love with her daughter and her parents for giving them that perfect day.

But Tiffany knew that a wonderful day with her family wasn't enough to put her life right. She felt as though she had been thoroughly "ass-whupped" to get to the point of wanting to stay clean and was grateful that Acton provided a forum for her to learn about recovery and herself. She had started to love herself, had become more at ease with life in general, was happy that her word meant something, and that her family was giving her another chance. Because of all these things, she could see a future but understood that she had much more work to do to maintain her sobriety and transition into society.

Early on the day of her twenty-four-hour pass, Deborahh dressed and headed toward the administration building. Ralph, her john-turned-boyfriend, was due to pick her up and spirit her away from Acton. It was her first day of freedom in several months and she didn't want to miss a minute of it.

The grounds were deserted; it was Saturday, before 7:00 A.M., and cold.

Suddenly Pete materialized in front of her. Her heart skipped a beat. They had been fighting and she hadn't spoken to him in days. Even so, she ached for him.

The day after their first encounter in the canteen, they had had a repeat performance. Then Pete got mad because she didn't have money for cigarettes. He lashed out, saying she'd given him the clap. Deborahh stopped talking to him and he went ballistic, telling everyone who listened that she was a disease-carrying whore. When she still refused to talk to him, he threatened to tell Ralph about their relationship.

Deborahh didn't take Pete's threat seriously since he benefited almost as much from her relationship with Ralph as she did. The older man provided sweets and even cigarettes, though he knew she didn't smoke. Deborahh believed that Ralph was happy if she was happy, and usually Deborahh was happy when Pete was happy. So, as far as she was concerned, the arrangement would work as long as Pete stopped being stupid.

Deborahh knew that Pete was jealous of Ralph. He had once begged her not to marry Ralph. She had laughed. Even though Ralph was much older, didn't have Pete's body, and wasn't as cute, he promised more than Pete could ever give: security, companionship, and respectability. Without money, a pension plan, or medical insurance, Deborahh had to be practical. Ralph might lack some qualities, but he loved her, could help her financially, and would stand by her.

Big Red, the resident telephone operator, came out of the building. He jokingly offered them the use of the administration building, saying he would be point man.

Deborahh's body heated instantly; she craved Pete more than she had ever craved drugs. The next thing she knew, she and Pete were inside and Big Red was outside, standing guard. Her desire increased at the thought that Ralph was on his way. The idea of having sex in the administration building also excited her and the way Pete pulled her into a side room almost made her heart stop.

Excitement completely crowded out fear and reason. As always, they remained standing. Pete entered her from behind and quickly finished. It wasn't great sex, but the circumstances heightened the thrill of the experience. Also, Pete would soon be leaving the center so she knew it might be their last sexual contact.

A car rumbled toward the building. Deborahh smoothed her skirt and rushed outside as the engine cut off. Although she had told Pete all about Ralph and, in fact, teased and sometimes taunted him with the things the older man could provide her, she had not told Ralph about her Acton husband and wanted to keep him ignorant. Ralph was a nice man and had stayed with her through bad times, even when she had stolen his checks and forged his name. She didn't want to hurt him now by revealing her relationship with Pete.

She hurried to Ralph's car and slipped into the front seat, still seeping semen. Within seconds, they were heading toward the exit, away from her life at Acton.

Deborahh didn't know what she wanted to do with her day of independence. MacArthur Park, her office and home for several years, was a big draw. But she was afraid to test her resolve by returning to the spot where she had used drugs and prostituted herself. After months of confinement, she felt too shaky to be left to her own devices, especially at her old haunt. She wanted Ralph to say no, to say he wouldn't take her to MacArthur Park. But Ralph refused to monitor her. Instead, he offered to drop her off at the park and pick her up a few hours later, in time for dinner.

That was how Deborahh ended up standing on Wilshire Boulevard, peering into the park like an anthropologist observing a foreign culture. She had piles of dollars in her pocket, courtesy of Ralph, and her options were many: she could remain an observer, walk away entirely, or take her bundle of money and plunge into the park. She lingered, poised on the edge of the pit, damning Ralph for putting it all on her. But at the same time, she knew that her life was hers and only she could decide her future.

Deborahh began walking toward Alvarado Street, remaining on the perimeter of the park. After a few minutes, her head cleared and she knew that she didn't have to decide a thing. She didn't want to use. She didn't want to return to prostitution. There was really no decision to be made. This test wasn't even much of a test. The old neighborhood had deteriorated in the past few years and appeared almost desolate compared to the time in the late 1980s when it was a homeless city, packed with every type of item or service possible: clothing, food, alcohol, cigarettes, dope, sex, music, cell phones, calling cards, and even recycling. Those were the days of minimal police presence.

Although the park appeared empty in contrast to the previous decade, there were plenty of homeless crackheads remaining. Neither the increased police presence nor the park cleanup crews could move fast enough to eliminate the human depravity or the trash generated. In addition to bottles, bags, batteries, Styrofoam, and other bits of garbage, there was plenty of discarded clothing, abandoned appliances, stolen property, and shopping carts.

At the heart of the park was a lake bounded by willow trees. Benches overlooked a fountain. A statue of World War II hero General Douglas MacArthur kept watch from the northwest corner. The Rampart substation housed binocular-wielding cops who sent cars or bicycles to harass the dopers in an almost ritualistic game. In another part of the city, the grass might be filled with parents pushing strollers, children romping with dogs, or kids playing catch, but in the middle of an older section of Los Angeles, amidst run-down offices and discount stores, the park was not an attraction to the middle class. The brackish water of the lake reflected the grim lives of those who medicated with drugs near its edges.

Deborahh walked through the park, but it all looked different from a sober perspective; there was nothing alluring, nothing attractive about the place. Absent her friends, many of whom were either in prison or dead, and the park's former vitality, the site seemed sad. She was offered dope, including a huge dime bag, as well as several dates, but she didn't want the dope or the dates, even though she found the propositions flattering. She picked up a few messages and left some messages and, after gossiping a bit, moved on. The only thing she took from the park was a bunch of hangers that she planned to use for her overburdened closet back at Acton.

After her stroll through the park, Deborahh used Ralph's money to shop her way up the Alvarado Boulevard thrift stores, snagging shoes, makeup, perfume, and more clothes.

By the end of the afternoon, she was glad to see Ralph and happier still to leave the park. She and Ralph ate dinner, got a motel, and watched cable. She tried to keep him awake for sex but finally gave up and also slept.

The next day, Ralph drove her back to Acton. She was happy to return. Deborahh's twenty-four-hour journey was anticlimactic after all the anticipation, but she had learned one thing: she could face her former life and refrain from using. Furthermore, she didn't want drugs. The only thing she had to have was Pete.

Helen, one of the four remaining women who came from Twin Towers with Deborahh, chose to take her pass on her birthday. Her first weeks at Acton had been difficult. Her angry mask kept people at a distance. Slowly, that changed and she began to be more communicative and outgoing.

By the day of her pass she was almost happy—until she arrived in downtown Los Angeles. An Acton van dropped her off at the Veterans of America building with eighty dollars in her pocket and a craving so bad that she felt as if someone had hit her.

Helen shook her head violently and muttered, "This is not happening."

She quickly began to pray and the feeling evaporated. When she looked around, she saw people hanging, people hitting a crack pipe. Her next thought was, "These people is crazy. They be taking me on a suicide run."

She hurried away and went to find her mother, knowing that would be a challenge, too. As soon as they met, her mother said, "I need money."

"It's not happening like that today, Momma," said Helen.

In her mid-fifties, Helen's mother was deep in her own addiction and wanted nothing from her daughter except cash to buy drugs. Helen wasn't out to convert her mother to recovery, but she also didn't want to aid her addiction.

"I'm hungry," her mother said stubbornly.

Yielding, Helen took her mother to breakfast, but the older woman ate only two bites. She wasn't hungry for food; she needed drugs. Finally, Helen handed over five dollars for "cigarettes." Both mother and daughter were angry when they parted; her mother was mad that Helen didn't give her money right away and Helen was upset that her mother was still trying to manipulate her.

Helen's next challenge was going to her house. As soon as she opened her door, the dope man was standing beside her. Helen told him she was five months clean, but he persisted, asking if her momma wanted it. Helen told him to leave.

The remainder of the day was spent declining beer and drugs. The one happy period was with her best friend, a dope dealer, who got rid of her clients and said she was happy for Helen. The biggest disappointment of the day was that her sister failed to show up. Although her sister had smoked crack in the past, she was now clean—except for a little weed now and then. Helen had really looked forward to seeing her again and was hurt by her absence.

Helen ended her visit to the outside world by staying at a cheap motel because she didn't want to stay at her own house. The next day she took the bus back to Acton, grateful to return to a place where people didn't use. Mentally, though, she could not escape the outside world and it depressed her even after she returned to the peacefulness at Acton. She retreated to her bed.

Although Helen had a rough experience, she, like Deborahh, learned that she could stay strong and resist using. Both women also got an inkling of what their lives would be like after leaving Acton. Tiffany and Patty seemed to have an advantage during their twenty-four-hour pass because they got to spend time with their families, yet while Tiffany understood the day was a magical step away from reality, Patty appeared to believe that returning to her family would solve all her problems. Neither woman had been confronted with temptations, so neither knew how they would react once they returned to the reality of everyday living. Patty, the only one of the four women who was not court-sent, seemed to be the only one under the illusion that her life would be easier after Acton. The others—and

Eddie—knew that Acton was merely a beginning and that if they were going to remain clean and stay out of trouble, they still had much work ahead of them.

17

EXIT DREAMING

Eddie was anxious to leave Acton, but he had nowhere to go because the Clare Foundation, his only home, had turned him down.

When he learned that he couldn't return to Clare, Eddie was angry. He blamed the Acton counselor in charge of submitting applications to Clare, even though it wasn't her fault that he had been denied admission. It was actually Eddie's fault because he had lied on the application.

Although Clare's rejection was difficult to accept, Eddie was somewhat mollified after getting a cheerful postcard from some of the guys he knew at Clare. The goodwill from his fellow recoverers showed Eddie that he had been rejected by policy, not by people.

Eddie's initial anger eventually turned to resignation. Soon he was ready to let it go and find someplace else. Recovery, he kept telling himself, is wherever you are. His major requirement was that he find a place quickly.

He was frustrated by Acton. He found the jailhouse pos-turing, the barely suppressed violence of some of the residents, tiring. At Clare it had been his job to help men overcome their jailhouse mentality, but at Acton he felt surrounded by people with negative attitudes. Eddie was also sick of the weather; the bitingly cold nights and increasingly chilly days were beginning to affect him. There was no way that he wanted to be in the desert when the snow arrived.

He was anxious to meet again with his counselor and get help finding a place to stay. Eddie vacillated between wanting to leave immediately and waiting to find another program. On a morning when his frustration level was high, Eddie attended the 11:00 A.M. AA meeting. He listened intently as a man echoed his feelings, his exact sentiments, about wanting to get away from Acton. The man said he then asked himself where he would go if he left, and he knew he would get in a wreck. Eddie felt that those words were meant for him. He was fed up enough "to book," but had no place to go and knew he would end up in trouble. Eddie decided he better stay at Acton at least one more day. But he had to make plans.

Bundled in a heavy plaid jacket and wearing a base-ball cap pulled low over his head, Eddie trudged to Rehab Services immediately after lunch. Counselor Jeff had agreed to call Beacon House in San Pedro. When Jeff couldn't reach the right person, he told Eddie that he would call back in two hours.

Reluctant to leave Jeff's office without a new place to go to, Eddie asked, "What about the L.A. Task Force? Is it a program?" Eddie had heard good stories about the East

L.A. place. Supposedly it was connected with the sheriff's department, which volunteered to help those in recovery by playing handball and sponsoring other activities. Before hearing that, Eddie thought the sheriff's job was to draw a paycheck and kill people. Eddie liked the idea of the East L.A. place because it was close to USC, the spot where he had once gotten his teeth fixed. It was also familiar territory while San Pedro was not. He didn't want to be stuck somewhere he had never been, somewhere far from the world as he knew it, somewhere like Acton.

"Why are you so anxious to go to another program?" Jeff asked. The underlying message was that Eddie seemed capable of taking care of himself.

"I need to go to a *program* because I'm not going to get another job until I get my self-esteem up and I won't do that until I get my grill fixed."

Jeff nodded. "East L.A. is a program. I've talked to people who went through there. It's a good, structured program."

Jeff called the East L.A. Task Force. He couldn't reach the proper person there, either, so Eddie grudgingly left, but returned two hours later. Jeff finally contacted someone at Beacon House and said, "I've got a good guy that would like to get into your program. He's scheduled for discharge in a few days, but I can hold him over two to three weeks."

Eddie's heart sank at those words. He wanted to go immediately.

"His name is Eddie," continued Jeff. "And he's a good guy and he'd be an asset to your fellowship and your program down there."

Jeff listened for a few minutes, nodding and writing on a notepad. When he hung up, he handed Eddie an application, taken from the aftercare binder. "Fill this out completely. I'll take it when you've completed it."

"Hey, Jeff," Eddie said, trying very hard to remain calm and not beg. "What about East L.A.?"

"We'll call," Jeff said, not responding to the urgency underlying Eddie's question. "For Beacon, it gives you a little bit of an edge if I call down. If we think someone is not working a good program or is pulling our leg, we'll send him someplace else. If you go to Beacon, we'll see if we can get a copy of your TB test. You'll also need a copy of your ID and social security card. Print real nicely. Try to answer everything with complete sentences. Fill in all the lines with something so it looks complete, a full effort."

Eddie nodded. Taking the application with him, he left, momentarily forgetting about East L.A. He just needed to get somewhere. And soon.

Deborahh was weary of Acton, too. Nevertheless, she continued the necessary steps to program completion. She joined a dozen people in the Recovery House for a sober-living class led by Cassandra. Deborahh took a seat next to Inez, the raccoon-eyed woman who had come from Twin Towers with her. Chairs were placed around the perimeter of the room, facing the table where Cassandra perched.

Counselor Cassandra's baseball cap and oversized jersey divulged her relaxed manner even before she spoke.

She said, "Give yourselves a hand for lasting this long. Most people you came in with aren't here."

Deborahh could barely remember some of the women who had come from Twin Towers with her. Yolanda had been discharged quickly for having sex in her dorm room. Drugged, mentally ill Uta hadn't lasted much longer. Marissa was another discharge due to violation of the policy that forbade sexual contact. The other four were there, though. Inez was sitting next to her, angry Helen had returned from her twenty-four-hour pass, and occasionally Deborahh crossed paths with mannish Nancy or tiny Ana.

Cassandra continued. "You've taken a major step in getting this far. Hopefully, you've gained tools to use when you go back out there." She hoisted a book, *Living Sober*, in the air. "This book really helped me in my first months of recovery. It gives concise, direct answers to what's going on. Look for it in serenity shops. It's AA approved material and good."

She told the residents that they would be reading aloud, any part of the book they wanted, and sharing.

Deborahh refrained from broadcasting her feelings about the stupidity of sharing, but a "Shit!" remained corralled inside her mouth. She respected Cassandra's experience. In fact, she knew that if Cassandra had been her counselor, she wouldn't have gotten away with her relationship with Pete. Deborahh felt that she could learn from Cassandra and only wanted to hear what the instructor had to say. She didn't want to share with others or hear more from the brainwashed Acton residents.

A volunteer read:

Looking out for over-elation. A great many drinkers (whether alcoholics or not) change an internal state of discomfort to one of enjoyment by the single act of taking a drink. This method of fleeing from pain to pleasure has been described as "escape" drinking . . . At such times (even after several years of sobriety), the thought of a drink may seem quite natural, and the misery of our old drinking days temporarily dims. Just one drink begins to seem less threatening, and we start thinking that it wouldn't be fatal, or even harmful.

"Can anyone identify?" asked Cassandra.

"I'm scared," replied a resident.

"Shit!" Deborahh muttered.

"How many of you drank or used at weddings or holidays?"

Most hands went up.

"A lot of people say"—Cassandra switched to a whiny voice, mimicking an addict— "'I don't see why I can't drink. I'm a methamphetamine user. Drinking wasn't my thing.'"

Cassandra looked over the quiet classroom, knowing she had their attention. "A man argued with me for twenty minutes, saying he was a methamphetamine user and he didn't see why he couldn't have one drink at a party. He left Acton, stopped at a liquor store to celebrate, and wound up in jail."

Cassandra paused for dramatic effect and then said, "Never was his thing." Another pause and she continued, "Disease is in the mind. I was clean for six years from meth and coke. Then, at a wedding, I had a drink. Was it a good thing to drink?"

"No," answered several people.

"Would it have been a good thing to have weed?"

"No," repeated the group.

"You're right. I substituted alcohol for my drug addiction. I got drunk and it opened the door and within a day I was lost. It took three years for me to get back to recovery. If you're a dope fiend and plan to take a drink, think about it. You're robbing yourself of the benefits of this program.

"Does it make sense to go from a loaded gun to a gun with one bullet and start clicking while saying, 'Got less bullets now'? How many times have we believed our own lies and gotten mad because people called us on it? I was embarrassed about going to a bar so often that I justified my right to drink by claiming I got a job writing for the TV show *Cheers*. The waitress then told the others, 'She's just a drunk like the rest of us.' And I had the nerve to get mad."

The residents chuckled.

"We alcoholics and addicts think we can talk and function like we're everyone else, but we're crazy. We start thinking, 'I been going to AA for three months, I think I deserve a drink or a joint.' That's insanity. If I could take two drinks and be okay, then chances are I won't need to go to meetings in the first place.

"Don't just look at your obsession. You might stay away from meth or coke, but sometimes addiction can come in the back door like a drink or a joint. We're happy, think we're doing okay with our obsession, and then have a drink and it's all over."

Deborahh nodded. She well understood obsessions and that if you had the willpower to subdue one obsession, something else took its place. The layer of fat girding her waist reflected her latest obsession. Instead of dreaming about drugs like many addicts, Deborahh's dreams focused on food. She envisioned herself in a bakery, greedily searching through piles of cake boxes. Her daydreams also were populated with thoughts of food and many of her waking minutes involved eating.

"What if we can have a drink, but get back to our fellowship before we get sucked into the insanity?" asked one man. "What's wrong with that?"

"Have a drink, but go back to AA?" Cassandra asked.

The room erupted in laughter. Deborahh and Inez leaned toward each other, sharing the joke.

"I've seen people die that way," Cassandra said. "They think they can always get back. But they've been in and out of recovery and keep getting sicker."

"What about when you don't want to try to stop or you're afraid you'll fail?" asked a resident.

"Until we surrender completely, we don't have a chance of recovery. We can share the joy of recovery only if we surrender.

"When we *plan* to drink once a year or two drinks at Christmas, it doesn't make sense. Why would I do something twice a year, something that will kill me?"

"But I have a love for it," someone said. "I don't hate the sight of beer."

"I don't hate beer, either," Cassandra said. "I have respect for it because it kicked my ass."

Deborahh laughed along with everyone else.

Cassandra asked for a volunteer to continue reading from *Living Sober*. Deborahh read, "*Sure enough,* one *drink would not be* [bad]—*for the average person. But our experience with a drinking problem shows us what that one supposedly harmless, fateful drink would do to us un*average *people. Sooner or later, it would persuade us that one more could do no damage, either. Then how about a couple more?*"

"Whenever I wanted to justify myself," Cassandra said, "I would go to the Bible. Jesus turned water into wine. But nowhere in the Bible does it say Jesus said I could drink up all the wine."

Laughter rippled through the air again.

"And that's what I would have done if I had that first drink." Cassandra looked at each resident and ended the class, saying, "You guys be good to yourselves."

Deborahh thought that some classes, like Cassandra's, were entertaining, but she still hated the whole Twelve Step crap. She often escaped those meetings by committing drive-by's or using one of the pens in her vast collection to forge an approval on her program card. But she couldn't avoid all meetings. So one cool morning she entered the Hill House classroom for a women-only Cocaine Anonymous meeting and quietly took a seat. Her sedate clothes—blue jeans skirt and white turtleneck topped by a large shirt—bore testimony to her determination to remain unobtrusive. She was under the impression that if she melted into the fabric of Acton she could serve her final days with ease.

She disliked the CA fellowship and only attended that one meeting in an effort to keep Counselor Alicia happy.

Weeks ago, after getting sick of the fights and melodrama, Deborahh had given up attending the regular CA meetings, claiming that they "prove that if you put a bunch of niggers together and took away the dope, there was nothing left but attitude." She had gotten so fed up that she finally walked out, telling the meeting secretary, "Suck my dick, bitch." She had briefly considered switching her fellowship to Narcotics Anonymous, but there was too much reading and "those NA people believed that if you hadn't done heroin, you had no business being there." Simply by elimination, Deborahh had ended up in AA. She felt that "none of it is a realistic way of dealing with stuff from the street. It's all brainwashing. And most people don't know how to spell Higher Power much less what it means." But at least she could tolerate the calm seriousness of AA.

Boisterous conversation rifled through the air as more women drifted in and settled into chairs forming a ragged circle. Tiffany, wearing all black, from her Keds to the scrunchy holding her ponytail, complained that her new parole officer wanted to move her out of the Antelope Valley. Raccoon-eyed Inez entered, moaning about her sore foot, claiming she'd hit a rock. "What kinda rock did you hit?" someone wisecracked. Helen limped in with the aid of crutches. She had begun to recover emotionally from the disastrous day on pass, but had sprained her ankle and wasn't in a happy mood.

Deborahh ignored the maelstrom and opened a Frank Yerby novel, balancing it on her lap. She knew that the only way she could refrain from laughing during meetings was to immerse herself in another world. This time it was the American South before the Civil War, where handsome men wore ruffled shirts and stickpins, where white men of humble origins crossed paths with the gentry, slaves, and Hispanics, and where sexual tension reigned.

Tiffany brought the meeting to order with the serenity prayer. The group, minus Deborahh, chanted the words that had become a part of the Acton mantra: "God, grant me the serenity to accept the things I cannot change, the courage to change the things I can, and the wisdom to know the difference."

Talking fast, repeating the phrase for the thousandth time since her arrival at the rehab center, Tiffany intoned, "Hi, my name is Tiffany. I'm an addict." After reading from the CA liturgy, Tiffany turned the spotlight over to a woman who read from chapter five of the Big Book.

Next, Helen, the woman who had to contend with her drug-addicted mother while on pass, took over the meeting, droning, "Hi, my name is Helen and I'm an addict." She began reading the Twelve Steps: "Step One: We admitted we were powerless over alcohol—that our lives had become unmanageable."

A chorus of voices announced the next step: "Two!"

Helen resumed without missing a beat: "Came to believe that a Power greater than ourselves could restore us to sanity."

"Three!" the refrain answered.

"Made a decision to turn our will and our lives over to the care of God *as we understood Him.*"

Deborahh shifted her book, reading, "*Slave niggers,*" he boomed. "*Bragging 'bout what you cost! Can't buy a man! Ain't no price set on a man. Buy things like you, buy fool beast niggers like you, but not no man. I been slave, I slave now, but my heart free. Don't nobody own that but God!*"

"Four!" shouted the group.

"Made a searching and fearless moral inventory of ourselves."

"Five!"

"Admitted to God, to ourselves, and to another human being the exact nature of our wrongs."

"Six!"

"Were entirely ready to have God remove all these defects of character."

"Seven!"

"Humbly asked Him to remove our shortcomings."

"Eight!"

"Made a list of all persons we had harmed, and became willing to make amends to them all."

"Nine!"

"Made direct amends to such people wherever possible, except when to do so would injure them or others."

"Ten!"

"Continued to take personal inventory and when we were wrong promptly admitted it."

"Eleven!"

"Sought through prayer and meditation to improve our conscious contact with God *as we understood Him,* praying only for knowledge of His will for us and the power to carry that out."

"Twelve!"

"Having had a spiritual awakening as the result of these steps, we tried to carry this message to alcoholics, and to practice these principles in all our affairs."

Deborahh tuned back in for a moment and muttered, "What's the point?" In a way, she could see how the

Anonymous program worked for some people—after all, it was even more powerful than religion. The Twelve Steps were definitely a brainwashing of the most efficient type, but Deborahh didn't need her brain washed. Furthermore, Alicia's rejection of her effort to work on Step One still rankled. Perhaps Deborahh hadn't undertaken the task as seriously as Alicia would have liked, but she hadn't written bullshit, either. For the idea of powerlessness she had drawn a picture of herself in handcuffs. In answer to the question "What about drugs did you enjoy?" she had written that she liked watching The Three Stooges, especially when the comics hit each other in the head.

The only other time that Deborahh had paid attention to the steps was when she decided that she needed to work a Pete Anonymous program. After Pete left Acton, Deborahh had pulled out her Twelve Step book—which she had won in a raffle—and opened it for the first time. As a joke, she admitted that she was powerless over Pete, but she couldn't get past the first step because the second one involved that Higher Power thing again and she wasn't about to go there.

Two more women drifted into the room as someone began reading the Twelve Traditions: "Our common welfare should come first; personal recovery depends upon AA unity . . . Tradition Two: For our group purpose there is but one ultimate authority—a loving God as He may express Himself in our group conscience."

By the last of the Traditions, some women intoned the words with the reader, "Anonymity is the spiritual foundation of all our traditions, ever reminding us . . ." Everyone but Deborahh joined in the last few words, loudly proclaiming, ". . . to place principles before personalities."

The group clapped.

Deborahh, her garnet and zircon ring flashing as she moved her hand, looked at her watch.

Tiffany resumed control of the meeting. "Hi, my name is Tiffany and I'm an addict. We encourage newcomers to ask questions. There should be no cross talk at meetings. All the speakers have a three to five minute limit."

One speaker focused on men. "I found out you can't give them no kind of attention. Puts me in a position: 'you mine.'"

"That's crap" and "That's right," women muttered.

"I don't believe in boyfriend-girlfriend," continued the speaker. "I believe in courting. I don't believe in shacking up. They trying to talk to me about after Acton. I don't know what I'm doing after Acton."

Several women cheered.

"People make me laugh," she continued.

"Good to laugh" and "Hmmm, hmmm," answered the group.

"I'm happy on the inside. I didn't come in here to be happy on the inside. I was ugly inside."

"All right!" someone shouted.

Deborahh looked up briefly, pretended to be involved by adding a "Yeah!" She then resumed reading, "*I am yours,*" *Conchita wept, "in my heart I am yours."*

Tiffany announced that she was going to speak about Acton. "I know everything that goes down in this place. You came up here to figure out your mother-fucker self. As far as these men go, you need to sit back and watch before you jump up in it. Learn from watching. Listen to what he's sharing about—like his wife. I've sat in the same meeting thirteen weeks and seen so many faces saying the same things. Then they get fucking rolled because they got involved with some dude who didn't give a fuck anyway. Makes me feel bad because I want to help you. Whoever the fuck sent you, you're here. It's the only time you'll ever have ninety days to work on yourself. No rent. No need to feed yourself. No need to feed your fucking kids . . . Sit back and look at yourselves. Be bigger people. Each one teach one."

"That's it," several women said amidst much clapping.

"That's it!" Deborahh muttered. "Five more days."

"Our time is up," announced Tiffany.

"Ohhh," Deborahh said, faking regret. She read one short line in her book— *"Good God"*—and closed it.

Tiffany said, "We'll close with a prayer."

Deborahh grabbed her initialed program card and raced for the door. The sharing was bad enough, but she drew the line at prayers. She hadn't always been a heathen; she went to church from the time she was born until she escaped that family tradition, but she couldn't shake the unease that enveloped her when she thought of day-long Baptist Sunday services. Deborahh had already passed the threshold before the prayer began. She knew the first prayer would be followed by a joining of hands while the group intoned the Lord's Prayer. And at the very end of the meeting everyone would shout, "Keep coming back." As far as Deborahh was concerned, she never wanted to go back.

18

EXIT PLANNING

Stella stood in front of a room full of residents, sunglasses perched above her stringy hair. Without preamble, she began the Exit Planning class. "I hope you've got a better exit plan than when I got here. My sponsor taught me: make plans, leave the rest to my Higher Power. A lot of us have a second shot at life. Now we gotta decide what we want to be in life for real this time. It's a long-term thing, what you're gonna be when you grow up. You can be a fireman. A man. Not a user. How many of you are going back where you came from?"

"I was, but my sponsor said no."

Stella nodded. "I got the hell out of Dodge. I used to live in Reseda. The dope man would come to my house. He hunted me down. I lived in the back of a head shop the last three years of using. In tie-dye glory, I came out to Acton eight years ago. I got here and there were rednecks, cowboy hats. At a meeting, there was a horse outside. I'm serious. I thought: 'Oh, shit.' . . . Let me tell you about

Acton. Those people ended up not being as redneck as I thought. They ended up being my support group. Then Cassandra walked in with her Ingleside hat and I knew she could relate.

"When I left here, I stole a blanket 'cause I had no money available. No sober-living. I stole a blanket—and later made amends." She had made amends by collecting blankets, gloves, and clothes and donating them anonymously to Acton.

Stella continued. "I went to a girl's house and slept on the floor. I got a job and got a room and kept going up, better and better. I don't want to tell you where I am now . . ."

Stella was nearly homeless again. She had a job, but keeping a roof over her head was increasingly difficult. She had recently moved into a friend's garage—after living briefly with her girls and a man and his son in very cramped conditions. Now, she and her younger daughter shared four wooden walls and a space heater. Her older daughter opted to live with a friend. Stella was upset that her oldest wouldn't live with them, believing that the kid was breaking up the family. The girl was only eighteen; surely she could stand a little adventure in her life, thought Stella. Besides, Stella almost had a house. She'd thought she would close the previous week, but was now certain that escrow would close in only six more days.

"How many of you are going to sober-living?" Stella asked.

Most raised their hand.

"Why not the old neighborhood?"

"I thought I'd make a complete change," offered one resident.

"I'm gonna have you fill out these forms and you don't get your card back until you're done. It's on you," Stella said, passing out four pages titled Personal Exit and Recovery Plan. The handout forced residents to consider the future of their housing, financial situation, recovery, health, social life, and leisure time away from drugs.

"I believe you're a child of God or you wouldn't be here. Most of us didn't make it. You're intelligent. We don't get game plans and don't follow through most of the time, but God gave us brains. If I see something totally weird in your answers I'll check you because I love you. This stuff is going in your chart, it's going in your file. You don't get to leave unless you have an exit plan. How many of you guys have visited your sober-living?"

Three people raised their hands.

"I always suggest that you save your pass to visit your sober-living."

"Yech!" came an anonymous protest.

"I can't recommend a specific sober-living this month. They might be okay and next month they're all loaded. Call them and ask what their policy is on relapse. If they say three times . . . click! You want a place where they're strict. Ask if it's Twelve Step based."

"I'm going to a place where it's Acton alumni. Is that okay?"

"Just because they're Acton alumni doesn't mean they're not using. I've seen sober-living where they find a corner for you and put women out there. Lots of predators hang around the fringes of newcomers. You're vulnerable and they know that. Be a monk."

Stella turned to the next section of the handout. "Financial plans? How are you going to support yourselves? Don't take on too much too fast or you're open to relapse. What's the first thing you gotta do?"

"Meetings," answered a resident.

"What's the first thing you have to worry about? . . . Staying clean. Make a gratitude list. It sounds so corny, but it helps. Make a gratitude list and a priority list. God, fellowship, family, and then comes friends or job. If you're doing something wrong, chances are you're messing up your priorities.

"The first job I got I lived in the Antelope Valley and you'll have two hundred people go for one minimum-wage job. I had no car. I took a bus. My job was to find a job, nine to five. It took one and one-half months. I got a job, temporary, part-time, minimum wage. And damn I was so grateful to get it.

"Now you need to decide what to put on your application. Just because we got clean and sober doesn't mean we got stupid. It's a double-edged sword because we try to be honest. When shit came up missing, who did they look at? The addict who got out of Acton."

"So what should we put?"

"I'm just telling you my experience," Stella said. "You know what I do on job applications? I put my fellowship symbol up there, real tiny. Anybody who needs to know will understand it or ask me about it. But that's just for me. What do you do when it asks if you've been convicted? It's against the law to lie, but you're in a bind. If you say yes, they may not want you. If you say no, you can get fired."

Stella switched subjects, moving on to the Recovery portion of the form. "I know before I go into a Mexican restaurant what I'm going to drink because what goes with Mexican food?"

"Margaritas," offered one resident.

"Right! What goes with pizza?"

"Beer."

Stella nodded. "At baseball games what do you eat? Beer and peanuts. So you need a game plan. When someone comes up with a bag, what do you tell them?"

"Thank you."

"No!" Stella said. "Do I tell them I've been in treatment for ninety days? No, because at the end I'll take the bag and say thank you. I tell them, 'You don't have enough.' They'll say, 'Sure I do. I got this and that.' I tell them, 'You don't have enough because I'll get loaded and pretty soon you won't like me no more.'"

Stella went on to talk about outside support and sponsors. She told them that if they got into trouble, they should call her *before* they used. "If you're using, I'll hang up on you. I don't talk to pipes. I don't talk to bottles. You call before you get in trouble.

"I was clean and sober for six months but didn't feel right, so I called my sponsor and asked what's happening. She said, 'You don't have chaos any longer. That's called serenity.' I didn't like that feeling, so I ran out and stirred up stuff."

The following week, Stella still seemed to be stirring up stuff. Escrow had not closed on her house, she was still living in a garage, and her finances remained precarious. On Monday, she announced that the muffler of her beater car had blown and her auto insurance was due. She worried about which to pay, asking everyone she could get to listen which they would choose. Her question contained a hint of beggary, but the other counselors had gotten tired of lending her money that they knew they'd never see again.

The next day, Stella said that her car was in the shop and "the muffler is taken care of." She didn't mention her car insurance, but said that over the weekend she and her daughter "decided that we wanted Christmas lights. I've wanted hanging icicles for three years. So we decided that we wouldn't eat and get them. Over the weekend we blew my entire paycheck. Seven hundred dollars. But we *had* to get the lights."

A few minutes later, Stella sat in her office, trying to figure out how to order Christmas presents for her daughters. She had seen "these beautiful rings" in a catalog and wished she had a credit card so she could get them sent immediately. Stella called the catalog company and ordered the rings, telling the salesclerk that she would send a check as soon as she could. "I'm in escrow so I can't give you the new address. I don't want to jinx the deal. Here's my work address."

During this chaotic time in Stella's life, she worried about how she would be portrayed in the book. "I was starting to get embarrassed," she told me, "but then I thought, 'This is life.'" It definitely was Stella's life. Even for her, though, she was unusually erratic. I didn't know if she was back to using drugs, but her behavior was disturbing.

———

Deborahh sat on her hastily made bed, writing a letter on a yellow legal pad. It was 1:40 P.M. and she had fulfilled her obligations for the day, allowing her time to concentrate on the only thing that interested her: Pete. Even though Pete had completed and left the program, much of Deborahh's life still revolved around him. She no longer cadged cigarettes for him or did his laundry, but she wanted to keep him emotionally afloat with twenty-plus-page letters. He was already drinking and using a little weed, so she hoped her missives connected him to something outside of himself. Deborahh felt silly for letting it slip that she loved him before he left, but she ignored that mistake and hoped he would, too. Now when Pete called she teased him by saying, "Hi honey . . . wait . . . who is this . . . Ralph?"

Pete was still jealous of Ralph and didn't want her to sleep with the old man any longer. Deborahh asked what he could give her in exchange and he had no reply. As Deborahh expected, the "big man" was intimidated.

Ralph, however, was not easily daunted and Deborahh liked that about him. She appreciated the quiet, steady support he provided. And in return, she was proud that she had never fucked up his work or disgraced him, once even going so far as to dress in dowdy clothes to make a good impression on his mother. Deborahh also had worked hard to make his house look great. Whatever others might think of their relationship, she believed that it worked for them. She looked forward to a clean life with Ralph, although she told him he would have to stay up and have sex because fucking was the only thing she could still do.

Deborahh glanced at the bed across from hers. One room-mate was lying on her blankets, reading. The other two beds in the cubicle were momentarily empty, which Deborahh was grateful for. One of her new roommates was a religious nut, the kind Deborahh couldn't tolerate. Deborahh claimed that if the roommate farted, she thanked Jesus.

Above them, hanging from the light fixture on the ceiling, were a sprig of mistletoe and a lone ornament. Deborahh smiled when relating how easy it was to swipe those items and some tinsel from the Recovery House. Contrary to her own prohibition on stealing, Deborahh had decided that it wasn't Christmas unless she boosted something. Now her bunkmates benefited from her burst of holiday cheer.

Deborahh couldn't wait to get out of Acton and see Pete again. He had gone to Clare, just like she planned to do, but had not stayed at the aftercare facility. Instead, he was living with a cousin only two blocks away. That sounded perfect to her. Deborahh had heard that at Clare it wasn't as easy to escape meetings, but she was eager to go. Not only would Pete be nearby, but she knew the facility would keep her out of trouble until her court date. Plus, she had been excited to learn about Clare's thrift store. They might make her work—which was okay since she was experienced at alterations, having helped with weddings and the medieval Renaissance Faire—but the real attraction was the clothes that she could acquire.

She planned to get a respectability outfit.

Her closet was still crammed with more clothes than she could wear in a month, but now her selections were veering toward what she called "decent, middle-aged lady kinds of things." Her transformation occurred after she decided that she was too fat to dress in her old manner. "After all," she reasoned, "what's the point of being a big, fat hoochie?" So, she had sacrificed her high heels and fishnets in an attempt to achieve a proper, more dignified appearance; now it was dresses to her knees and stockings.

The new clothes were just one example of how Deborahh had changed in her ninety days at Acton. At first, she had been rebellious, a reaction to the way Rico had overwhelmed her and because she feared the program would make her get too involved. But she had stayed away from Rico and had refrained from involvement with everything except Pete.

Deborahh still thought Rico had an ass in the middle of his shoulders, but she also realized that her problems with him stemmed from the fact that she knew he was one person she could not manipulate. He had her number; he knew her without knowing her. She flirted with a couple of the other male staffers but stayed as far from Rico as possible. Not realizing that all the counselors and most of the staff knew who she was, Deborahh thought she was keeping a low profile. At the Thanksgiving dinner, in an attempt to remain anonymous, she moved from where Mr. Clark and his family were serving. She suppressed her urge to be snide to a particular counselor that she didn't respect, knowing such behavior would get her ass kicked out. She had refused to join the residents' council, and had declined to take a job or be a literacy volunteer.

Despite her dislike of the Acton program, Deborahh was proud that she had almost made it through. She knew that she didn't have another drug run in her and was happy that she could find a way out of her former life. She claimed that she had done it through sheer grit. The county had provided a place for her to live, but she believed that she was doing well in spite of the classes and meetings and counselors and other do-gooders, not because of them. Once Pete had asked her if she had to notice everything and talk to everyone. Ignoring his fit of jealousy, Deborahh had replied that she had to pay attention, especially since she was nearsighted, because no one could watch her back like she could. That sentiment seemed to sum up her stay at Acton.

Tiffany sat with a male co-leader at the front of a small classroom, ready to begin the resident-led Step Study group. The stark white walls contrasted with the nighttime darkness that could be seen as residents entered the room.

The study session was one of the many activities that Tiffany continued to pursue to the end of her Acton stay. She opened a copy of the book, *Twelve Steps and Twelve Traditions,* an Alcoholics Anonymous publication. She suggested that they read one paragraph and discuss how it applied to their lives. Tiffany began with a passage from the Step Two chapter: *"Sometimes AA comes harder to those who have lost or rejected faith than to those who never had any faith at all, for they think they have tried faith and found it wanting . . . the dilemma of the wanderer from faith is that of profound confusion . . . He is the bewildered one."*

After finishing the text, Tiffany spoke from her heart. "I never lost values. I lost morals, but regarding lost values, I knew what honesty was and good people, but I chose not to hang with them. I was always working hard. I didn't jack people off. I worked my fucking ass off and worked harder than I should of. But I never lost the values of life—the ones I was raised with. But being such an honest fucking crack fiend didn't save me from other shit."

The group applauded Tiffany's confession.

A greasy-haired white man began to talk. "Both my parents are Methodist ministers, but they couldn't help me from feeling despair, hopelessness, and abandonment. I didn't have the guts to put a gun to my head so I used a syringe. I played Russian roulette by shooting up with the same needle as people who have AIDS. So, only by the grace of God, I don't have AIDS. I made a mess of my life. I had a fucked-up lifestyle. Now I take several showers a day, and all I can see is black nastiness washing off me."

A Hispanic man in his mid-forties began to cry as he spoke. "I was robbing on a daily basis. Kmart. Walmart. Three hundred dollars a day. I don't want to . . . I was fucking scandalous. I'd be hanging with straight-out murderers. I can't take that shit back. I was fucking sick. Just to get what I got. There's people who fucking died because of my shit. I don't want to go there any more."

After several more confessions, another Hispanic man had the last word. "I always worked all my life. Never forgot where I came from. If I didn't go to church, I couldn't go to the movies. I became clean. I don't feel like using. But I don't know about tomorrow . . . Your stinking thinking will take you back to where you came from . . ."

Tiffany was proud that she got Southsiders, the Hispanic gang members, to participate in the Step Study sessions. The Southsiders tended to stay apart from others at Acton. One of Tiffany's many missions while at the center was to get them involved in positive activities. She felt as though she had done a good job connecting them to something outside their small clique.

By the Step Study meeting, Tiffany was already thinking ahead, to her life after Acton. She planned to live in a sober-living facility and go through the Twelve Steps with a sponsor. She had started the steps while at Acton but didn't feel as though she was getting anywhere. At Acton it was too easy to say, "Hi, I'm Tiffany and I'm an addict." She knew things would be different in the outside world, but that didn't stop her from formulating big plans. She had decided to go to college, get a degree in counseling, and use her energy to treat drug addicts.

19

LAST DAYS

Patty's last two days were a blur of activity.

Tuesday morning she started at the Admissions Office, picking up paperwork for a treasure hunt of signatures attesting to her good standing at Acton. Minutes later she tracked down the head of housekeeping and got the woman to sign a statement saying that Patty owed no household supplies. Next, Patty visited the financial office.

Three residents were crowded into the tiny office, waiting in line. Patty shifted from foot to foot, sniffling and wiping her nose on the plaid jacket she wore above a blue turtleneck, jeans, and black boots. The short feathers of her newly cut hair bobbed every time she bent her head and the silver bracelet on her wrist fell out of sight when she lifted her sleeve to her nose.

One of the residents finished his business and left. The line inched forward. Moments later the front door burst open and Owen poked his head inside. He entered the office while yelling to someone outside, "She's right here, you knot-head."

"Who?" Patty asked.

"You." Owen closed the door and moved closer to Patty, as if cornering his prey.

Patty didn't budge. After weeks of telling Owen to leave her alone, she still didn't know how to deal with him at close range. She knew they had no relationship, could have no relationship outside of Acton, and preferred that he go away, but a part of her still liked to flirt and she couldn't cut him off forever. After all, Owen had proposed marriage to her. She didn't take the offer seriously since it was one of six she had gotten from various men while at Acton, not to mention countless propositions. Nevertheless, Owen's attention flattered her and an ego boost was always welcome.

A staff member working at the side of the room witnessed Owen's entrance and stepped toward him. "Can I help you?"

"I'm waiting for a ride." Owen said.

"Then go down to admin and wait there."

Owen grinned at Patty, exposing his gold tooth.

"She politely told you to get out," Patty said, trying to keep the glee from her voice.

Owen skulked out of the office, but nine minutes later, as Patty left, she found him on the stoop outside.

"I just want a hug," Owen said.

"You're going to get me in trouble." Patty tried to avoid touching him.

"No. I just want a hug."

Patty threw her arms around him and quickly withdrew. Then she yelled, "It's been fun!" She danced away from Owen, saying she had to go to the library for another signature. She had checked out six books during her stay and still needed to return two.

Inside her dorm, Patty looked at her tiny area. Since her arrival, she had added new things to the bed stand. A self-esteem book written for single mothers joined her cherished Bible. Other prized possessions included a picture of her daughter, cards from several people, and a flowered frame containing a photo of Patty with her youngest child. Patty snatched up her two library books and exited.

Owen was waiting outside.

"I said good-bye to Julie," Owen said.

"Did you kiss her?" Patty asked.

"Yes."

"I'm jealous."

Moments later, Patty was in the library, exchanging phone numbers with the female resident working behind the counter. When Patty finished penning her phone number, the woman asked Patty to write a good-bye in her NA book, a custom similar to that of high school students leaving their sentiments in friends' yearbooks. Soft music played in the background as indecipherable work noises issued from the Learning Center located in the next room. One resident busied himself with a pile of newspapers. Five others read at two tables shoved together. They all ignored Patty's excited utterances to her Acton friend.

"Are you coming to my graduation?" Patty asked. Although attendance at the completion ceremony was required, many residents found ways to avoid it.

The woman said she would be there.

"I'm anxious and I'm scared," Patty said. "I'm a woman of God and I put my faith in God."

"You'll be fine," her friend replied.

"It would be nice if they start early," Patty said.

"You'll be out in time for the holiday."

Patty smiled. Graduation was early, on Wednesday rather than Friday, because it was Thanksgiving week. She *would* be home for the holiday, just as her daughters requested. Patty had talked her counselor into letting her exit a week early. Most counselors frowned on such a practice, believing that residents should be held to their 90-day promise, but Patty had sweet-talked her way into an early release.

She headed to her counselor's office, needing that signature, too. Tiffany, who was working as the receptionist, nodded toward Patty's papers and asked, "What's that for?"

"Graduation."

"You're boning out . . . ?"

"Now I've got all they had to offer me," Patty replied, somewhat defensive that she was leaving early.

"Now *I'm* just upholding responsibilities," Tiffany said.

Diane invited Patty into her office, where a cat lounged on the sofa.

"When I get out," said Patty, "I'm going to NA and AA. Rico voted me least likely to stay, but I proved him wrong. I'm going with my family tomorrow. Your name is going to be in my speech. You'll be there in my heart. What do you suggest I do?"

"I don't believe in trying to get our anxiety level down," Diane said. "When we have anxiety, it's an energy. Accept anxiety. It's energy. It will make you more animated. Acknowledge it when you get up. Saying it takes away the negativity."

"I'm excited," Patty said. "I'm glad I decided to stay. Last week I was thinking, 'What's a graduation?' and I almost went home with my family."

"Good decision," Diane replied.

"People here want to nitpick. The SIP part taught me to grow. In the beginning I was flirtatious. Now that I'm a woman of God, I don't want to be looked at that way. I cried in Bible Study last night because I don't want to come off that way no more. When I confess to God . . . it helps me to grow. Admitting it is a way of dealing with it. A couple of guys in Bible Study say, 'Patty, you have changed.' But there's still a couple of guys . . . I've earned a lot of respect. In three months, I feel like I've grown compared to a six-month program. I found an awesome relationship with God."

"You've worked really hard," Diane said. "But don't work hard on making your anxiety go away."

"I have plans two days after Christmas. My daughter would like the two of us to go to Kansas City to see my best friend and my sister."

"Are you going to be able to follow through financially?" Diane asked.

"Yes. I'm using Christmas money for tickets."

"How long will you be gone?"

"Five or six days," Patty said. "How long do you think I should take?"

"Do any of these people use?"

"No. My sister never used. My best friend is clean off cocaine for ten years."

"Does she go to meetings?"

"I don't know."

"Tell yourself you'll go to one meeting. Not only is a meeting going to be supportive to your recovery, but you'll see a new meeting in a new state."

"My daughter's father is trying to push me," Patty said.

"To move in?"

"Yes. But I'm trying to stay by myself one year."

"It's a control issue," Diane said.

"Before, I was okay with being miserable. I've come a long way to where I am today. It's awesome. I never have to go back there. I haven't had an obsession to drink since I got here. Do you believe God can take that desire away? I feel He healed me. I don't feel I'll ever have that problem again. I think it won't ever come back. Is it okay to feel that way?"

"Yes. God has the charity to do it. But there's no guarantee that your obsession won't return. It might just be a craving."

"I have faith in God. He will take craving away."

"He'll take obsession away," Diane said. "But a craving can come from nowhere. Bodies have memories. But that won't hurt your relationship with your Higher Power."

Patty nodded. "I love you."

"I love you," Diane said.

Minutes later, Patty found Rico in front of the Admissions Office. She told him, "You're the one who got me here. I remember on the phone you asked me if I really wanted recovery."

"I remember that day," Rico said.

Quinn, a resident who had become Patty's friend, approached Patty and Rico. "I have the word for the day: Growth."

Rico nodded. At the beginning of Quinn's stay, Rico had provided her a word every day for encouragement. At some point in Quinn's recovery, she had reached a turning point and could furnish her own motivation. Now she contributed a daily word to Rico.

"What's the acronym?" Rico asked.

"GROWTH. God Responsibility Opportunity Willingness Trust and Honesty. Or Hope."

Later that afternoon, Patty and Quinn met at the reception area of the Recovery House, where Quinn worked afternoons, taking over from Tiffany. They were in a room that once had been a kitchen. Quinn sat behind a desk, reading the first draft of Patty's speech. Patty hovered nearby. Across the room was a turquoise-and-yellow tiled counter. Rock music played in the background.

"I want to mention each name," Patty said, agonizing over how to include her children in the speech. "I have individual relationships with each of them but don't want to say something specifically to each one . . . To my three beautiful daughters and to my handsome son . . . To my four beautiful children, Mandy, Janie, Bobby, and Lara . . . They're my world, but I don't know how to say that. Should I put that?"

"If that's what you want," Quinn said.

"I want to put them with God. I think I need to write more to my children. And I really want to say something about God in there . . . I'm tired."

"God is going to help us stay healthy and strong."

"What would you put? My oldest daughter doesn't want amends so this is my chance to make amends."

"You just said a really loving thing: you are my world."

"This thing is for newcomers. That's why I stayed: for newcomers . . . Not enough people go to Bible Study."

"Tell them that," Quinn said.

"Everyone says stay out of the mix."

"I didn't," Quinn said. Quinn had recently gone through the ceremony but needed to remain another two weeks to complete her court-mandated stay.

"What did you say?"

"Stay focused. Surround yourself with positive people."

"I'm not going with nobody for a year," Patty said. "Sometimes I'm sad about the way I was. I was like that because I was a housewife. I did it to get attention, validation. Just outside of Bible Study, a guy came up to me and asked me to take a walk. He told me to put aside God. Just so he could get his groove on. That made me think."

A few days after completing his Beacon House application, Eddie sat down to talk to me. The wintry weather was bothering him. It was too chilly to spend much time outdoors and he had gotten a cold. Despite taking a sinus pill, he was stuffy and miserable. He desperately wanted to leave Acton immediately, but he was worried that he might have to go to a sober-living house rather than a treatment program. He had at least one state disability check coming to him and was considering using that money to camp out at a sober-living place until a program admitted him. His only absolute requirement was that he not end up on the street.

I asked Eddie if he had gotten anything out of Acton. He said he "did get some stuff out of Acton," but didn't elaborate. Instead, he said, "My ex-sponsor knew the right path and told me to come up here and listen, don't get involved. Otherwise I might have given up. When I came in I was confused. I had let myself down.

"If I don't go to a program, I'd go straight to a gang. I still know people in Norwalk. Many are in jail. People there are still in trouble, still using and going into prison. There's nothing there for me . . . My sister is there . . . I'll leave it alone . . . When I feel comfortable, I'll go back."

Eddie claimed that "using doesn't even occur to me. I got no obsession. I don't dream about it. I'm too old. I tried it and it didn't work. The whole deal was to fit in and it wasn't there. I partied my days and it's over with . . . I'll go to AA . . . I'm just gonna suit up and live life peacefully. I just want to be comfortable. Not worry about who I burnt."

Before we parted, Eddie gave me a copy of his Step Three thoughts:

Made a decision to turn our will and our lives over to the care of God as we understood Him. I've tried to live my life runing things my way and it never worked for me. I always got in trouble or hurt people that I loved. So I learned to turn it over to my higher power. Last year wall at work I came into contact with a lot of people who dident know of twelve step programes and what they represent. So when I tried to handle the problems that I ran into my way I always failed. I had to turn it over and let it go so it wouldent fester inside of me. In my life today my higher power plays a big part taking the anger and hurt away from me so I can fuction in todays life. I know one of the worst things I can do is stuff feeling inside of myself. I have to let them go and ask my higher power to relieve me of this. I also, everday ask him to keep the absettion [obses-sion] from my mind and body away for just this day. and so far it has worked. I know that I have the willingness and the open mindeness to stay sober & clean. I just have to apply myself ever day.

The day after sharing those words, Eddie left Acton as quietly as he had arrived. The same van that transported him to the center whisked him away. He said no good-byes. He didn't attend his completion ceremony. His counselor later told me that Eddie had gotten his wish and had been accepted by a program.

20

GRADUATION

Almost three months after Danika's completion ceremony, Patty's big day began much the same way. Residents hustled to clean and decorate their cabins, those graduating scrambled to find the perfect outfit, and the area outside the canteen had been set up for the ceremony. Now, though, the summer heat had morphed into late autumn weather. The bright sun, low in the sky, emitted little warmth. A cold wind whipped through the trees, driving the low clouds into thin streaks. A few leaves were turning yellow or had already fallen to the ground, but most of the trees were still brimming with green foliage.

By three-twenty in the afternoon, the chairs were almost filled and several residents had made themselves comfortable on the grass. Small groups of their relatives huddled together near the front of the stage, looking uncomfortable and out of place amidst the scores of recovering addicts. Patty's extended family was there: parents, children, the father of her youngest child, three sisters, a niece, nephew, and grandmother.

A small band of residents completing their stay at Acton arranged themselves in two rows of chairs facing the assemblage. Patty wore a black velvet cocktail dress with a big bow on the back, almost like a pair of dark angel's wings. Black stockings and high heels complemented the outfit more suited to a night on the town than a sober ceremony in the desert. Patty shivered as a gust of wind passed.

Tiffany, her long hair loose and uneven at the ends, was the master of ceremonies. She had completed the 90-day program, but she was in her fourth court-mandated month and had chosen to wait until the week before her departure to go through the ceremony. Instead, she presided over this ceremony and called the newcomers forward, asking them to sit in the front three rows.

When the opening formalities were finished and it was Patty's turn to speak, she approached the podium, hugging a jacket that someone had slipped to her. She looked at her family, proud that they had come, proud that they were proud of her, and proud that she had something to be proud of. Cheers resounded. There was much clapping and even more whistling. Patty smiled nervously and said, "Hi, my name is Patty and I'm an addict. I have a little bit of a cold, but I'm okay."

"You can do it, baby girl. Be strong," came encouragement from the audience.

"This really touches me . . . because of the happiness." Patty sniffled, failing to hold back tears. "I'm really home and it feels okay."

Applause filled the air.

Patty looked at her children. "Kids, I'm so happy." She then glanced toward the Acton residents. "To the ladies: I love you all—and I mean that." Patty turned back to her children. "I do love you and you're going to make it. To my parents . . ."

She was crying and couldn't get any words out. Her mother waved. The residents clapped again. Finally Patty said, "Children, I love you so much."

There was scattered applause. Patty then faced the residents. "You can find out a lot about yourself here. I suggest you put God first, fellowships, and then self. God is wonderful. God bless."

She returned to her seat amidst cheers, whistles, and clapping.

Toward the end of the ceremony, Patty introduced her family to the assemblage. "This is part of my family. My loving mother. She has seven children. She don't get enough credit."

Patty's mother spoke. "I'm so happy for Patty to get into this program. This will be the first Thanksgiving to be with Patty for many, many years."

During our last conversation, Patty had said she had learned a lot at Acton. "I love myself today. I don't need a man to validate me. Before, I always put myself second to men . . . but alcohol was first. Now it's God, my fellowship, me, relationship. Before I got here it was drugs, relationship, and then me. Not God."

On the subject of God, Patty claimed that she had mellowed out. Bible Study taught her that if a person "raced full bloom into the Lord, you'll get tired and fall down. You can't be so hallelujah and burn out. That's what I used to do. Now I'm steady. People said I was really tripping on the Lord. The chaplain called me a fireball for the Lord. People got tired of it."

Patty's immediate plan was to sleep on the couch at her parents' house. She hoped to go back to school and find a job. She wanted to get her own place in Simi Valley and feed the homeless through her church. She also intended to repair her relationship with her family. "Families need healing from this disease," she said, ". . . all the pain we caused. Addicts self-medicate, but families weren't medicating. They need to heal."

Patty also said, "I'll hit a meeting in the afternoon after I get home. And go to Red Lobster. I'd like to get to the beach and walk with my family."

When I asked how Patty now felt about drugs, she said, "It turns my stomach. Talking about it makes me sick." She grabbed her stomach. "I don't like talking about it at all . . . I have to do this day by day, minute by minute . . . I can't lose contact with God, fellowship . . . Once I do that I'm a goner and I know that."

By the following week, it was too cold to hold the completion ceremony outdoors so Deborahh's was in the cafeteria. Excitement rippled through the large room. Rows of chairs faced a temporary podium, set up beside a huge bingo board and near a Christmas tree, its multicolored ornaments competing with red, white, and green lights and a giant aluminum star. The windows behind the podium revealed waves of mountains beneath a deep blue sky, its lower edges smudged by a layer of wispy clouds.

Deborahh and two of the women who came from Twin Towers with her, raccoon-eyed Inez and mannish Nancy, congregated in front of the tree, along with the other dressed-up residents undergoing the completion ceremony. The trio had a right to be proud; they had survived the court-ordered program in spite of themselves. None of them would have chosen treatment, but they had persevered, even when the others in their group had fallen. Yolanda, who'd had sex in her dorm, hadn't lasted twenty-four hours. Drugged Uta, not much more than that. Marissa, who'd had sex throughout the center's grounds, had been expelled after several weeks. Helen, who'd had a rough time during her twenty-four-hour pass, and Ana were required by the court to remain an additional thirty days. Of the Twin Towers group, only Deborahh, Inez, and Nancy had been released by the court after ninety days and had earned the right to stand before their peers and announce that they were ready to move on with their lives, to venture into the world, to test their commitment to recovery in less supportive situations.

As the three o'clock hour approached, more and more people crammed into the room, escaping the biting wind. The chairs filled while residents and counselors competed for leaning space against the walls, giving them a quick getaway or easy access to the door for a cigarette break. Small family groups stood near the graduates, awkwardly talking to their addict relatives, clearly happy that their son or daughter or grandchild or parent had completed the Acton program, but also uneasy about the future. So many promises had been broken, so many lives shattered and relationships mangled. But this was a day of repair, of healing, of taking a giant step forward, and of celebration, so they all focused on the positive. Warily.

Tiffany, again the master of ceremonies, introduced the new residents and then called the completers to the podium one by one. The first residents, including Nancy and Inez, gave short speeches and thanked God.

Then, it was Deborahh's turn. Her effort to look good paid off: a black patterned overlay topped her scoop-necked white dress, showing off her body to great advantage. Her black choker and the red, sparkling bow in her hair accessorized her outfit nicely. The overall effect was demurely sexy.

"Hi, my name is Deborahh and I'm an addict . . . I MADE IT! I'd like to give a shout-out—even though I'm not supposed to do that—to my roommates, my bunkies in Z. Especially Beth. I can't mention guys' names because that would be SIPing, but you know who you are. Thank you to Danny." Deborahh felt free to mention his name because she knew a gay man wouldn't get in trouble for her words. "I'll be out of here on Monday and back to the real world. Thank you very much."

Deborahh was beaming by the time she sat down and continued to smile through the remainder of the ceremony.

The day before completion, I had asked Deborahh if she had learned anything during her Acton stay.

"I've learned a lot of stuff since I got here," she replied. "I can go to sober-living and get tested. That'll impress a judge. I've learned stuff that will help me get off probation. I learned that brainwashing can be subsidized."

Deborahh still considered Acton the lesser of two evils. She said that there were many times when she almost got caught doing something forbidden, but was happy that "God didn't fuck with me this time."

Despite her rebellious words, Deborahh recognized that she had been given another chance at life. She was a good example of how Acton fulfilled its promise even to people who seemed to resist. Ninety days had given her time to reassess her life. She had decided not to return to prostitution, had taken her counselor's advice and no longer referred to herself as a hooker, and did not intend to return to drugs. Deborahh was looking forward to finishing her probation and expunging her criminal record. She was even considering getting a job and again becoming a contributing member of society. Whether she knew it or not, whether she wanted to or not, Deborahh exemplified the hope of Acton.

For me, these completion ceremonies also marked the end of my journey at the center. It was time to make sense of the stories I'd been told, the lives that had unfolded before me, and what ninety days at Acton meant.

After months of listening to Acton counselors and staff, in classrooms and private situations, I thought I understood many of the lessons that residents were supposed to learn and the tools they were to take with them. The biggest and most important lesson was AA's Step One: *We admitted that we were powerless over alcohol [or drugs]—that our lives had become unmanageable.* Until there was complete surrender, there was little chance of recovery, and until there was admission of the problem, the addict wouldn't look for or find a solution.

Another important lesson was to change their behavior, to get out of the drug mindset and behave like a "normie." The tools that Acton provided to help residents change their behavior were numerous. First, residents had three months to focus on themselves, get to know themselves, and invest in themselves. They were supposed to open their minds and be honest about their feelings and their past. After acknowledging their past, including poor choices and drug use, it was important that they talk about the behavior that led them to Acton, then "drop their burdens," and move on. Another tool involved replaying memories of the bad effects of drug using. Rather than glamorizing their past, they needed to accurately remember the reality of using or drinking and how drugs had produced few good highs and quickly left them feeling worse, lowering their self-esteem, and causing physical and emotional pain.

Although counselors taught residents to pay attention to themselves and their immediate environment, they also explained that self-knowledge alone wouldn't save them. Necessary tools involved creating their own road maps and learning to use their resources wisely. Residents were told not to go back to their old neighborhoods or hangouts. Counselors advised residents to find a sober-living facility so they could be with others who also had the goal of recovery. Plus, residents were encouraged to attend anonymous meetings, share at meetings, and find a sponsor, someone in AA or CA or NA who had years of sobriety and could capably guide a newly recovering person.

Additionally, residents needed to learn their triggers, and if they couldn't avoid situations that reminded them of drinking or using, they had to create a game plan for coping with such situations. The game plan should involve calling their sponsor *before* picking up a bottle or a syringe. Furthermore, as Eddie had already learned the hard way, residents needed to be aware that taking only one alcoholic drink—even if they were strictly heroin users—could send them back to full-blown drinking or using. They had to be careful not to substitute one obsession for another.

Another lesson counselors taught was that addicts were often attracted to the wrong people and that relationships could be serious pitfalls. Residents were warned not to move too fast with members of the opposite sex, that jumping into a relationship was risking relapse. The idea was to focus on themselves and their recovery, not another person.

Above all, the wisdom that Rico had imparted during orientation was important: do *whatever* it takes to remain in recovery.

With these lessons in mind, and knowing that Acton defines success by whether or not the resident stays in the program a full ninety days, I thought about who could be considered a success. Using the Acton gauge, the successful included prostitute Deborahh, porn star Danika, big lie Curtis, and homegirl Tiffany. Technically, Vietnam vet Eddie and religious Patty didn't stay the full ninety days, and even though they had finished all required classes, they fell into Acton's unsuccessful category. The other unsuccessful residents included crazy Jason and sleepwalking Matt. Jason was caught streaking naked through the women's dorm and discharged after twenty-eight days. He was earnest in wanting to forge a new life, but was young, had no self-control, and hadn't been at Acton long enough to learn the lessons necessary for recovery. Matt had voluntarily left the program very early. Perhaps he had achieved his personal goal of kicking heroin—the drug that kicked his ass—and was using cocaine and marijuana only, but his goal was not Acton's.

Americans at large have a different measure of success than Acton. They consider success to be foreswearing drugs and becoming a productive member of society. Using that standard, I wondered who would succeed.

Those who left early, Jason and Matt, seemed to have no chance of remaining drug-free. For Patty and Danika, it also appeared unlikely that they would refrain from using. Patty thought prayer and the embrace of her family would subdue the drug demons, but as far as she had come, she seemed unsteady, and I thought she needed additional care. The fact that she had not chosen to go somewhere with a strong recovery atmosphere, like a sober-living house, did not bode well. Danika, too, made a bad choice, deciding that the way to earn money for herself and her dependent husband was returning to adult entertainment. She seemed to be deluding only herself by claiming it would be just one more job. Stella's assessment was that women in the adult entertainment world didn't feel good about themselves and took drugs to dull their shame. Both Danika, who had finished the program and was considered an Acton success, and Patty made choices that indicated they were headed, again, in the wrong direction.

I thought that some of the Acton graduates had a good chance of succeeding by both Acton and societal standards. Eddie, thoroughly beaten by his last relapse, was determined not to make the same mistake. He had regained some of his old confidence, knew the type of place where he would thrive, and was intent on bettering his life. Before arriving at Acton, Tiffany had left behind the drama of prostitution, drugs, and violent Cuban drug dealers. She had tried to learn every rehab lesson and was determined to create a new life as a drug counselor. Curtis, who had spent years in prison and needed forgiveness from his big lie, had only come to Acton so he could keep his meal-ticket girlfriend, but he had gained self-assurance and learned that he could become independent. He seemed poised to make the right choices and redeem himself.

Even Deborahh appeared likely to stay clean and had a good chance at succeeding in the world outside Acton. She hadn't known what to expect from the center and was initially intimidated by Rico, but she had learned how to navigate her way through the center. Though she claimed that she wasn't listening and that Acton's program was worthless, she had absorbed more than she thought. Early in her stay, she had decided not to return to prostitution or drugs. She had used the center as a time to think about how to stage the next chapter in her life. She intended to go to another recovery program, one that would allow her to get a job, earn money toward her own apartment, and move on. She hoped to expunge the misdemeanors from her record, and continue her affair with Pete while becoming Ralph's wife and working hard at Ralph's business.

I was convinced that Eddie, Tiffany, Curtis, and Deborahh had benefitted from Acton. I believed that they would prove the center a success, confirming the benefits of rehabilitation to both themselves and society.

Most of the counselors had come to Acton through different paths and represented a variety of experiences. Yet, most were in recovery and all understood well the ravages of addiction. They also knew the precariousness of recovery and the fragility of life, and had a keen appreciation for their current lives and how far they had come. There seemed to be no doubt that Rico, Walt, Jeff, Suzanne, Mike, David, and Cassandra would remain clean and sober. All of them remembered well, and some of them missed, the excitement surrounding the procurement and use of drugs. However, they had learned how to channel that intensity into other pursuits, primarily helping others in recovery.

I believed that Rico would continue using his tough-love approach to help Acton residents and would also continue to stay clean. Walt had been clean longer than the other counselors, was nearing retirement, and wouldn't jeopardize his recovery. Laid back Jeff, who had been in and out of several programs, including Acton's, before choosing life over the threat of a drug overdose or dying during a drug deal gone bad, was content working at Acton. Suzanne was far enough away from her alcoholic blackouts that she didn't seem in danger of relapsing. Mike, who called Acton "Jurassic Park After Dark" and viewed himself as the zookeeper, was happy to continue challenging residents' behavior.

David still awakened each day eager to get to work because he knew something interesting would happen. He could recount in amusing detail his days of living behind a Dumpster and getting shot while pilfering pizzas, but now he concentrated his drug-using dramas into helping others get clean. Cassandra, like the others, had had a rocky road to recovery, but was primed to continue helping substance abusers get and remain clean.

Stella, though, was different. She was close enough to her drug days to miss the adrenaline rush. Her family life was chaotic and her financial status precarious. Although in some ways she appeared to thrive in that situation, even Stella could have too much drama. Homeless, living without her dog and older daughter, she was struggling with her health and work. She seemed on the verge of disintegration, and I doubted that she would stay clean if she didn't remember the lessons she imparted to others.

In sum, I worried about Stella's future, but I thought the other counselors would continue to do well. I believed that Jason and Matt would go back to using until they matured and made a sincere attempt at recovery. I had serious doubts about Patty and Danika's ability to remain drug-free even though they thought they were committed to recovery. I was confident that Eddie, Deborahh, Tiffany, and Curtis would stay clean. Those four seemed to have soaked up the Acton lessons, formal and informal, and had made plans to use those lessons to create a new life. They had found hope in the hell of drug using, and I fully expected them to stay away from alcohol and illegal substances.

—

Before I began the Acton study, I had several questions and a couple of concerns. I had wondered what drug treatment was like, how addicts recovered, and about Acton's role in aiding recovery. I had also worried that I might not find people as interesting as Joe and Al, the residents I had met years previously. It turned out that my concerns were unwarranted; I was not the least bit disappointed. Contrary to my apprehensions, I did meet interesting people and rather than refusing to talk to me or preventing me from observing their activities, residents flocked to me, eager to tell their stories. The counselors, too, were gracious and invited me to interview them, observe their classes, and sit in on meetings.

I also learned the answers to my initial questions about what happens during the treatment process and Acton's role, and I had a better understanding of recovery. I fully appreciated that it was a process, that relapse was often part of that process, and that for most addicts, recovery was both a complicated and individual route. I recognized that recovery wasn't just a matter of willpower; it involved a variety of factors, including the individual's motivation to recover, to do *whatever* it took to stay clean. What happened after treatment was also a key factor. These variables meant that only time would tell whether my predictions were accurate, what Acton's impact was on the lives of those I followed, and, most important, whether treatment was successful. I would have to wait to find out if the seeds Acton planted would take root, grow, and blossom into renewed, vital lives.

21

TEN YEARS LATER

Most of the residents that I followed were homeless and few had a permanent post-Acton place to stay. Between that and the fact that their primary focus was supposed to be recovery, I did not maintain continuous contact with anyone except Deborahh. The others lived their lives and pursued whatever activities they chose, either forgetting me or putting any thoughts of The Writer, as most knew me, and my book, out of their minds. As a consequence, when I attempted to reestablish contact, it wasn't easy to find them. Phones had been disconnected, family or friends had moved, or the residents had disappeared into the haze of Los Angeles County and its more than nine million residents.

Deborahh's story after Acton was the easiest to reconstruct, but for me the most difficult to tell. She went to another treatment facility where she continued to flout the rules and pursued her drama-filled life. Pete, her "Acton husband," was in a nearby program, so she saw him every night. Ralph, her ex-john-turned-boyfriend, lived twenty miles away, but visited and gave her money. Deborahh considered it a perfect arrangement, and when Pete asked her to stop seeing Ralph, she said, "Are you crazy? He's supporting us both."

She was unhappy with the "Oprah Twelve Step fantasy" that she had to pretend to adhere to while at the new program and hated listening to staff members insist that she was a dry drunk, a relapse waiting to happen. They told her that she had to feel recovery, to wait for a miracle, but Deborahh thought the miracle had already happened: she had been clean for six months and had a healthy fear of being back in the vicinity of her drug activities.

She got an unpaid job at her program's bargain center, allowing her "to shop all day." Even though she continued to gain weight, she enjoyed swiping clothes that fit her new "camouflage lacy tent style." Although Pete didn't treat her very well, she reveled in the drama of seeing him while Ralph tried to start his multi-million dollar project. Calling herself a gold digger, Deborahh thought that remaining with Ralph was the chance of a lifetime. As soon as his project took off, she hoped to be a corporate officer in the company and planned to marry him.

A few months later, Deborahh had a meeting with her probation officer and was excited to learn that she was no longer under threat of surprise drug testing. She claimed that she had always assumed that she would go back to using once she was no longer under court supervision. Instead, she attended an AA meeting on the anniversary of her first drug-free day and was proud that she earned a one-year cake and chip. Both the "birthday" cake, shared by all at the meeting, and her personal poker chip-sized piece of plastic, stating "AA, 1-year," were commemorations in honor of her recovery. Deborahh later surmised that what kept her clean was remembering the misery, hopelessness, and frustration of constantly chasing the pipe.

Deborahh attended the Acton Alumni Reunion ten months after leaving the center. Although she had sent me long handwritten letters detailing every aspect of her life, it was great to see her again. She had gained more weight, but she looked wonderful. Her infectious laughter floated across the familiar desert grounds as she delightedly talked to counselors who had been skeptical that she would stay clean. Deborahh told me that she didn't have the heart to tell them that she had only paused in her drug use and that she was sure she'd use in the future, but I didn't believe her. Deborahh's bravado was a tiny act of defiance in the face of the system, and in spite of her protestations, I thought the system had changed her.

By Christmas, Deborahh was living in a hotel, paid for by Ralph, near MacArthur Park, her old "home." She had said good-bye to Pete, tiring of his continued drug abuse and inability to return her love. Then Ralph's project fell apart and he had no money to support himself or her. Deborahh was mad at Ralph for leading her on and madder at herself for believing him.

Without Ralph's money, Deborahh had to move out of the hotel. She stayed with friends, then at a county "voucher motel," and later a homeless shelter before securing a spot in a transitional program. The transitional program allowed her to live free as long as she worked and saved money. She obtained a job at Macy's and worked for three weeks before her background check revealed her arrest record and she was fired. Despite the setback, Deborahh declared that once she got the desire to get off her ass, it was easier to act. She lost twenty-five pounds, contacted a sister she hadn't talked to in ten years, and started going to weekly AA meetings with some of her friends. She was also excited that she had only a few more months on probation and needed only $900 to pay restitution to erase the misdemeanors from her record.

A short time after getting a temp job that stretched into a two-year position, she met Jay. Her first description to me was that he had a drop-dead body, wore a suit to work, and was affectionate, fantastic in bed, and interested in a long term relationship with her. It exactly fit Deborahh's perfect man. Unfortunately, he was an alcoholic. Deborahh and I had switched from letter writing to emails when she got her temp job and one of her first emails mentioned Jay's new job and the fact that he took his first paycheck and true-to-form went drinking. Deborahh proclaimed him The One but didn't trust his drinking. Nevertheless, within a few months they had gotten an apartment together.

Deborahh had been clean for almost three years when she learned that her mother wanted to reestablish contact. As soon as she heard that news, hostility and anger toward her mother thawed. At that point, Deborahh decided that she was really getting her head on straight and noted that she would be officially clean for three years on her mother's birthday.

She soon began paralegal school, excelling at her studies and earning all A's for the first three semesters. Then, her temp job ended. Deborahh collected unemployment for a while and began unpaid paralegal internships. The first organization did a background check and told her not to return, but she was very happy interning at a non-profit, claiming that she could answer all the questions posed by other interns. She was able to get five misdemeanors dismissed and was looking forward to the next year when she thought she could get her record sealed. Jay, who she continued to call "my Man," was drinking heavily and still living with her. Then he stole her credit card and she decided that he had to leave at the end of the month. She thought anyone would be better than a drunk who didn't even take her out. Despite the problems with Jay, the last email I received from her was an optimistic one. She was soon to celebrate her fifth anniversary of sobriety. Her last words were, "Not bad for a crack head, right?"

A few months elapsed before I realized that I'd lost track of Deborahh. She had consistently written twenty-page letters at least monthly in the beginning and long emails every few months for the previous two years. She had promised to stay in touch no matter what, but her email address was the only contact information I had and by the time I realized she was gone, the account was closed. With the help of a private investigator and some Internet searching, I discovered that she had died a few months after her last communication. I was stunned. It was hard to believe that someone as youthful and vibrant as Deborahh could die so quickly. Acton counselors who had thought Deborahh wouldn't make it a year clean wondered if she had overdosed. I didn't believe it. I paid for a copy of her death certificate which noted Lou Gehrig's disease as the cause of death.

Ten years after first meeting Deborahh, I was able to track down her sister, who told me that Deborahh had passed out while at work. A doctor put her in the hospital for two days. A few weeks later, Deborahh couldn't get out of bed and her speech was slurred. The sister made Jay take her to the hospital. Deborahh couldn't speak, but kept writing, "I want to go home." She never left the hospital.

Deborahh's sister called her a force of nature. It was an apt description that had been eluding me for years. She *was* a force of nature.

At the first Acton alumni reunion after Patty left, Owen, the man who tried to lure woman of God Patty into a relationship at Acton, claimed that she was under her mother's thumb and he had been unable to talk to her. I thought I might get a similar rejection if I called Patty's mother, so I wrote. After failing to get an answer, on one of my trips to Acton I decided to drive to Simi Valley. I thought that if I showed up in person, Patty's mother would see that I wasn't a drug addict and talk to me.

I found the house and knocked on the door. There was no response. I returned to my car and contemplated the drive back to the Antelope Valley as well as the thousands of miles I had come. I decided to call. A woman answered and wanted to know who I was. When I said my name and that I knew Patty at Acton, the hostile answer was, "I don't remember anything at Acton." Realizing I had Patty on the line, I told her I was "the writer" and she replied, "Oh! Did you finish the book?"

I asked if I could visit with her, but she said she was going shopping with her daughter. I asked if I could just say hi. Patty gave me her address. It was one block away— apparently I had transposed two numbers. I hopped in my car and raced down the street, hoping she wouldn't change her mind. As I exited my car, I saw Patty running. For a moment I thought she was trying to get away from me, but seconds later she launched herself into my arms and gave me a big hug.

I talked briefly to Patty and her daughter. Patty said she had relapsed after Acton but had been clean for four years. Her daughter confirmed that Patty was doing well and that they finally had a good relationship. On my next trip to Simi Valley, a year later, I learned the full story.

Patty had gone to her mother's home after leaving Acton. Looking back on that choice, she says she "was doomed." She was unhealthy, depressed, and had no support group. After Christmas, Patty ignored her mother's advice and went to Kansas to visit a friend. She was okay until New Year's Eve, when she drank beer. The next day she didn't remember where all the empty bottles came from and snuck out in the snow to get more liquor. When she got back from Kansas she tried to stay sober, but her life continued downhill and she was "ten times crazier than before." Patty says that the disease was bigger than her and she just "couldn't put it down."

She and her boyfriend, Ned, got a trailer and moved in with their four-year-old daughter. They soon started doing methamphetamine. Realizing that she had become "a monster on meth," Patty asked her mother to take her daughter. Patty and Ned soon lost their trailer and she began living outside in the nearby mountains. Sometimes she hung out in the park near her mother's house, where Patty's kids occasionally glimpsed her as they rode by.

Two years after Acton, Patty's older daughter got married. Patty cleaned up and took a date to the wedding. Her date, and probably Patty, too, smelled like marijuana. She had spent so much time apart from her daughter that, except for family members, no one knew who she was or recognized her as the mother of the bride. Patty was upset by that, but was devastated when her son-in-law told her to leave. "It still hurts not to be in the pictures or part of the wedding." On that day, she asked herself, "How many more days of this do you want, Patty?"

Within a few months, Patty was arrested for possession of drugs. She said, "I spent thirty days in jail and hated it." The court gave her a mandate: either go to jail or devote a year to treatment. Patty chose to get clean. She spent ninety days in a treatment program, followed by nine months in a sober-living facility. At the end of the year, she earned a one-year chip. At that point, Patty felt as though she had become a totally different person and was happy that people no longer seemed afraid of her.

At one point, I was able to talk to Patty's boyfriend. Ned told me that he was arrested during the time that Patty was in treatment and he expected to spend the next several years in prison. While in jail, awaiting sentencing, a newspaper article about a church kept appearing in front of him. Several times he tried to throw it away, but it kept returning to him. Believing that was a sign from God, he "accepted Christ back into my heart" and committed himself to getting clean. Soon afterward, he was freed from jail.

Ned wasn't sure why he was released, but he thought it was a miracle.

After Ned's release, he and Patty reunited and married. Together they dedicated their lives to God. Ned began a motorcycle ministry. Patty was honored to be a deaconess of the church and began learning to ride a Harley-Davidson. She secured a job as a courtesy clerk at a grocery store and was promoted to deli manager. One Sunday a month she fed the homeless—in the same park where she had spent time while using drugs.

Despite Patty's cheerful outward appearance, the first time I sat down with her, eight years after she left Acton, she still struggled. She held a lot of anger inside her. She was still angry at Ned for his abuse when they were loaded and revealed to me for the first time that she had been abused and abandoned by men before she met Ned.

Two years later I saw Patty again. She was still clean, although she appeared more stressed than the previous time I had visited her. She had recently switched jobs to shed her managerial responsibilities. "I don't know how to process stress well," she told me. "I'm still trying to do that." By then she owned a Harley, had three grandchildren with a fourth on the way, and declared that she was still ditzy. She also continued to have anger issues.

Until that time, Patty had been involved only with church members, but she had recently gotten an AA sponsor and had become involved with recovery people. She didn't like to do step work, but continued to pray and wrote in journals. She was starting to attend group therapy and felt that was helpful to her continued recovery.

Despite her inner turmoil, Patty declared that she was happy. She had "freedom, true friendship, the ability to really be a mother to my youngest, and I'm able to help my parents financially." She even had times of peace. After seven years of remaining clean and sober, Patty knew that recovery was something she had to work to maintain and that it was a lifelong process, but she felt as though she was on the right path, saying, "I walk with integrity now."

Jason, the self-described "psycho" who was discharged for running naked through a woman's dorm, has proven impossible to contact. He had given me his mother's address, so he should have been easy to find. I sent unanswered letters to both Jason and his mother. When they weren't returned, I wondered if perhaps the mother had moved, so on one of my trips to Los Angeles County, I went to see if she still lived in the same house.

It was a worn neighborhood just off a well-traveled street. As I got out of my car, I saw a mail carrier leaving the house I sought. I asked the carrier if Jason's family lived there. Immediately suspicious, he asked, "Who do you work for?" When I told him that I didn't work for anyone, he said he couldn't give me that information.

Undeterred, I went to the door and knocked. No one answered. I knocked again. It sounded as though someone was inside, but no one came to the door. I wrote a quick note addressed to Jason's mother asking her to tell her son that I wanted to talk to him. I raised the mailbox lid to wedge my note inside and saw that the just-delivered name belonged to Jason's mother. I was happy I had confirmed her address. Unfortunately, I never heard from Jason or his mother.

Eddie, the Vietnam vet, was also elusive. For years I tried to track him down but was unsuccessful. Neither his contacts at Clare, his pre-Acton facility, nor people at Beacon House, his after-Acton program, were able to provide a way to reach him. His parents died before I met him and he had been out of touch with his sister for decades, so Eddie had not been able to give me the phone number or address of family members, which meant that I was at a dead end.

Although I believe that Eddie remained clean, I have no way to verify it. I hope to find him some day and learn about his post-Acton life.

In addition to the four residents that I had followed from admission to discharge, there were four others that I had tracked and was interested in learning about post-Acton.

Homegirl Tiffany had been a model resident and I expected that she would do well after leaving the center. I wasn't disappointed. I didn't see her again until seven years after she graduated from Acton. We were both back at the county facility. I was visiting and she was, amazingly, a counselor.

After finishing the Acton program, Tiffany had spent a year at a sober-living facility. She had secured a sponsor and attended meetings. When the year was up, she moved in with her boyfriend. They soon married but divorced nine months later. Despite the collapse of the marriage, Tiffany kept her married, Latino last name.

Marriage was one of the few things that didn't work out for Tiffany. She successfully completed nurses' aid training, and did so well that she decided to tackle a drug counseling education. She also volunteered and served as an intern at Acton, working under the direction of counselors Alicia and Jeff. Three years after getting clean and first walking into Acton, Tiffany was hired there as a counselor. She bought a condo and, in her words, "learned how to be an adult." She also enrolled at the University of Phoenix, expecting to get her bachelor's degree by the end of the year.

Tiffany's transformation was accompanied by a physical makeover. She was no longer the chunky girl with weird hair. Instead, her sparkling eyes looked out from stylishly cut and highlighted hair. She was slim due to a gastric bypass operation that helped her shed seventy pounds. Her unconventional streak revealed itself in her multiple-pierced ears and the colorful tattoo that covered her right shoulder and spread halfway to her elbow.

I sat with Tiffany in her office at Acton. It seemed like a strange time-warp. I had spent many hours in Stella's and Jeff's offices. It felt the same sitting in Tiffany's office. Residents popped in to ask quick questions and the public address system issued occasional announcements. Posters reflecting Tiffany's taste in décor dotted the walls: "One by one the penguins steal my sanity," "FUCK DRUGS," and "And your whiney cry-baby opinion would be . . . ?"

Tiffany seemed pleased with where she was, but she still possessed a restless energy. She had made amends to herself and her daughter and continued to go to NA meetings. She even attended meetings at Acton to show the newcomers how the Twelve Step program worked. She was happy to see her daughter twice a year. Though the teenager was overweight, as Tiffany had been at her age, her daughter was making wiser choices and didn't smoke cigarettes or weed.

As Tiffany was telling me about Stella's latest escapades, another resident interrupted. "I'm having a bad day." The resident explained her problems and ended by saying, "I'm sorry I'm laying this on you."

"That's okay," Tiffany replied. "You just need to hold on. Ride it out." Though Tiffany was sympathetic to the resident, I sensed a slight impatience. I wasn't sure if it was with the resident or because I was there, preventing her from doing her job as well as she might have done without my presence. The resident nodded and left, saying, "Sorry I'm bugging you." Later in my conversation with Tiffany, she told me that she only had women residents on her case-load and that they were needy, damaged, and took up a lot of her time with fighting, bickering, and bitching.

When I asked about her plans for the future, she bub-bled with enthusiasm. After finishing her bachelor's degree, she wanted to get a master's in Business Administration and a master's in Social Work. She thought it would take her eighteen months to get the MBA and three years to get the MSW. She then intended to become a social worker. She had decided that she didn't want to problem solve, as she was doing at Acton. Instead, recognizing how important it was for those in recovery to integrate back into society, she wanted to plug people into the right place, help them gain the services they needed. Tiffany planned to use her MBA knowledge to open a business, perhaps in the trucking/ transportation industry or in vending machines. She was also thinking of moving back to New Mexico, maybe to live with her sister. At the same time, she was applying for a certificate of rehabilitation, the first step in gaining a pardon from the governor for her felony drug possession.

Tiffany felt that, though she had had a rough life, the journey was worth it. If she had never used drugs, she might still be a phlebotomist in New Mexico. As it was, she saw the future as one of endless possibilities. And she couldn't have done it without Acton.

Three years later, a decade after completing the Acton program, Tiffany was still clean, working as a drug abuse counselor for a California state prison.

Unfortunately, porn star Danika was impossible to find in person. Her presence on the Internet, however, was strong ten years after Acton. I found mini-biographies noting her real name, birth date, and birthplace. Photos of her ranging from provocative to raunchy were on several websites. Danika was advertised on one porn site as a "smoking hot blonde." She was featured in several videos on demand. Another site offered 212 titles for sale that Danika starred in during the first five years after Acton. Recent releases indicate that she continues her porn career even though she is close to forty years old. There is a website showing a free video featuring fifteen minutes of hard-core sex between Danika and a "prom" date. I was sad to see her on the Internet and missed the vulnerable, sweet woman who wanted to help others. The fact that Danika continued to make pornographic videos is not definitive proof that she returned to drugs, but it is enough for me to believe that Acton's lessons had no lasting effect on her.

Curtis, the man who felt he had to make amends for a lie, was another Acton resident that I expected to do well. I reached him through a call to his mother. She was suspicious and wouldn't say if she was in touch with Curtis, but minutes after our conversation, he called me. He had remained clean the first five years after Acton, obtaining a job as a cemetery caretaker and staying out of trouble. After knee surgery he became hooked on prescription drugs, which led him back to the streets where he was arrested and jailed. Afterward, he "went to Warm Springs and got into the Big Book." By the time I caught up with him, ten years after I met him, he had been clean, again, for almost a year.

When Matt, the jittery man accused of sleepwalking, took his disability check and left Acton, his future didn't look good to me. As expected, he returned to his old neighborhood in Venice, and in his words by "that evening it was all over." He bought some cocaine and was immediately back in his old world. The following year, he met a woman who would become his wife. On a vacation, she introduced him to the quiet of Utah, and he was entranced by a place without helicopters, sirens, or traffic. He gladly moved out of Venice to a quieter part of Southern California, a move that he attributes to saving his life. Nevertheless, he sold pot and continued to use cocaine and marijuana.

Exactly nine months after 9-11, Matt became a father. At that point, he switched from illegal drugs to alcohol. Two years later, he and his wife had a second daughter. To continue his substance abuse, Matt would wait for his children to go to sleep before drinking, but by that time in his life, he had to consume a fifth of alcohol to get drunk. Although he had a tolerant wife, two children, money, and cars, he wasn't happy. He had the shakes every night and recognized that the quality of his life was deteriorating. He tried to quit drinking, but couldn't.

When his older daughter was four and a half, Matt disappeared from his family's life and resumed using cocaine and other chemicals. For three months he went back and forth, between home and the streets. After an arrest for DUI and possession, he attended a diversion program, but was in and out of that, too.

A year after his arrest, Matt realized that he was ruining his life and decided to get clean. He began attending Twelve Step meetings, got a sponsor, and started a twenty-seven-week study program to go through the entire Twelve Steps. As soon as he finished that, he started the steps over again.

Nearly a year after getting involved in NA, ten years after his brief Acton stay, Matt was clean and sober. He attended Twelve Step meetings four to five times a week and except for remaining drug-free, his main focus was his family. "My girls are everything to me," he said. Mornings he took them to school and at night he either drove straight home or to a meeting and then home. Facebook photos of

Matt, his wife, and children at Disneyland are snapshots of what appears to be a close-knit, happy family.

During one phone conversation I had with Matt, he was playing X-Box with his wife. He managed to answer all my questions while playing the game and offering advice to his wife. When his kids came into the room, Matt continued talking to me and playing while saying to his daughter, "Give me a kiss, Sweetie . . . Mommy and Daddy are trying not to get our characters killed."

Matt claims that he's not a big church goer, but he does attend with his family. He and his sisters, one of whom has been in recovery for twenty-four years, enjoy each other's company and spend time together. They don't invite Matt's father, "a stone-cold alcoholic," or his mother, who had relapsed with painkillers after eleven years in AA.

From everything I could tell, Matt had changed a lot in the time since his short stay at Acton. He had a steady and responsible job. He had a family he adored. He was clean and sober. Most importantly, he was determined to stay that way. Matt had changed physically, too. At Acton he was, as he said, "sucked up, strung out." He's 6'1" tall, but weighed only 115 or 120 pounds. Thanks to medical care while at Acton, Matt discovered that he has an over-active thyroid. He began taking medication for that and for high blood pressure. He had put on about one hundred pounds and his graying hair no longer resembled the shaved, skin-head look he had when he entered Acton. He had also blacked-out his Aryan-themed tattoos.

Although he still seemed to have a lot of energy and could do several things simultaneously, Matt had matured. He felt as though he had freedom from his addiction. He wasn't just "resting up." Previously when he got clean, he still romanticized about using. In our last conversation, he said, "I get a queasy feeling when I think about it." He believed that addiction was a disease and said he had seen the progressive nature of it. Matt claimed, "If I feel squirrely, I laugh. If I hear a voice saying 'have a couple of beers,' I laugh." Matt's sponsor told him that when his head starts talking to him, suggesting he drink or use, he should say "Thanks for sharing" and then go to a meeting. Matt said he knows that he can't afford to "mess around" any more. When I asked if he was done using for good, Matt said, "I believe so . . . yeah . . . it doesn't interest me anymore."

In addition to finding out what happened to the former residents, I wanted to conduct follow-up interviews with the Acton staff to see how they fared. I started with Stella, but piecing together the last decade of her life wasn't easy. She had quit her job at Acton, worked as a treatment counselor for a prison, and then quit that job. I had heard two types of rumors about Stella: she was using and not attending Twelve Step meetings, or she wasn't using but was exhibiting the erratic behavior of users.

Six years after the Acton study and a short time after Stella had stomach surgery, I visited her at her house, the house I had doubted that she would get a mortgage loan to purchase. It was an ordinary tract home in a nondescript neighborhood. She proudly showed me the add-on rooms that were created so that she could turn the place into a sober-living facility. Stella was vague about her recent past and told me that she didn't think it was important to attend Twelve Step meetings. I didn't know if she was drained from the surgery or by life, but she wasn't the same Stella I remembered.

As I was leaving, Stella insisted on giving me her ten-year chip. It is a beautifully crafted piece of wood showing the rings from the trunk of a fifteen- to twenty-year-old tree. One side of the two-inch chip is imprinted with a large "NA" in black ink, shadowed in blue. On the other side, it states "Congratulations, 10 years." I objected to taking the chip, but Stella was adamant. Finally I agreed on the condition that I could return it after she attained another ten years clean and sober. Stella said that she didn't think she would live that long. "How long have you been clean?" I asked. She wasn't sure, so I asked, "Are you clean today?" When she said yes, I told her I would return the chip to her in exactly ten years.

The following year when I was in the L.A. area, I tried to find Stella. No one knew where she was, but there were rumors that her current boyfriend was trying to sell her house. I went to the house. There was no for sale sign and no one was there, but a neighbor gave me Stella's boyfriend's phone number. The boyfriend told me Stella was in a Malibu treatment center.

Two years later I caught up with Stella. She was living in the San Fernando Valley with a successful businessman. She looked great. She sounded great. And she was clean. We went to lunch and she insisted on paying. After lunch, we stopped at a coffeehouse where Stella's elder daughter was the manager. Karen, Stella, and I sat outside on a busy street, sipping iced drinks, while talking about their drug using years. Stella said that she had relapsed because the stress had gotten to her. The deaths of her sponsor, brother, and sister, and losing her husband were overwhelming. For a long time she was insane without using. She knew that all the drug-using symptoms were there because she had stopped doing spiritual maintenance, which caused a spiritual malady.

Stella said that she "went out" (used drugs) for three to four years. During that time, Karen began using, and the two of them even drank together. Stella claimed that at first her using was under control. When she realized how bad off Karen was, she "swooped her up" and put her into a rehabilitation facility. By the time Karen got clean, Stella had gone full tilt into using and Karen was pissed. She told her mother to "get clean—or whatever" and stopped talking to her. Sometime later, Stella contracted pneumonia and her doctor said, "I think you're allergic to cocaine." Karen then "swooped up" Stella and got her into rehab.

After rehab, Stella knew she couldn't go back to her house in Palmdale, to her old situation. Instead, she moved to the San Fernando Valley. The first few months were especially tough. She didn't feel welcome at her initial NA meeting, one populated by rich San Fernando Valley housewives. At another NA meeting, she heard a woman named Elizabeth talking and "everything clicked for me . . . the message of recovery was strong and clear. It was a spiritual thing. I was perceptive and aware. I didn't buckle with the weight of it." Elizabeth told Stella that she had been an Acton resident years previously and remembered taking classes from Stella and Cassandra. In an ironic twist, Elizabeth became Stella's sponsor.

At the time of the coffeehouse conversation, Stella had been clean for more than two years. Both she and Karen seemed content and I was happy that Stella was back to being the woman I first met: caring, giving, and slightly kooky but honest about herself. Once again, she had big plans with only a vague sense of how she would accomplish them. The roof on her Palmdale house needed replacing, but she didn't have the money. She was using the house as a sober-living facility and hoped to move more women into the place so she could earn enough money for a new roof. After that, she wanted to go to Mexico and help American addicts who she said flocked there.

Stella's dreams were big, but I knew that if she maintained her focus, she would get there. I once doubted her; she had been homeless and said she was going to buy a house. She proved me wrong, and though the last few years had been rough, I believed in her. I looked forward to the day when I could give back her ten-year chip.

Rico got his wish to work at Warm Springs, the mountainous facility that housed men only. He loved working at "Miracle Mountain" and was proud that he had become the first Puerto Rican administrator at the Antelope Valley Rehabilitation Centers. He was the first resident to get clean at the centers and become an administrator. He was right to be proud; it was an implausible and extraordinary journey.

Ten years after the Acton study, Rico was dressing down a bit to "be more inviting to the clients and to meet them where they are." He no longer wore his recovery symbol every day or told the clients how long he had been clean and sober. Instead, he invited the residents to look at what "brings us together."

One day I stood with Rico as he handed out mail.

"How you doing, today?" he asked a resident who'd gotten a package.

"Pretty good," the man replied.

"You're doing fantastic!" Rico told him. "Who sent your package? . . . Go call Mom and tell her thank you. Not tonight. Now."

He turned to another resident. "You better not be smoking. That's probably why your resistance is down. Everybody's puffing. Cigars, cigarettes. Why come here to resist a fatal disease and then commit suicide on an installment plan one puff at a time?"

When a resident who had received no mail asked where his birthday present was, Rico said, "Your birthday present is your sobriety."

The man walked away smiling.

Twenty years clean and sober, Rico still attended meetings and strongly believed the AA tenet that service to others is important. He also frequented the national AA convention.

Counselor David quit his job at Acton soon after my time there to start a treatment program at a private recovery center near downtown Los Angeles. He put as much energy into that program as he did at Acton and the facility flourished. He had been there almost two years when a former client accused him of holding her captive and sexually abusing her. David later found out that his employer's daughter had induced the client to make the false accusation.

When he showed up at the first hearing on the case, the judge asked why he had no legal representation. David replied that it was because he was not guilty. The judge was upset with him and declared that she would either find him guilty or he would never work in the treatment field again.

David was suspended from his job at the recovery center and for the next year and eight months his career was in limbo. During that time he volunteered at a Lancaster youth group four days a week. Also his mother died, his brother died, and the father he never got to know died. David viewed his mother as his best friend and it was "a big deal" to him that he had been clean the last fifteen years of her life. He knew that he caused her a lot of stress and thought he might have contributed to her early death, so he was happy that she got to see him clean.

At David's hearing, the charges against him were dismissed and the judge apologized. David knew that he could be bitter about the situation, but he felt as though it strengthened his relationship with friends and God.

Next, he began a counseling service for drug addicts and got county referrals. He was happy with his life, so when a former colleague asked him to work for a Catholic group, David initially said no, but was then persuaded by the chance to work with neglected and abused children.

Before he started working with the children, he was told that maybe 5 to 10 percent of foster care clients had experimented with drugs. David thought the estimate was low, and his belief was confirmed when he met with the young-sters. To get the kids to open up in ways that they wouldn't with other adults, David played the part of entertainer, teacher, and psychologist. He would do almost anything to achieve an open dialogue, not caring if he looked foolish. He once created a stir by dressing in wig and makeup to get the teenaged girls to think about self-image.

Even after almost two decades of remaining clean and sober, David was still wary about drugs, believing they would send him back to a life of substance abuse and thiev-ery. When he had knee surgery and his doctor insisted that he would need Vicodin, David was equally adamant that he wasn't going to use it. "No. You don't want to give it to me. You give it to me, first thing you know you'll come home and find me sitting on your couch."

"Why would you be doing that?" the doctor asked.

"I'll need you to help me carry your shit out the door."

David's life was very different from the one he had while he was using. Even after all the bad things that hap-pened to him, he thanked God for every experience. He delighted in the simple things; he had a front-door key and a refrigerator with food. For him, serving others and making a daily difference in their lives was important. He attended Anonymous meetings two to three times a week. He was still a great story teller and seemed to get in more predicaments than the normal person, but then David had never claimed to be normal. He was, however, the rare indi-vidual who was blessed to be in exactly the right place and knew it.

"I've been on a joyride since I got clean," David told me. "I've been on a pink cloud."

———

Jeff, Alicia, and Cisco were still working as Acton counselors. Karen was the counseling administrator. Walt had retired and lived in Northern California. Mike, creator of the Magical Michael Monkey, quit Acton and was working at another treatment facility.

Lynne, the Antelope Valley Rehabilitation Center's first female administrator, moved to Acton's sister center, Warm Springs, and headed that facility until she retired after thirty-eight years with the county. Suzanne became the assistant administrator at Acton and then served as the acting administrator.

I hadn't seen Joe, my initial inspiration, in years. I knew that he had become a counselor at Warm Springs before I began the Acton study. During the years after the study, I heard that he had started a sober-living facility. Some people said he had obtained a master's degree. Others said it was just a rumor and that he hadn't gotten an advanced degree.

Seven years after the Acton study, I traveled to the center to attend the annual alumni event. I hoped that I would be able to connect with Joe some time that week, so I was excited to see that he was at the reunion. He was on the program and spoke—immediately after Tiffany. Afterwards, I found Joe amidst a crowd of people. He introduced me to the people with him, saying they were residents from his treatment center. I stood in shock for a few moments, taking in the fact that Joe had accomplished far more than rumors indicated. Opening a sober-living facility meant renting or buying a house and then making certain that the residents in recovery remained clean and sober. A treatment facility was on an entirely different level. Joe wasn't just housing people in recovery, he was taking in addicts and helping them recover.

Joe then told his clients something I had long forgotten. He said that one day, years earlier, he and I had been talking. He had been grumbling about the fact that Dr. Rioux, his mentor at Acton, was pressuring him to go to school. Dr. Rioux told Joe that he was capable of doing anything he set his mind to, that he could get a bachelor's degree, maybe even a master's degree. Joe had complained to me that it was too much pressure; it would take years to accomplish those things. According to him, I then said, "Joe what will you be doing with your life anyway?" Joe told his clients that the comment stuck with him and was additional motivation to aim higher.

Later that week, I visited Joe's treatment center. He had purchased two houses side by side and was running a full-fledged treatment facility, setting up a wide range of classes and programs, and hiring a psychologist and other professionals to teach. I teased him about turning the entrepreneurial skills he had developed as a pimp into something grand and beyond my imagination. Joe showed me his master's degree certificate and told me that he was teaching university classes. I was impressed—and in awe. I know that Dr. Rioux would be proud.

Two years later, I had lunch with Joe and Rico. They were talking about treatment modalities. I was struck by the topic and the tenor of the discussion. It was so different from the first conversations I had with Joe. He had the same passion and energy, but the wild-eyed, arm-waving Joe was gone. We weren't discussing literature or philosophy, but he was still interested in learning. Joe said that he loves the feeling of being useful and contributing to something. He claimed that he's living better and contributing more than ever before. He attributed much of his success to Dr. Rioux, the role model who "inspired him to aspire," and others who constantly told him that he had more to offer the world.

22

HOPE

The question looming over this study is: How successful is the program at Acton? Before examining the answer, a bit of context about addiction and treatment in the U.S. is important. In 2012, only 1 percent of individuals addicted to drugs or alcohol (or both) received treatment at a substance abuse facility. That left 20.6 million addicts—7.9% of the U.S. population—untreated. The economic and health costs of substance abuse are estimated at $428 billion per year. Loss of productivity, increased crime, court and prison expenses, and a strained health care system are only some of the costs that untreated addiction adds to an already stressed American economy.

The "war" on drugs, which has cost more than 2.5 trillion dollars in the past forty years, has focused the bulk of its resources on enforcement. As a nation, we should reach an understanding that addiction is a public health issue. We should also redirect money away from law enforcement—both global efforts to battle drug trafficking and the imprisonment of illicit drug users—to prevention and treatment. Large scale studies have proven that drug treatment benefits addicts, that there is a societal need to combat substance abuse, and that drug treatment provides an estimated return of four to seven dollars for every dollar spent.

This small inquiry adds to the proof that drug treatment is beneficial. Of the eight people whose journey through Acton that I followed, four finished the 90-day program and succeeded by Acton's standards. By the other easily measurable definition of treatment success—staying clean and becoming a productive member of society—at least three of the eight were clean after a year. That number is larger than the amount Rico predicted when he said that only two out of twenty would be clean in a year and one of them would be him. At the five-year mark, the same three were clean. Ten years later, Deborahh had died from causes unrelated to drug use, Curtis was clean, but had a three- to four-year relapse, leaving only Tiffany as the remaining person (that I can verify) who stayed clean the entire ten years after removing Deborahh from the group. However, after a decade, Curtis *was* clean again, Patty had been clean for several years, and Matt had been clean for almost a year, so at least four of seven were clean after ten years. The percentage may be higher, but I have no information about the remaining three people.

Although these two definitions of treatment success (remaining at Acton for ninety days versus abstaining from using drugs) have the advantage of being concrete and measurable, I find them unsatisfactory. Simply getting through the 90-day program isn't enough. Patty could have stayed an additional four days and she would have been considered a success by that standard, even if she relapsed the day she departed. Likewise, demanding total abstinence and expecting all addicts to lead a more productive life is an ideal, but it is not the most practical definition. Addiction is complex; each addict has a different background and simplified definitions of success don't take into account the problems underlying each individual's addiction.

Using my core group of eight residents plus five counselors (thirteen total), I re-examined what they had told me about their pasts and grouped their probable reasons for abusing drugs into five categories: (1) severe mental stress (childhood abuse or traumatic experiences); (2) family history of substance abuse; (3) emotional pain (such as feelings of abandonment or the end of a relationship); (4) social reasons (such as insecurities, trying to fit in, an attempt to relax, or have fun); and (5) physical pain. Most people had multiple possible reasons for substance abuse. Only Rico had one; his was emotional—he says he crossed an invisible line between drinking and using after a serious relationship ended.

An astounding percentage of the thirteen experienced severe mental stress. When I first started going to Acton, I was surprised to hear that many addicts had been sexually abused when young and that sexual abuse perpetrated against males seemed almost as prevalent as against females. No one employed the abuse as a reason or excuse for drugs, but the disturbing pattern seemed clear to me. Of the eight residents that I followed, four told me about sexual abuse, one about physical abuse, and Eddie's Vietnam experiences qualify as severe mental stress. The

other two didn't mention abuse, and since I didn't specifically ask about it and don't have access to them, I'll never
know for certain if they were abused or not. But even 80
percent is far too high. Most of the counselors who were
former addicts didn't mention childhood abuse, but when
I later asked, I discovered that all of the five except Rico had
been either sexually or physically abused. Most people told
me that their families don't know or won't acknowledge
the abuse. Deep wounds caused by abuse and the unwill-
ingness of others to recognize their exploitation seem to
perpetuate the victim's pain, causing lingering anger and
low self-esteem.

Another pattern was the high number of addicts who
had a family history of alcoholism or drug abuse. Of the
eleven counselors or residents whose background I know
well, eight had a family history of addiction. Usually it was a
parent or grandparent, although one person claimed that
eleven of twelve aunts and uncles died of alcoholism, and
all eight aunts and uncles in another family were alcoholics.

At least half of the residents and counselors suffered
from some kind of emotional pain, one-third used drugs
for social reasons (mostly due to social awkwardness; only
Deborahh claimed to use drugs purely for fun), and one
attributed drug use to physical pain. From this sample of
drug addicts, it appears as though addiction arises out of
something much different than a hedonistic desire to have
fun or even an attempt to fit in. A desire to dull mental
and emotional pain through self-medication, along with a
family history of substance abuse, appears to be the rule
amongst drug addicts. It would seem, then, that expecting
substance abusers to stop using and immediately begin

leading productive lives is unrealistic. A 90-day program like Acton should provide residents with the tools to move forward, but it is only the first step in a lifelong recovery process.

I surveyed six counselors who were at Acton during the time of my study, and while all believe that abstinence is the ultimate goal, each gave me a different definition of treatment success. One counselor said that Acton's program would be considered successful if the resident went to a Twelve Step meeting on his or her first day out, continued going to meetings, got involved in a Twelve Step fellowship, and stopped using. Another counselor said that staying sober isn't enough, that residents should start participating in life (through work, continuing their education, and establishing a stable family life) and pass on what they've learned. Another counselor expressed a similar viewpoint, stating that an Acton stay would be successful if the resident changed his or her mindset so he or she did not go home or return to old habits, that, instead, the resident would have a career change—from addiction to something productive.

Three counselors mentioned that success involves "planting the seed." These counselors all had the same sponsor, and more than two decades after her death, they revere her wisdom: "We plant the seed, God waters it, and when the shit gets deep enough, it grows." These counselors had slightly divergent things to add to their "seed" definition of treatment success. One thought success involves increasing self-esteem and providing positive contacts (such as exposure to Twelve Step programs or classes) that give them the tools to eventually make the commitment to recovery.

Another counselor believed that if Acton residents abstain for a while after leaving treatment and adjust their lives, "a little for a short time, even if they relapse," but eventually "come around," that's success, too. One counselor omitted abstinence from the definition of success but included the criteria that the residents learn about themselves or learn where they can get help, acquire the tools to recover, no longer get caught up in the criminal justice system, cease being a menace to friends or family, and gain hope.

This last definition is more complex than the others, but it better takes into account the complicated nature of drug abuse and the problems underlying addiction. Measured against this definition of success, all of the Acton residents that I talked to years later were examples of treatment success. Deborahh, who only reluctantly stopped using drugs, not only stayed out of jail but was working to expunge the misdemeanors and felonies from her record. At Acton, she learned where to get help and gained hope that she could leave behind the life she thought she was mired in. Even Matt, who spent nine of ten years abusing drugs, had fewer run-ins with the criminal justice system and was able to stay off heroin and start a family.

There are many components of the Acton program that contribute to residents' success. Several former residents told me that they found role models at Acton. Others said they were happy to see former addicts who had made it because it gave them hope. Establishing a close relationship with a counselor or staff member and knowing that someone was behind them was also important to several people. The Twelve Step program was a frequently mentioned positive Acton component. The classes and tools residents got were helpful. According to these former residents, the classes promoted self-esteem, gave residents opportunities to learn more about themselves, and provided an education about what drugs do *to* people—not *for* people.

Two people mentioned something that normies take for granted: the food. For many Acton residents, the kitchen produced the first nutritional meals they had had in a long time. One ex-resident cited the cook, Carlos, as someone to thank. The variety of activities were also important. One person was happy to have the chance to play golf for the first time; another to attend Bible Study. Some were excited to be able to keep busy with healthy activities. Others were grateful to have aid with leads and admittance to aftercare facilities, one of the most important services Acton provided.

All of these things are important and were made more effective by two key Acton components: the physical setting and the 90-day length of treatment. A large percentage of the Acton residents are city dwellers and they benefit from getting away from bad situations and enjoying the serene, rural atmosphere at Acton. More than half of the former residents that I followed appreciated that Acton was a calm place. One person said that Acton "gave me a safe place to get away from it all." "Time to think" was another important factor. The 90-day stay in a drug-free environment, one loosely structured and not overloaded with scheduled activities, helped them begin to restore their mental and physical health.

Most successful residents had nothing negative to say about Acton. Others claimed that the only negative thing was that ninety days wasn't enough. One person thought the classes were a waste of time. Another claimed that the Twelve Step meetings were a waste of time. Two people thought that some of the staff didn't have a clue about addiction and made the process of recovery harder than it was. These few complaints did not overshadow the positive things that former residents had to say about Acton.

This study illustrates that by any definition of treatment success, residential substance abuse treatment works and at Acton it worked well for some people. Deborahh, Tiffany, Rico, David, and Joe, all first-timers in treatment, got clean and never looked back. Except for Deborahh, all the first-timers were so committed to recovery that they made a life-long career change and chose to work in that field.

Treatment was successful for Stella and Curtis, too. Even though they relapsed after several years, they were later able to stop using and get their lives back.

Treatment works even for people who do not seek it when entering Acton. Tiffany, Rico, and David knew that they needed something different and Acton showed them how to change their lives, but Joe, Deborahh, and Curtis weren't expecting to get clean. They looked at Acton as an obstacle course they had to follow before returning to their old lives, yet they found something different: a way out of using and the motivation to quit.

For Patty, it took another treatment stint, that time a year-long program, but ultimately she found her way to sustained recovery.

Treatment appears to have been less successful for Matt, but by the one counselor's expansive definition of treatment success, which included fewer run-ins with law enforcement and close family ties, he, too, benefited from Acton and got clean.

The stories in this book focus on those benefitting from treatment, but I also benefitted from the study. My questions had been answered. I better understood the treatment process and Acton's impact, from intake through the residents first post-treatment decade. Additionally, I had gained insight into the underlying causes of addiction and the difficulties of breaking free.

But much more than satisfying my curiosity about treatment, I discovered a subculture that thrives on service and inspires people to aspire. The men and women who chose to be counselors after escaping their own addiction are excellent role models to residents and to the rest of us. They show us the value of treatment, not just the classes and meetings, but the idea that there is life, vital life, after addiction and in recovery.

A story about Rico sums up the major lesson that I learned from the Acton experience. Rico often traveled to New York to see his ailing father. When a seat mate asked what he did for a living, Rico said he was in sales.

There was always the follow-up question: "What do you sell?"

Rico would reply, "I sell hope."

ACKNOWLEDGEMENTS

This book would not be possible without the aid of the entire Acton community. Clearly, the residents whose lives are portrayed here deserve my gratitude. There are dozens more who also opened their hearts to me, but weren't mentioned in these pages. Sincere thanks to all of them. I learned something from each resident and appreciate their candor more than they can imagine.

Dr. Richard Rioux and Joe were the initial inspiration for this book, but many Acton staff members were unstinting in their efforts to aid me. Stella was the first person to offer to help in any way she could. She meant it and allowed my constant presence. I am in debt to her and many others, including but not limited to Alicia, whose good deeds proved very helpful (she knows what I mean), Cassandra, David, who often kept me guessing, Diane, Jackie, Jeff, who let me in on his meditations on life, Karen, Mike, Mr. Clark, and Walt.

Rico earned my thanks for allowing me to witness not only his day-to-day activities, but his hilarious lunchtime banter with Joe. A special thank you to Suzanne, who welcomed me into her home, and Lynne, who allowed me to use, for weeks at a time, her guest room and her best and only air-conditioned car. I will never forget the laughter the two of them inspired over many meals. I can't thank the Acton community enough. They are the kindest, most giving people I have ever met.

Endless thanks to my writing colleagues whose critiques helped improve my work. They include, but are not limited to Ken Ackerman, Carolin Crabbe, Lawrence J. Ellsworth, Cynthia Gayton, Gina Hagler, Joe Harrison, Beth Kephart, Clyde Linsley, Lloyd H. Muller, Sky Phillips, James Polk, David O. Stewart, Johanna Willner, Nina Willner, and Mary Wuest. An extra big thank you, for going above and beyond, to Carla Joinson, Adelaida Lucena de Lower, and Michael Williams.

I would also like to thank those who were there at the beginning and offered moral support along the way: my family, especially my parents, and my friends, especially Lorre Jereb, Doug Dodd, and Alicia Rodriguez.

RESOURCES

Where to go for Treatment Referrals

Substance Abuse and Mental Health Services Administration
(www.samhsa.gov) 1-800-662-HELP (4357)
Practical Recovery (www.practicalrecovery.com)
1-800-977-6110
RehabHotline (www.rehabhotline.org) 1-888-876-7760 or
1-800-559-9503

Support Groups

12 Steps (www.12step.org)
Al-Anon Family Groups (www.al-anon.alateen.org) – support
site for families and families of teens
Alcoholics Anonymous (www.aa.org)
Chemically Dependent Anonymous (www.cdaweb.org)
1-800-CDA-HOPE
Christian Recovery International
(www.christianrecovery.com)
Cocaine Anonymous (www.ca.org)
Computer Based Intervention
(http://collegedrinkerscheckup.com)

Crystal Meth Anonymous (www.crystalmeth.org)

Marijuana Anonymous (www.marijuana-anonymous.org)

Nar-Anon Family Groups (www.nar-anon.org) – for family
and friends of drug addicts

Narcotics Anonymous (www.na.org)

National Asian Pacific American Families Against Substance
Abuse (www.napafasa.org)

National Association for Children of Alcoholics
(www.nacoa.org)

Rational Recovery (www.recovery.org)

S.O.S. Secular Organizations for
Sobriety (www.cfiewest.org)

Where to Get Further Information

Addicted.com (www.addicted.com)

American Society of Addiction Medicine
(www.asam.org)

Centers for Disease Control and Prevention
(www.cdc.gov/pwud/addiction.html)

National Institute on Drug Abuse (www.drugabuse.gov)

Office of National Drug Control Policy
(www.whitehouse.gov/ondep)

Substance Abuse and Mental Health Services Administration
(www.samhsa.gov)

U.S. Department of Veterans Affairs (VA) (www.va.gov)

Women for Sobriety Inc. (www.womenforsobriety.org)

National Alliance of Methadone Advocates
(www.methadone.org)

Drug and Alcohol Prevention Network (www.drugnet.net)
1-800-315-2056

Books for Further Reading

Amen, Daniel G., MD and David E. Smith, MD. 2010. *Unchain Your Brain: 10 Steps to Breaking the Addictions That Steal Your Life.* Mindworks Press. (www.amenclinics.com)

Beattie, Melody. 2003. *The Language of Letting Go Journal: A Meditation Book and Journal for Daily Reflection.* Hazelden.

Bradshaw, John. 2005 *Healing the Shame that Binds You.* Deerfield, FL: HCI Books, Inc.

Chopra, Dr. Deepak, and Dr. David Simon. 2007. *Freedom from Addiction: The Chopra Center Method for Overcoming Destructive Habits.* Deerfield, FL: HCI Books Inc. (www.chopra.com/freedomfromaddiction).

Covington, Stephanie S. 2011. *A Woman's Way through the Twelve Steps & A Woman's Way through the Twelve Steps Workbook: A Women's Recovery Collection.* Hazelden.

Dorsman, Jerry. 1997. *How to Quit Drinking without AA: A Complete Self-Help Guide, 2nd Edition.* Harmony.

Eisenberg, Arleen and Howard Eisenberg. *The Recovery Book.* 1992. Workman Publishing Company.

Gadhia-Smith, Anita. 2011. *From Addiction to Recovery: A Therapist's Personal Journey.* iUniverse.com.

Gant, Charles. 2009. *End Your Addiction Now.* Garden City Park, NT: Square One Publishers.

Haroutunian, Harry and Steven Tyler. 2013. *Being Sober: A Step-by-Step Guide to Getting To, Getting Through, and Living in Recovery.* Rodale Books.

Khaleghi, Morteza and Karen Khaleghi. 2011. *The Anatomy of Addiction: Overcoming the Triggers That Stand in the Way of Recovery.* Palgrave Macmillan.

Kipper, David and Steven Whitney. 2011. *The Addiction Solution: Unraveling the Mysteries of Addiction through Cutting-Edge Brain Science.* Rodale Books (http://davidkippermd.com/treatingaddiction.html).

Kuhn, Cynthia, Scott Swartzwelder and Wilkie Wilson. 2008. *Buzzed: The Straight Facts About the Most Used and Abused Drugs from Alcohol to Ecstasy (Third Edition).* W.W. Norton and Company.

Lawford, Christopher Kennedy. 2014. *Recover to Live: Kick Any Habit, Manage Any Addiction.* BenBella Books.

Shapiro, Rami. 2009. *Recovery–the Sacred Art: The Twelve Steps As Spiritual Practice (Art of Spiritual Living).* Skylight Paths Pub.

Trimpey, Jack. 1996. *Rational Recovery: The New Cure for Substance Addiction.* Gallery Books.

Urschel, Harold. 2009. *Healing the Addicted Brain: The Revolutionary, Science-Based Alcoholism and Addiction Recovery Program.* Sourcebooks.

THE TWELVE STEPS

1. We admitted we were powerless over alcohol—that our lives had become unmanageable.
2. Came to believe that a Power greater than ourselves could restore us to sanity.
3. Made a decision to turn our will and our lives over to the care of God as we understood Him.
4. Made a searching and fearless moral inventory of ourselves.
5. Admitted to God, to ourselves, and to another human being the exact nature of our wrongs.
6. Were entirely ready to have God remove all these defects of character.
7. Humbly asked Him to remove our shortcomings.
8. Made a list of all persons we had harmed, and became willing to make amends to them all.
9. Made direct amends to such people wherever possible, except when to do so would injure them or others.
10. Continued to take personal inventory and when we were wrong promptly admitted it.
11. Sought through prayer and meditation to improve our conscious contact with God as we understood Him, praying only for knowledge of His will for us and the power to carry that out.
12. Having had a spiritual awakening as the result of these steps, we tried to carry this message to others, and to practice these principles in all our affairs.

Made in the USA
Charleston, SC
07 September 2014